I'll Make You a Gardening Wizard Overnight!
Derek Fell

DEDICATION

For my wife, Carolyn and my three children, Christina, Derek Jr and Victoria

Carolyn has always partnered me in my gardening endeavors and because of her special insights I asked her to make comments on the manuscript. These I have included throughout the book. The children all enjoy gardening. In their younger years they willingly served as models for many of my photographs.

© 2010 Copyright

ACKNOWLEDGMENTS

A big thank you to Harry Smith who taught me to photograph plants and gardens, to O'Dowd Gallagher who taught me to write; and David Burpee who taught me how America gardens.

CONTENTS
I'll Make You a Gardening Wizard Overnight
By Derek Fell
Photography and illustrations by Derek Fell

xi . . . . INTRODUCTION: *The Wizard of Cedaridge Farm*

About the Author; Focus of the book; The promise of making a person a gardening wizard overnight along with a visit to the author's experimental organic garden and studio through four seasons.

1 . . . . CHAPTER 1: *The Wizard Guarantees Healthy Results*

Health benefits; How vegetables promote longevity; The wisdom of organic gardening; Understanding hardiness zones; Start small; Choosing a site; Improving shade; Testing soil; No Dig gardening methods: Lasagna Gardening; Square Foot Gardening; Edible landscaping; Boring grass or flavorful vegetables? Designing your plot; Small, Medium, Large vegetable garden designs for maximum returns; How to save $2,000.00 from a 10 x 20 ft space; Growing vertically; Foundation planting; Raised beds; A No-Aching Back garden; Hydroponics; Espalier; Succession planting; Inter-planting; Four season gardening; Winter vegetables.

33 . . . . . . CHAPTER 2: *The White House Vegetable Gardens*

The Gerald Ford Garden; the Michelle Obama Garden; The basic difference between the two – Gerald Ford's to fight inflation; Michelle Obama's for health reasons. Planting plans for each type of White House garden.

39 . . . . . . CHAPTER 3: *Get Started with the Best Deals on Garden Tools*

Where to acquire garden tools inexpensively; Spade, rake, hand trowel, wheelbarrow, back pack sprayer, garden hose, soaker hose, sprinkler. Planning your garden budget - cost of supplies if purchased from a discount department store like Lowe's. Examples of savings over store-bought vegetables. How to save $2,000.00 with a 10 x 20ft plot.

47 . . . . . . CHAPTER 4: *The Wizard's Secret Soil Formula for Incredible Edibles*

The value of compost; How to compost; Free compost materials; Micro-organisms; Booster feeding; Lateral growth; How to make a compost bin; A secret formula for compost tea; Commercial composts; Green manuring; Crop rotation; The value of earthworms. Make your own worm farm.

57 . . . . . . CHAPTER 5: *Inside Tips for Free Garden Supplies & More*

Free seeds (saving your own), Free starter pots; Free mini greenhouses; Free spray bottles; Free potting soil; Bottom heat; Direct seeding; Pre-germinating seed; How to avoid stretched seedlings; How to avoid root bound transplants; Frost protection; Hybrid seed; Heirloom seeds; Patented seeds; Seed rack versus seed catalog versus internet; Seeds versus transplants.

CONTENTS *continued*

65 ..... CHAPTER 6: ***No Weeding, Sure Feeding, Automatic Watering***
Shallow rooted and deep rooted weeds; How to eliminate weeds; Mulching for cool soil; Mulching for warm soil; Free mulch materials; Winter clean-up; How to read a fertilizer label; Organic fertilizers versus chemical fertilizers. Granular versus liquid fertilizers; Compost tea – the super growth stimulant; How to water- watering cans, sprinklers; Drip irrigation (soaker hoses); An inexpensive automatic watering system.

73 ..... CHAPTER 7: ***The Wizard's Top Ten Secrets for an Amazing Garden***
The 10 Tips you need to become a gardening wizard. Some common garden questions answered.

79 ..... CHAPTER 8: ***How to Make Pests & Diseases Disappear***
Organic controls of various pests: slugs, Japanese beetles, bean beetles, cabbage worms, aphids, cutworms, flea beetles, corn earworm, squash vine borers, voles, deer and other foraging animals. Organic controls for diseases: sunscald, blossom end rot, wilt, corn smut, anthracnose, leaf spots, botrytis. Floating row covers (fleece), Making your own garlic/pepper spray. Symptoms, diagnosis and cure for common pest problems and diseases.

87 ..... CHAPTER 9: ***Variety Selections for Huge Garden Yields***
Giant vegetables, Rainbow vegetables; Early varieties; Heirlooms, GMO seed; Artichoke; Arugula, Asparagus, Lima beans, Pole snap beans; Edible soy beans; Shell beans; Beets, Broccoli; Brussels sprouts, Cabbage, Carrots, Cauliflower, Celerica; Celery; Chayote; Corn salad; Cucumbers; Eggplant; Fennel; Kohl rabi; Leeks; Lettuce & Mesclun mixes; Melons; Okra; Onions; Parsnips; Peanuts; Peas; Peppers; Potatoes; Pumpkin; Radish; Squash; Vegetable spaghetti; Sunflowers; Sweet corn; Sweet potato; Swiss chard; Tomatillos; Tomatoes; Tomato-Potato; Turnips and rutabaga; Watercress; Watermelons.

175 ..... CHAPTER 10: ***Sell Your Surplus for a Profit***
Selling surplus vegetables and fruits to local restaurants, at farmers' markets, at a roadside table or farm stand. Visit to a profitable organic farming enterprise. Tips on selling produce at a farmers' market.

181 ..... CHAPTER 11: ***How to Turn Your Hobby into a Tax Deduction***
IRS rules about deducting expenses as a legitimate business expense. The distinction between a hobby and a business. Expenses you may be able to deduct. How to obtain information about government subsidies for growing vegetables and starting a community garden.

185 ..... CHAPTER 12: ***Herbal Magic***
Designs for herb gardens (illustrations). How to grow the most useful herbs: aloe, anise, basil, bay laurel, chamomile, chervil, chives, cilantro, dill, garlic, ginger, ginseng, horseradish, lavender, lemongrass, geraniums, mints, parsley, rosemary, sage, savory, sorrel, sweet cicely, sweet leaf, tarragon, thyme. Cooking with herbs; Preserving herbs; Edible flowers.

CONTENTS *continued*

215 ..... CHAPTER 13: **Healing Ointments & Skin Creams**

How to grow plants that produce healing ointments and skin creams for a healthy, younger looking skin; Calendula salve; Herb infused oils; Aromatherapy; Herbal vinegars; Herbal soaps; Herbal potpourri.

219 ..... CHAPTER 14: **Grow Delicious Fruits & Berries for an All-Season Harvest**

Strawberries; Raspberries; Blackberries; Blueberries; Kiwi fruit; Apples; Pears; Plums; Cherries; Peaches; Apricots; Figs; Citrus; Growing these in containers; Growing fruits indoors over winter (citrus, tomatoes, strawberries).

239 ..... CHAPTER 15: **Container Gardens for Big Yields Fast**

Pro's and Con's of different containers – wood, metal, terracotta, plastic. Pots; Hanging baskets; Window box planter; Potting mixes; Making your own potting mix; Watering; Topsy Turvy planter; After care. Best vegetables for containers.

245 ..... CHAPTER 16: **Indoor Harvests Made Easy**

Vegetables and herbs to grow indoors. Sprouts. Light needs. Grow Light units for supplemental light. Other accessories.

251 ..... CHAPTER 17: **Children's Gardens**

How to involve children in gardening; the benefits to children of gardening; fun projects for children involved in growing fruits and vegetables.

261 ..... CHAPTER 18: **Gardening Myths You Need to Know**

Hydroponics, Coyote urine, companion planting; planting by the phases of the moon; an analysis of home remedies that work and those that don't.

265 ..... CHAPTER 19: **Recommended Reading**

Garden books for the compost pile. Garden books to treasure.

275 ..... APPENDIX: **Sources**

279 ..... INDEX

I'll Make You a Gardening Wizard Overnight!

Vegetable garden at Cedaridge Farm

INTRODUCTION
The Wizard of Cedaridge Farm

*"Derek Fell is a wizard at growing vegetables.
The size and quality must be seen to be believed."*
– **Scott Carlson**, *co-inventor of the Skyscraper Garden*

It may seem like a big promise, to turn you into a gardening wizard overnight. After all, gardening is like medicine. It is a HUGE subject to master. And that is why the older a doctor is, the more people respect his opinions. It's the same with gardeners. I started gardening when I was 5 years old, began working with Europe's biggest wholesale seed company when I was 19, and became catalog manager for America's largest mail order seed company at age 25. I have just turned 70, and so what I hope to achieve with this book is to tell you what I learned about gardening. I plan to do it by concentrating on the important parts, exploding a few myths, and make it as interesting as possible along the way.

It amazes me how many more people than ever before are seeking good gardening advice. The last time I checked there were *44 million requests for information about Recession Gardening* on Yahoo. There were *122 million requests for information about How to Plant a Garden.* There were *2.9 million enquiries about growing giant vegetables.* Yet the internet is a poor place for reliable gardening information because some people think that a little learning makes them an expert. Gardening is not an exact science, and there are many theories and variables concerning soil composition, hardiness zones, and variety selection that can make a big difference in the final result.

My publisher voiced his expectations for this book as follows: "I want you to deliver a book that a person can use to save grocery bills and discover some very interesting revelations that present easy to read tips many gardeners aren't aware of; The one garden book that jumps out and tells it all."

Today, there are many more reasons to garden than ever before. First and foremost are health benefits. Hardly a year goes by without health warnings about contaminated produce commercially grown. Growing your own produce avoids illness. Moreover, the fresher the vegetables (and what can be fresher than vegetables from your own garden?) the healthier your diet and the longer you are likely to live. The top ten foods for unclogging arteries and prevent heart disease are all vegetables such as tomatoes, spinach and broccoli, fruits such as strawberries and blueberries and nuts such as walnuts. It was primarily for health benefits that the First Lady, Michelle Obama chose to plant a vegetable garden at the White House in 2009.

There is also the ability to save hundreds of dollars over store-bought produce (a single tomato plant can save you $100.00 and more over one season), and the potential to earn income from selling surplus produce. A 10 ft row of pole snap beans can produce over 30 lbs of beans. At $3.30 a lb for organically grown green beans that's over $300.00 worth of product from a 10 ft. row. A space just 10 ft by 20 ft is sufficient to grow more than $2,000.00 worth of fresh vegetables - with the right choice of varieties and succession planting which I describe in the following pages.

My career as a journalist with the Shrewsbury Chronicle newspaper group in England started my interest in garden writing. As an investigative reporter and feature writer, the Shrewsbury Flower Show was a source of good news stories with its displays of produce in the horticulture tent – leeks as thick as my arm, onions as big as melons, sprays of blemish free, scented sweet peas and columns of blue delphiniums as tall as a person can reach. One of my favorite duties was to interview the award winners for the newspaper, and report HOW they produced a giant pumpkin or a prize winning rose. The subject of horticulture was endlessly absorbing and the key to exhibition quality results always seemed to be a secret formula the growers referred to as 'manure tea' (see page 52).

Later, while working in London with Hurst Seeds, who maintained a breeding program for flowers and vegetables, I realized there was another key element to beautiful flowers and award-winning vegetables – variety selection. Hurst employed two plant breeders and it was fun helping them to introduce their new varieties through advertisements and press releases. At this time I also took an interest in garden photography for publication in Hurst's seed catalog.

This catalog, showcasing the work of Hurst's breeders, won an award in Britain's Best Catalog Contest, and as a consequence David Burpee, dean of American seedsmen, invited me to join his company in Pennsylvania, the world's biggest mail order seed house. He was 70 years old, having inherited ownership of the company from his father at 19. As his catalog manager, with an office at Burpee's world famous research establishment, Fordhook Farm in Bucks County, I absorbed his knowledge of gardening like a sponge. Fordhook was a magical place, with hundreds of acres of flowers and vegetables grown for evaluation, and two sister farms in California. As soon as I qualified I became a US citizen.

When the great plant breeding wizard, Luther Burbank visited Fordhook from California he described it as the best of all his eastern object lessons, the farm of value to gardeners worldwide. Fordhook was the birthplace of famous vegetables such as the Fordhook Lima bean, Big Boy tomato, Iceberg lettuce (a different variety from the rather tasteless supermarket variety), Golden Bantam sweet corn, Golden beets, Fordhook zucchini squash and a host of other milestone breeding achievements.

ALL-AMERICA SELECTIONS. Six years with Burpee qualified me to accept an invitation to become executive director of All America Selections, the national seed trials and the National Garden Bureau, an information office sponsored by the American seed industry. All-America Selections tests vegetables and flowers grown from seed and makes awards for those that grow well in North America. The job involved a lot of travel, meeting with plant breeders all over the world and persuading them to enter their best home garden varieties. In three years I visited most countries of Europe, plus China and Japan and most regions of the USA, meeting growers and judges. This contact was necessary in order to find varieties that might otherwise be overlooked in the annual confusion of so many plant introductions.

Through the All-America Selections, and later as an independent consultant to seed and nursery companies, it was exciting to introduce to the world some of America's most popular vegetable varieties including the Sugar Snap pea, Premium Crop broccoli, Snow Crown cauliflower, Savoy King cabbage, Gold Crop yellow-podded snap bean, Red Acre cabbage, Fiskeby edible soy bean, Bright Lights chard, and Ace acorn squash. In 1974 when President Ford wanted more families to grow fresh vegetables in order to fight inflation, as head of the National Garden Bureau, Ford accepted my proposal for a White House vegetable garden, and he appointed me chairman of a White House Garden task force. When the Obamas entered the White House the subject of vegetable gardening was not only seen as a means to survive the recession, but also to promote a healthy diet.

After my time with All America Selections and the National Garden Bureau, a Chicago garden book publisher asked me to produce a series of garden books, and I have been writing garden books ever since - a total of 82 books and calendars, ranging from shade gardening to water gardening. In the Appendix is a complete list of these. My book titled *Vegetables – How to Select, Grow and Enjoy* (HP Books) won a Best Book Award from the Garden Writers Association.

CEDARIDGE FARM. In 1989 as my horticultural interests diversified it became necessary to establish a bigger test garden and so 20-acre Cedaridge Farm, a zone 6 garden in Pennsylvania, became my research facility. This allows me to better evaluate new garden varieties and a multitude of gardening techniques, like deer control, fertilizing and irrigation. The vegetable garden is the size of two tennis courts and it is surrounded by theme gardens such as a cutting garden, water garden, perennial beds and a woodland garden. The property has been featured worldwide in magazines, including World magazine, Gardens Illustrated, the Royal Horticultural Society's magazine, the Gardener's Journal, Birds & Blooms, the Green Scene, Nouveau, Flower Gardening, Fine Gardening and others. Kodak chose Cedaridge Farm to be the focus of a desk diary titled A Photographer's Garden. The cottage garden was replicated one year at the Philadelphia Flower Show and won three awards for design, including the prestigious Mayor's Trophy.

Cedaridge Farm allowed me to develop the amazing Tomato-Potato, a plant that grows tomatoes on the vine and potatoes in the soil, among the roots. Dozens of horticulturists from all over the world have visited Cedaridge to see my methods and appraise the results.

In 1990 the popular television shopping channel, QVC invited me to develop a garden show and for six years Step-by-Step Gardening sold millions of plants to television shoppers in one and two hour sessions. It was the first successful garden show for QVC. The success of the show was even reported in the New York Times and Garden Design magazine. Each show was live and completely unscripted, some of the segments filmed at Cedaridge Farm.

CEDARIDGE SOUTH. In May 2008, following a visit to Sanibel island, Florida, my wife and I decided to establish a zone 10 garden for further research and took on the challenge of restoring an overgrown, frost-free tropical garden. It is proving invaluable for testing tender plants that perform as perennials in Southwest Florida and Southern California, but can be grown only as conservatory plants or annuals further north. The property features a small citrus orchard, a banana grove, thirty mature coconut palms and various exotic fruits such as mango and papaya. A Zone 10 gardening book is already in progress.

Carolyn's Comments:

"Cedaridge Farm is not only our home where Derek and I have lived happily for the past 20 years, it is an outdoor studio for Derek to test new varieties, photograph the results and test different growing techniques. After a career in the fashion industry, designing men's fashions for fashion houses such as Calvin Klein, Pierre Cardin and Alan Flusser, I have devoted myself to designing gardens for private commissions, and also staging studio sets at the QVC shopping channel when they have garden shows. I have collaborated with Derek on several of his books, including two devoted to flower arranging.

At Cedaridge Farm Derek has his favorite spaces (such as the vegetable garden and water garden) and I have mine (such as several cutting gardens). Whenever we can, we travel together — to visit California plant breeders, several times to New Zealand, several times to England where Derek has a younger brother who is a magician, and an older cousin who has a sheep farm in the Yorkshire Dales. We have visited many parts of France to research his books on gardens of the Impressionist artists, and we made an especially memorable trip to Tahiti to research Van Gogh's influence on the Tahitian paintings of his friend, Paul Gauguin. There we occupied a thatched beach hut close to a similar beach hut that Gauguin occupied. We fell in love with the tropics and now have our own tropical paradise on Sanibel island, Florida, surrounded by a new garden of exotic plants and more test gardens to expand our horticultural knowledge. Not a bad life; in the good old USA!"

CHAPTER 1
The Wizard Guarantees Healthy Results

"The Agricultural College at Lincoln, New Zealand, is running excellent compost plots versus chemical plots... The results are astounding. The compost grown vegetables are far, far better in every way and are not attacked by pests and diseases as the others."
– Dr. W. E. Shewell-Cooper

Compared to many other nations the percentage of vegetables in the average American diet is extremely low, and nutritionists are worried about it because a diet that lacks the proper consumption of fresh vegetables and fruits results in malnutrition. This causes all kinds of health problems, including obesity (a prime cause of heart disease), diabetes (a build-up of dangerous levels of sugar in the system) and cancer. Although interest in eating more fruits and vegetables has increased in recent years the population (especially in urban areas) has a long way to go before the nation can be considered healthy.

THE WORLD'S HEALTHIEST DIET. Russian scientists studying longevity of villagers in the Caucasus Mountains of Southern Russia (where 5000 individuals were known to be more than 100 years old) have discovered a distinct link between plenty of vegetables in a person's diet and the ability to live to a ripe old age. With the combination of a vegetable-rich diet, moderate exercise (which the villagers get mostly from farming and gardening) and a pleasant disposition (which can also come from cultivating the soil) Russian scientists believe that a person can live to be 200 years of age. The world record is 175.

Among old people studied by the Russians, calorie intake of vegetable origin comprised 74% of a person's diet. In other areas of the world noted for longevity – in the Hunza region of Pakistan and Villacambe, Ecquador – calorie intake of vegetables is even more pronounced, at a whopping 95%.

If a bigger portion of the American population could emulate these healthy centenarians, imagine the benefits to the savings in health care. The medical profession acknowledges that eating vegetables avoids harmful cholesterol build up in the bloodstream. Also a diet rich in 'fiber' is as important to a healthy body as vitamin intake. No other food commodity, including meat, fish, milk and eggs – can match the balanced nutritional value that vegetables and fruit can bring to a diet.

Try to eat a green leafy salad with every evening meal for disease resistance and to avoid cataracts. For dessert eat a fruit salad – for example, a mix of fresh strawberries, blueberries and a tropical fruit like pineapple. Beans are an excellent source of low-fat protein, vitamins, minerals and fiber, including snap beans, lima beans, soy beans and shell beans. Add them to soups. Studies have shown that people who add exercise to a fruit and vegetable diet are also 60% less likely to suffer from Alzheimer's disease, a form of dementia. Use culinary herbs liberally at meals, especially herbs like parsley, chives, oregano, rosemary, thyme, basil, anise, garlic and hot peppers in order to build disease resistance. Just 1 cup of oregano provides as much disease resistance as three cups of spinach. Nuts and seeds also build disease resistance and have a stabilizing effect on blood sugar.

ORGANIC GARDENING. I think the first question in a beginner gardener's mind is whether to garden organically (using natural methods of soil improvement, fertilization and pest control) or whether to use chemical products, or a bit of both. I'm 100% organic and I advise you to do the same. Home gardens are not truck farms. When a farmer or professional grower has to make a living they will often resort to chemical controls as insurance and to ensure a blemish free product that will look attractive on the supermarket produce counter. For the home gardener, with a much smaller space to cultivate and with no-one else to please but himself and his family, there is no reason to use chemicals.

It's hard to believe that when the First Lady announced her intention to plant a vegetable garden and use organic methods, she received a letter from the Mid-America CropLife Association, a public relations arm of the agri-chemical industry chiding her on her decision, claiming her example would lead to massive unemployment in the agri-chemical industry and put many American farmers out of business. When I was appointed to a task force to plant a vegetable garden at the White House during the Ford Administration, the agri-chemical lobby was so strong, my first duty was to write a position paper addressing a concern from the USDA on whether home food production would, in fact, hurt the farmer. My paper presented evidence that on the contrary the farmer would benefit enormously from an increased home gardening movement because the nation was so far below its optimum level of vegetable consumption that a better understanding of the importance of vegetables to good health would benefit vegetable farmers in the long term .

When I first started to garden, a well respected garden magazine published this joke: "Turn over an organic gardener and you'll find a nut." I am an organic gardener and although I may seem a little eccentric in the way I am passionate about gardening, the image of an organic gardener has changed. Now it is the chemical user who is nuts. Organic gardening brings peace of mind.

I have been a speaker at several organic growing seminars where I deliver a talk and slide show revealing the organic methods used in my own garden. More than any other state, Pennsylvania has a heritage of gardening without potentially harmful chemicals. The offices of Organic Gardening magazine and their research farm are only an hour's drive from where I live and I have given tours of my facility to the Rodale staff. I knew the founder of Organic Gardening magazine, J. I. Rodale, and his son Robert. They were

Cabbage organically grown

inspired by the soil management practices of Sir Albert Howard, an Englishman who studied ancient organic growing practices in India. I visited and interviewed for *Horticulture* magazine the late Dr. W. E. Shewell-Cooper, an advisor to Britain's war-time Victory Garden initiative, and later director of the Good Gardener's Association whose flower and vegetable beds had not been dug in 14 years through composting.

When the first English Quaker farmers settled in the US, the only known methods of cultivation were organic. The Quaker religious sect was followed by the Amish, who came from Germany and settled mostly in the Lancaster area of Pennsylvania. The Amish earned a reputation in Europe as the best farmers, taking impoverished soil and making it productive through composting waste and manuring. They were the first to practice fertilizing by planting cover crops – leguminous plants like clover – to replenish nitrogen in the soil and till it under for aeration. Even today, the Amish use mostly organic methods – particularly organic fertilizers in the form of stable manure and compost.

There is abundant evidence that all home garden pest problems can be controlled with organic methods. Not so easy is the problem of protecting an entire commercial fruit orchard or a large acreage of sweet corn, and selling the product competitively. At the Organic Seminar, in Arkansas, I met several professional growers who had reduced their chemical spray costs up to 60% through the introduction of beneficial insect predators and the planting of disease resistant varieties. One orchardist cut the number of sprays from 22 a season to just two – one at petal drop in spring, and another two weeks later.

This resulted in a crop that was 95% free of insect damage. In Japan I saw an orchard that was 100% organic. The owner wrapped every single fruit in a clear plastic bag. It is laborious, but for an organic, chemical-free product the Japanese are willing to pay higher prices than we are used to in the US.

The introduction of horticultural fleece – an inexpensive lightweight fabric that covers plants like a spider's web – has been a boon to organic gardeners, for it can protect long rows of plants, and also cover an entire dwarf apple tree to keep out pests and disease.

As you read on you will learn a host of ideas for growing organically. Step one is to choose the right site and make the soil healthy. A healthy soil promotes healthy plants that resist insects and disease.

HARDINESS ZONES. For such a large land mass, the United States has a remarkably predictable climate. Although there are 11 hardiness zones extending from the top of Alaska (zone 1) to Key West (zone 11), most of the United States has frost in winter and hot summers with little rainfall. It is a very different climate from the British Isles, for example, which has a maritime climate. The proximity of the Atlantic Ocean to the entire British Isles produces more rainfall, relatively mild winters, and cool summers with lots of cloud cover.

North America's main mountain ranges – the Rocky Mountains in the West and the Allegheny Mountains in the East run parallel with a vast area of plains in between. This causes cold air from the Arctic to sweep down far south in winter, and for warm air from the Gulf of Mexico to funnel far north in summer. During winter months the warm Gulf and the cold Arctic play a tug-of-war game so that periods of extreme cold can alternative with periods of warmth. If the Allegheny Mountains ran East to West across the top of the US, instead of North to South then most of the US population would experience balmy weather like Florida in winter.

There is also a big difference between a zone 10 in Florida and a zone 10 in California. Zone 10 Florida can grow coconut palms because of warmer year-round temperatures. Its main growing season for vegetables (even warm season vegetables like tomatoes) is Fall, Winter and early Spring; California cannot grow coconut palms and its main growing season for vegetables is still Spring, Summer and Fall.

The most important dates to know for your climate zone are the first and last expected frost dates. It is difficult to learn this from a zone map because the maps almost always are printed too small to be a reliable guide. Rather, it is best to consult with members of local garden clubs, extension service personnel, and experienced old timers.

START SMALL. The biggest mistake beginner gardeners make is starting too large. A small space well cared for will yield more than a large space that is neglected. When summer days turn hot and humid the weeds can take over a large space and the chore of eradicating them can be discouraging, causing many people to give up. Early success with a small space – say 10-12 ft. wide by 15-16 ft. long – can be a big incentive to progress to a bigger space.

Chapter 1 - *The Wizard Guarantees Healthy Results*

Herb Garden, Cedaridge Farm

To begin your quest for a profitable, chemical-free vegetable garden, make a list of what you wish to grow; choose a level or terraced site and sketch out a planting plan showing the vegetable varieties that appeal to you. Choose a system. The old traditional method of straight, regimented rows can be wasteful of space and labor-intensive . You might prefer to try vertical gardening to save space (see the 'Skyscraper Garden' system, page 27), or planting in blocks in raised beds (see page 9).

SITE: Choose a location that drains well and provides at least 6 hours full sun a day. The more sunlight the better, especially for growing warm season crops like peppers, tomatoes and melons. To test for drainage dig a hole about 12 inches deep and pour in a bucket of water. If the water puddles and takes a long time to seep down, then you should consider another site or lay down drainage tiles to drain excess water away. A simpler solution may be to lay down a bed of crushed stones and build a raised bed above the indigenous soil. Truck in some screened topsoil and raise the level 6 to 12 inches. If you have an exposed site, constantly swept by winds, consider planting a hedge on the windy side for shelter.

SHADE. If the site is shaded by tall trees then you might consider trimming away some overhead branches. The removal of a single branch can mean the difference between a poor and acceptable yield. I once observed an experiment on tomato plants that showed 1/10th of a second more light per day could make a noticeable difference in growth rate and yields. If the site is shaded by a tall building or wall you might consider painting the walls white to improve light intensity through reflected light and using a light colored mulch like white plastic or shiny aluminum foil.

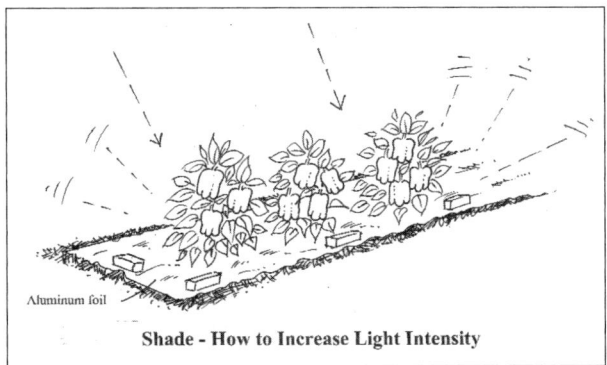

Shade - How to Increase Light Intensity

Know the nature of your soil. Scoop up a handful of topsoil and squeeze it in your hand. If it lumps together into an impermeable mass it is probably clay and will need a soil amendment such as compost to improve it; if it remains granular and trickles through your fingers it is undoubtedly sand. It also will need a soil amendment such as garden compost in order to give it moisture-holding capacity. A loam soil – one that crumbles in your hand – is ideal, but the action of heat, wind and rain can still cause loam soil to harden, and so the continuous addition of garden compost each season will keep it in good condition. Some desert areas have a soil called caliche that is so hard it may need a pick-ax to break it up. In difficult soil conditions like this build raised beds.

Sandy soils tend to be alkaline and clay soils tend to be acidic but only a soil test will tell you if any amendment is needed to strike a happy medium. Generally, in forested areas like the Northeast, soils tend to be acidic; while desert soils of the Southwest tend to be alkaline. Limestone soils (also called chalk soils) – where glaciers during the ice age scraped away the topsoil – can also be too alkaline for good growth. In general, vegetables prefer a slightly acid soil.

SOIL CRUSTING. If your soil forms a crust after you have prepared the site, it is an indication of clay soil with inadequate organic content. The crusting is a big problem for germinating seeds, especially fine-seeded vegetables like carrots and lettuce, preventing their emergence.

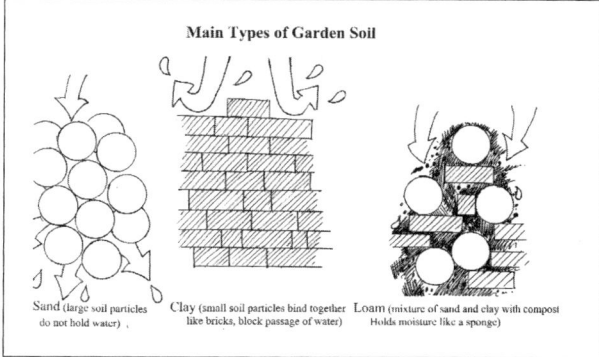

Crusting is prevented by amending clay soil with applications of compost and sand. However, do not apply sand to a clay soil without adding organic matter, as this sand-clay combination can end up with the consistency of peanut butter. Crusting will also inhibit the growth of transplants unless an organic mulch is applied to the soil surface. Examine your beds at timely intervals and break up the crust with a hand fork or hoe, taking care not to damage surface roots of your vegetables.

HOW TO CONDUCT A SOIL TEST. Visit any local nursery or garden center and they will give you a mailer with pouch for testing your soil at a local laboratory. You can use a soil test kit but a lab test is more reliable. Fill the pouch with soil from several parts of the plot you intend to open up, fill in the questionnaire telling the lab what crops you wish to grow, and back will come a computer printout telling you whether the soil is acid, alkaline or neutral, and what you need to do to make it a perfect planting medium. The print out will also show nutrient deficiencies and recommend specific amounts of fertilizer to correct any imbalance.

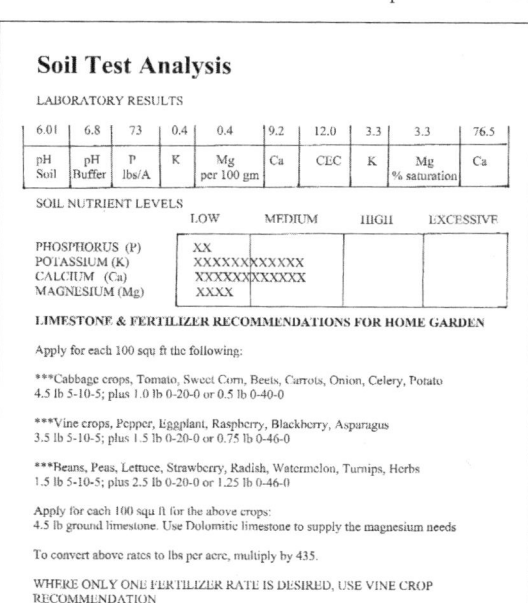

In the sample lab report shown here, for my garden at Cedaridge Farm when I first moved in, the numbers across the top largely tell the lab vital statistics to arrive at a recommendation. For example, you will see that the first two figures show an actual soil pH of 6.0 that normally would require no amendment, but the lab uses a more accurate rating called a pH buffer that takes into account the soil's composition. With a buffer of 6.8 that calls for the addition of some lime.

Note that under Nutrient Levels there is no listing for nitrogen. That is because nitrogen levels in soil are subject to rapid fluctuations – higher levels after thunderstorms when nitrogen enters the soil naturally through a chemical reaction in the atmosphere – and lower levels when the nitrogen is leached away through irrigation or rainfall. Therefore, the lab always assumes the soil needs nitrogen and gives its recommendation in the overall fertilizer analysis printed below the chart for each crop group.

Although the analysis gives recommendations for different crops (important to farmers growing commercially), for the home gardener it's sufficient to strike a happy medium, and so the report advises using the vine crop recommendation for all crops.

NO DIG GARDENS. Over the years some passionate gardeners have written about how to grow flowers and vegetables without digging the soil. As early as 1945 the late Dr. W. D. Shewell-Cooper, director of the Good Gardener's Association, in England, wrote about his No Dig methods in a book titled "Soil." In the US, the late Ruth Stout (1888-1980) wrote a book titled *The No Work Garden Book* (Rodale). I recall one reviewer saying: "I learned three ways to garden: the wrong way, the right way and the Ruth Stout way."

The wrong way is to constantly till the land and rely on chemical fertilizers to stimulate plant growth, which can leave harmful salt deposits that eventually poison the soil.

The right way is to double dig the existing soil down to two spade depths for adequate root development, place the indigenous soil on a tarp and mix in compost and other soil conditioners to create a raised bed.

Stout's book describes how you can lay newspapers over turf to kill the grass and weeds and compost directly on the area you wish to plant. She built her beds up in layers and planted directly into the compost, no digging needed. She would seed directly into the compost or use transplants, and cover the space between the plants with hay to deter weeds. She converted many people to her system of organic gardening.

Pat Lanza's book, *Lasagna Gardening* (Rodale) describes a similar system to Ruth Stout's but tidier and more practical for the small-space gardener. Mel Bartholomew's book *Square Foot Gardening* advocates planting vegetables in blocks within 4 by 4 ft. squares since it's easy to reach into the middle without stepping on the soil. He also advocates raised beds and using potting soils to avoid digging. Independently I have developed a system of no-dig gardening called Skyscraper Gardening by growing plants vertically in a narrow space (see page 27).

Mel Bartholomew advocates another no-dig system by placing a weed barrier over the soil and dumping over it a mix of 1/3 peat, 1/3 coarse vermiculite and 1/3 sterilized packaged compost – all available in bags from a garden center. The idea is to create a foundation of fluffy soil that has no weed seeds in it, and as you harvest a crop you replenish the space with garden compost to keep it suitable for succession crops.

The cost of Bartholomew's mix restricts it to small space gardening, in my opinion, and of course the commercial bags of peat, vermiculite and packaged compost – even to fill a 4 x 4 ft space - are not cheap. One way to avoid this cost is to sterilize finished compost

Chapter 1 - *The Wizard Guarantees Healthy Results*

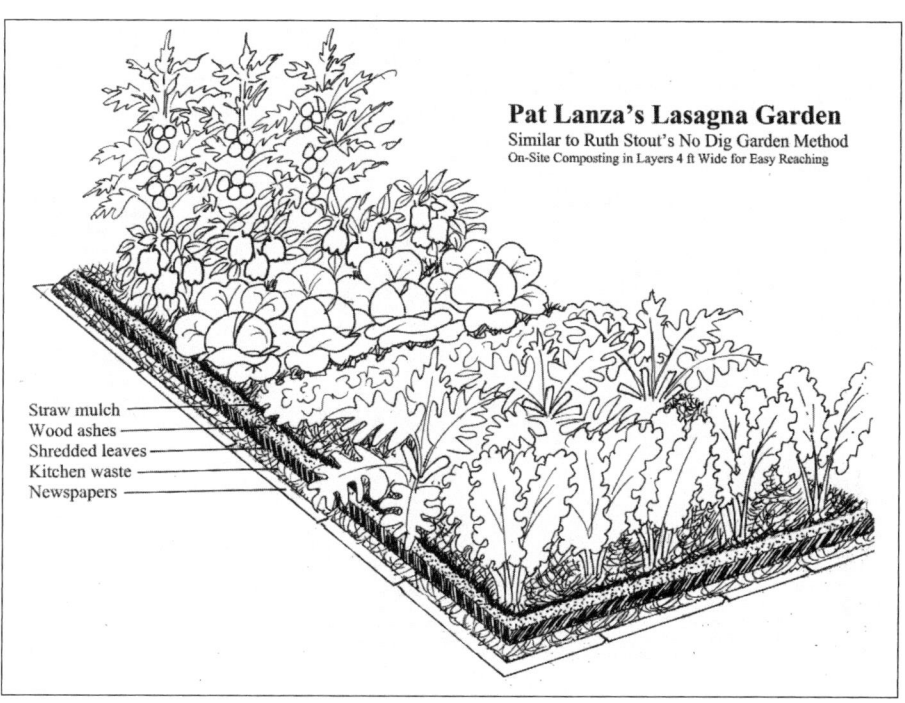

Pat Lanza's Lasagna Garden
Similar to Ruth Stout's No Dig Garden Method
On-Site Composting in Layers 4 ft Wide for Easy Reaching

Straw mulch
Wood ashes
Shredded leaves
Kitchen waste
Newspapers

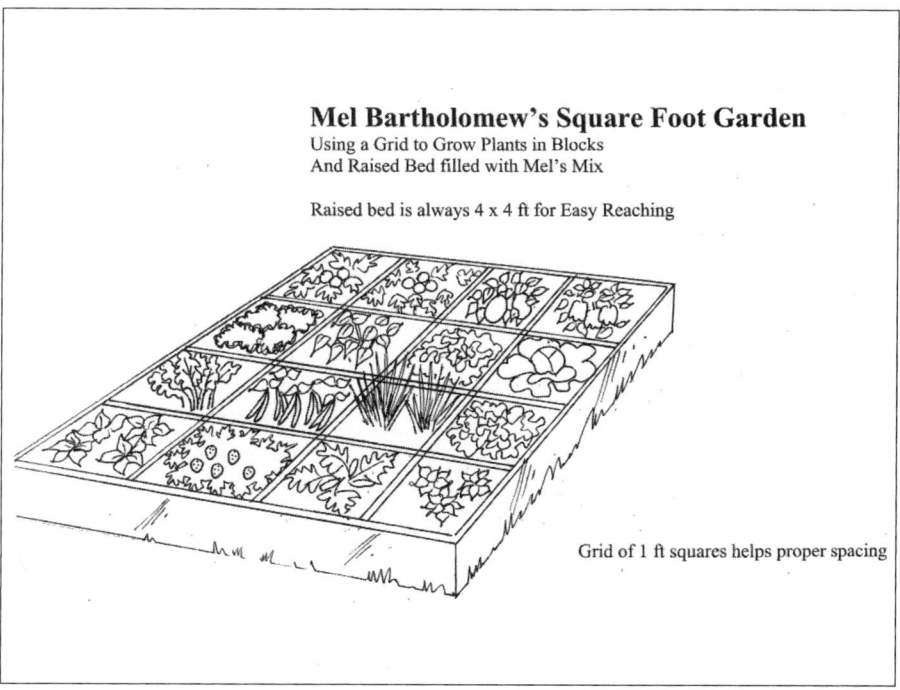

Mel Bartholomew's Square Foot Garden
Using a Grid to Grow Plants in Blocks
And Raised Bed filled with Mel's Mix

Raised bed is always 4 x 4 ft for Easy Reaching

Grid of 1 ft squares helps proper spacing

Square-foot garden on a patio

from your own compost pile by baking it in batches so all weed seeds are killed. This way you can dispense with the peat and the vermiculite.

EDIBLE LANDSCAPING. My good friend Roslyn Creasy brought the concept of edible landscaping into focus with her book of the same title. It shows how to incorporate many vegetable varieties into a home landscape without having a separate plot. For example, vining plants like cucumbers, melons, pole beans and grapes can be grown over a pergola or wooden canopy placed above a deck or patio. Many colorful vegetables like red lettuce, golden chard, bronze kale, and multi-colored peppers can be grown among flower beds, or mixed with flowers in decorative containers. Some vegetables or herbs - like thyme, parsley and bush basil - can be grown as a decorative edging to flower beds.

The largest edible landscape ever created is at the Chateau Villandry, in the Loire Valley of France. Here, the grounds of a castle are laid out in parterres (beds outlined by low boxwood hedges), the interiors planted with a different vegetable variety to create a beautiful pattern. One bed may contain all red-leaf lettuce, another blue kale, another silvery artichokes, another crimson chard, and so on. Because of the decorative appeal of the vegetables, Villandry is one of the most popular tourist destinations in France.

BORING GRASS OR FRESH VEGETABLES? Which would you rather have – a boring lawn to look at and slave over for nothing but good looks or a bountiful vegetable garden where your time and energy can help feed you and your family with healthy vegetables and fruits? A

Chapter 1 - *The Wizard Guarantees Healthy Results*

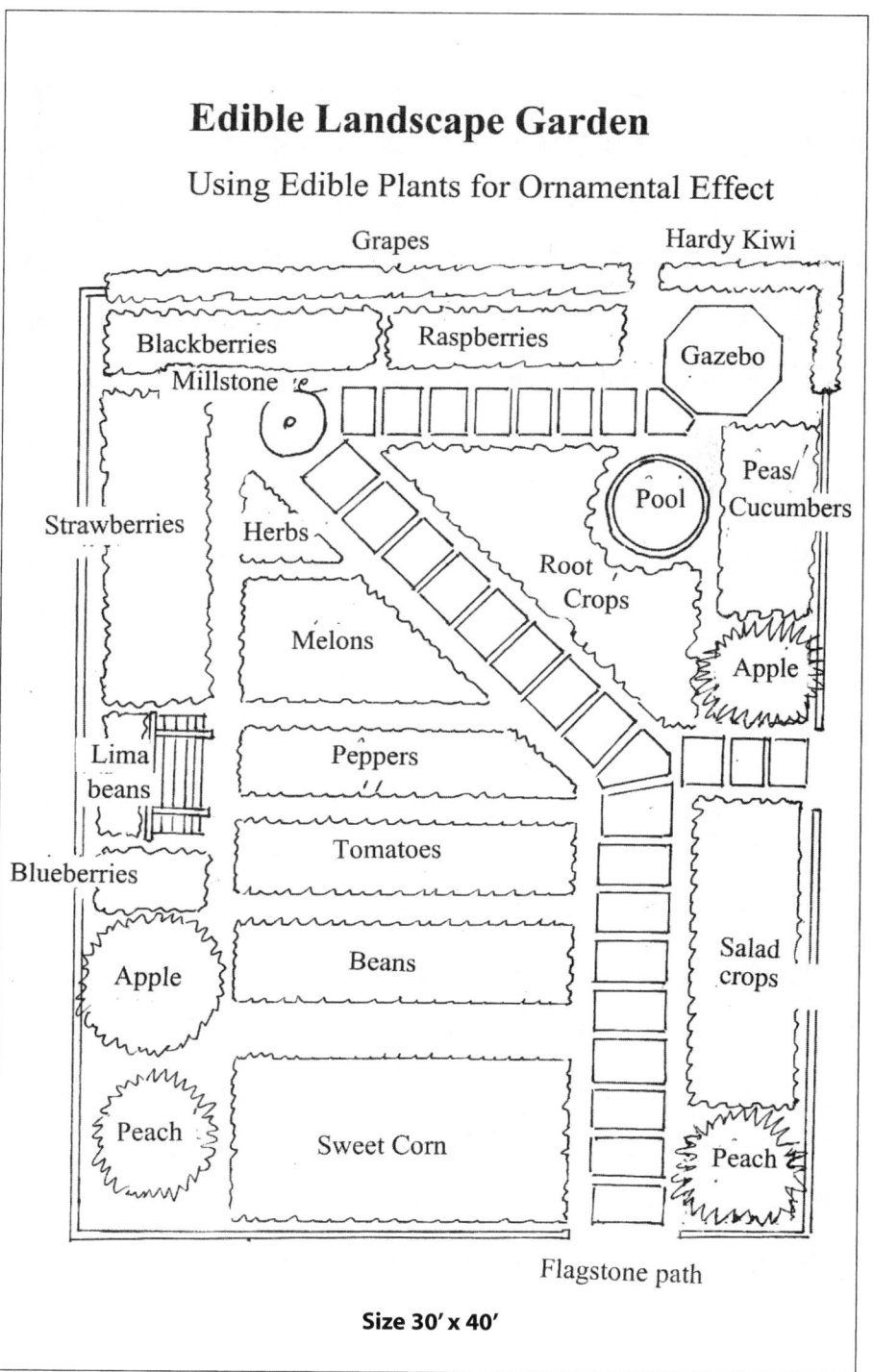

Go from a Bare Lot to a Food Factory

```
        Lawn



    Garage    House

         Path
   Driveway
              Lawn


        Road frontage
```

BEFORE

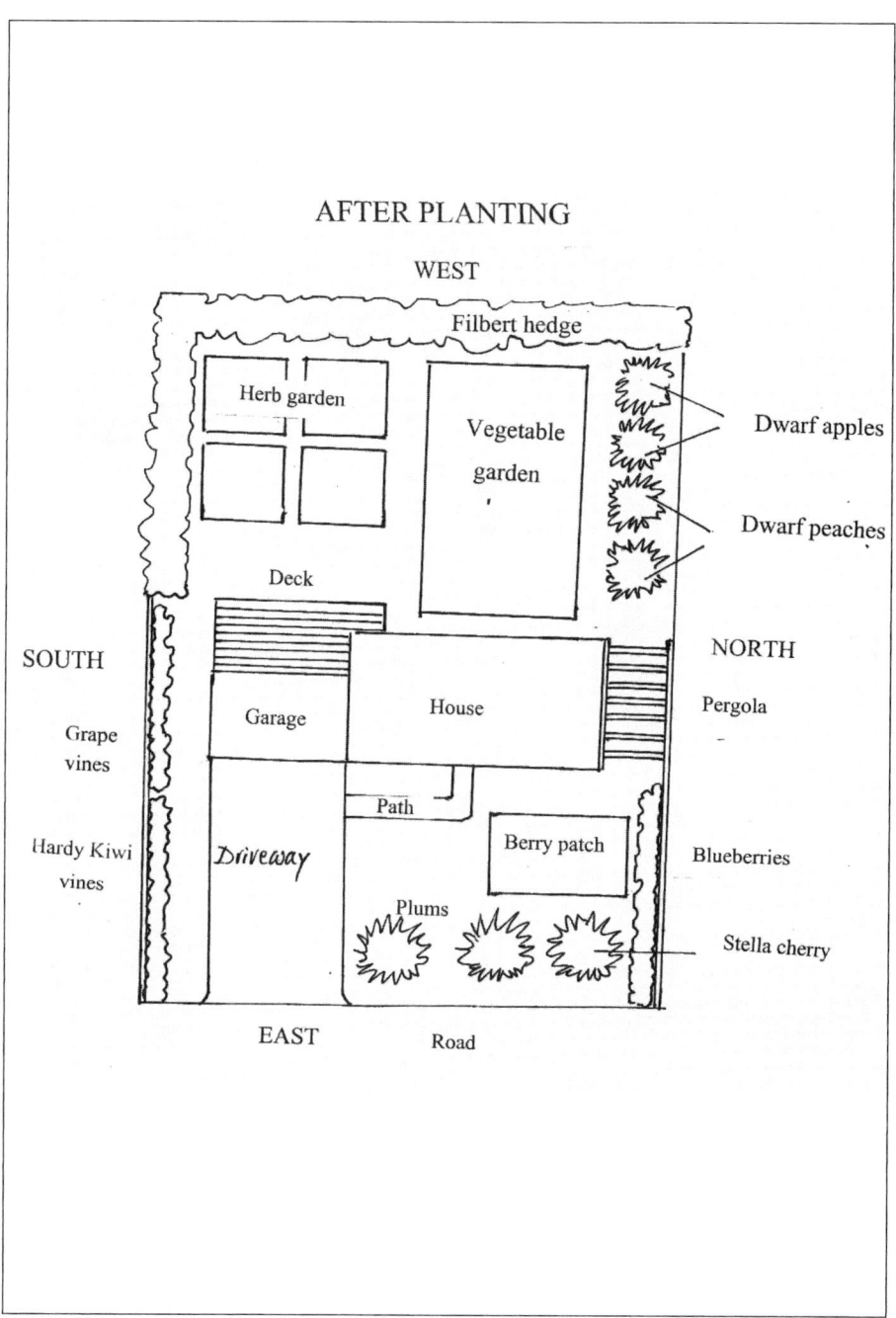

AFTER

Block planting of Buttercrunch lettuce

Lettuce in a quilt pattern to save space

lawn can be one of the most environmentally unfriendly features to have around the house. Think of the time and energy it consumes – mowing twice a week for 6-7 months with a gasoline engine that consumes fossil fuels and spews harmful gas into the atmosphere. Then there is the cost of fertilizer to keep it healthy, irrigation during dry spells to keep it green, weed-killers to keep it weed-free (I don't know of any organic weed-killers for lawns – only harmful chemical ones). Then you must keep it clear of thatch build-up, and contend with a host of potential pests like moles and grubs, plus a host of diseases that can make ugly bare patches. Devote more of your lawn to growing vegetables and the expense will be less, and you will have fresh, flavorful, healthy home-grown produce into the bargain. You don't have to dispense with a lawn completely. Just reduce the lawn area and you and the environment will be healthier for it.

RAISED BEDS. I have two raised beds, divided by a 2 ft. grass path, mostly for growing early salad crops and root vegetables. Soil in raised beds tends to heat up more quickly and you have greater control over its consistency. Each of my raised beds is 6 ft. wide by 24 ft. long, with a wooden divider mid-way along the length. Up-ended 2" x 12 ft wooden boards raise the soil level six inches. This promotes good drainage and allows me to fill the space with a mixture of screened topsoil (to remove stones and weed roots) and compost.

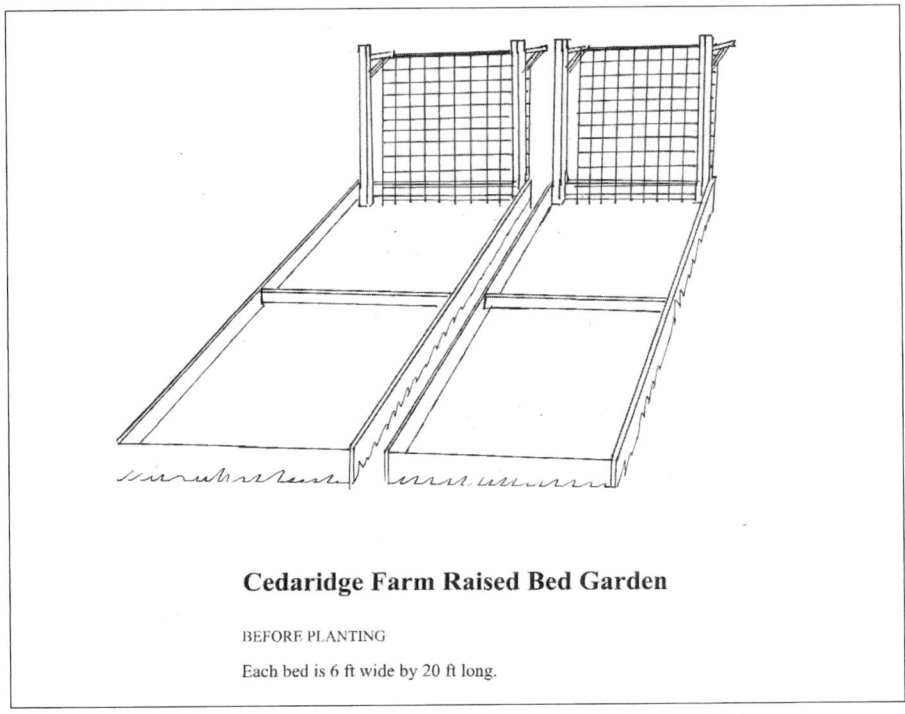

Cedaridge Farm Raised Bed Garden

BEFORE PLANTING

Each bed is 6 ft wide by 20 ft long.

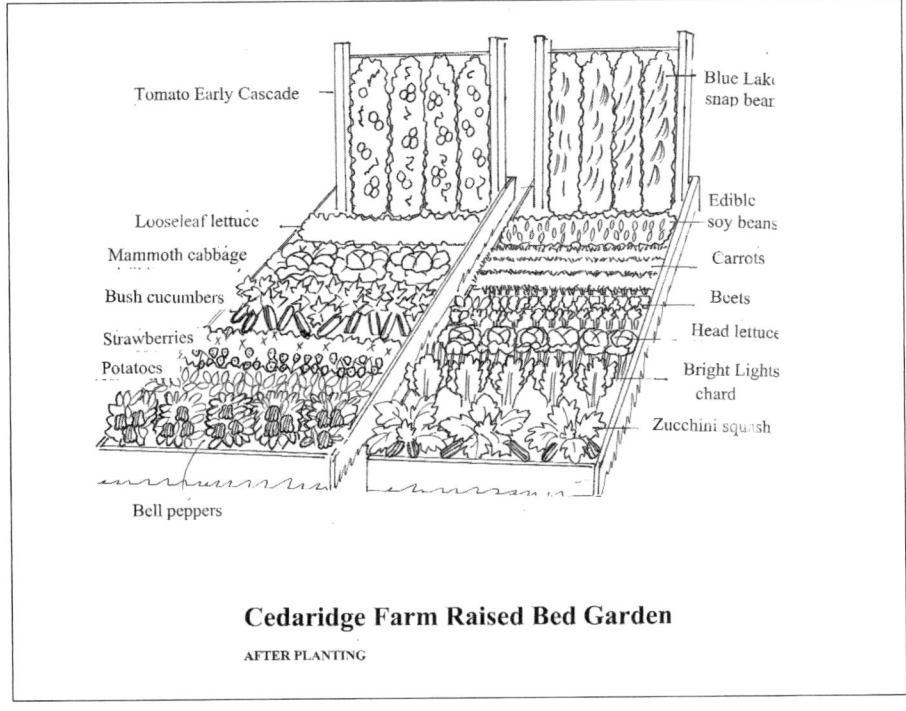

Cedaridge Farm Raised Bed Garden

AFTER PLANTING

Chapter 1 - *The Wizard Guarantees Healthy Results*

Raised bed with lettuce

A question I am often asked is whether to use treated or untreated lumber. I put the question to Huck deVenzio, of Wolmanized wood products, and this is what he advised, paraphrasing his answer:

> "Although studies have shown no harmful effects from using lumber protected with a preservative called CCA (chromate copper arsenate), public concern over the possibility of arsenic poison leaching into the soil caused wood preservative manufacturers to voluntarily switch to different preservatives for residential use. Our Wolmanized brand, for example, uses copper azole preservative consisting of two ingredients – copper (96%), which is sometimes used as a soil amendment and not harmful to mammals, and tebuconazole (4%), an organic fungicide that has been approved for food crops.
>
> "Nearly all the preservative injected into wood stays there. That's why treated lumber lasts so long. For those people who still worry about using treated lumber, we recommend placing a plastic liner between the walls of the raised beds and the soil. The advantage of preserved lumber is labor-saving, by not having to replace it from rapid rotting. Also, a person can use rot-resistant redwood, Western cedar or tropical hardwood."

VERTICAL GARDENS: If you need to save space there's no better solution than growing vertically instead of horizontally. Do the math – if you can grow a 1 ft by 10 ft row of snap beans vertically for a height of 6 ft. that's the equivalent of a 10 x 6 ft row cultivated horizontally, or 60 square feet of garden soil instead of 10 square feet using a vertical system. Not only do vining vegetables produce up to ten times more than a non-vining variety, the plants are generally ever-bearing AND the extra foliage cover from a vine produces better flavors than dwarf plants of the same vegetable. The following vegetables are suitable for growing vertically:

- Beans, Asian winged beans (self-climbing)
- Beans, Asparagus beans, aka Yard-long beans (self-climbing)
- Beans, pole hyacinth (self-climbing)
- Beans, Pole Romano beans (self-climbing)
- Beans, Pole snap beans (self-climbing)
- Beans, Pole lima beans (self-climbing)
- Beans, Pole runner beans (self-climbing)
- Beans, Pole shell beans (self-climbing)
- Chayote (self climbing)
- Cucumbers, climbing slicers (self-climbing)
- Cucumbers, climbing pickle (self-climbing)
- Cucumber, climbing yard long (self-climbing)
- Edible gourd, Chinese okra, aka luffa (self-climbing)
- Edible gourd, Chinese snake (self-climbing)
- Hop vine (self-climbing)
- Malabar climbing spinach (self-climbing)
- New Zealand climbing spinach (self-climbing)
- Melons, Cantaloupe (needs training)
- Melons, Crenshaw (needs training)
- Melons, Honeydews (needs training)
- Pumpkins, Mini (needs training)
- Pumpkins, Pie (needs training)
- Peas, Chinese snow peas (self-climbing)
- Peas, Shell peas (self-climbing)
- Peas, Sugar Snap (self-climbing)
- Summer squash, climbing Trombone zucchini (self-climbing)
- Tomatillo (needs training)
- Tomatoes, determinate (needs training)
- Tomatoes, indeterminate (needs training)
- Tomato-Potato (needs training)
- Watermelons (needs training)
- Winter squash, Acorn (needs training)
- Winter squash, Butternut (needs training)
- Winter squash, Buttercup (needs training)
- Winter squash, Vegetable Spaghetti (needs training)
- Yam, Chinese climbing (self-climbing)

Chapter 1 - *The Wizard Guarantees Healthy Results*

Pole lima bean, King of the Garden

Cucumber, Orient Express

Chapter 1 - *The Wizard Guarantees Healthy Results*

Bean, Pole Romano

Malabar climbing spinach

Pole runner beans and tee-pee support

Many fruits and berries will also grow vertically. Vines like kiwi fruit and grapes will climb unaided, while berry bushes with long canes will require help to climb, such as twist ties to secure the canes upright:

Blackberries (need training)
Grapes, Northern (need training)
Grapes, Southern (need training)
Kiwi vines, New Zealand (self-climbing)
Kiwi vines, Siberian, aka Arctic (self-climbing)

Passion fruit (self-climbing)
Raspberries, Black (need training)
Raspberries, Red (need training)
Raspberries, Yellow (need training)

ESPALIER: Many fruit trees have pliable branches that will allow them to be trained to an upright support or against a wall. This form of training is called espalier. Consider the following for espalier training:

Apples (especially 3-in-1 grafted apples)
Apricots (best planted against a wall to protect from frost)
Cherries (especially 3-in-1 grafted cherries or the self-fruitful Stella)
Figs (Brown Turkey and Black Mission are the hardiest)

Nectarines (best planted against a wall to protect from frost)
Peaches (best planted against a wall to protect from frost)
Pears (especially 3-in-1 grafted pears)
Plums (especially 3-in-1 grafted plums)

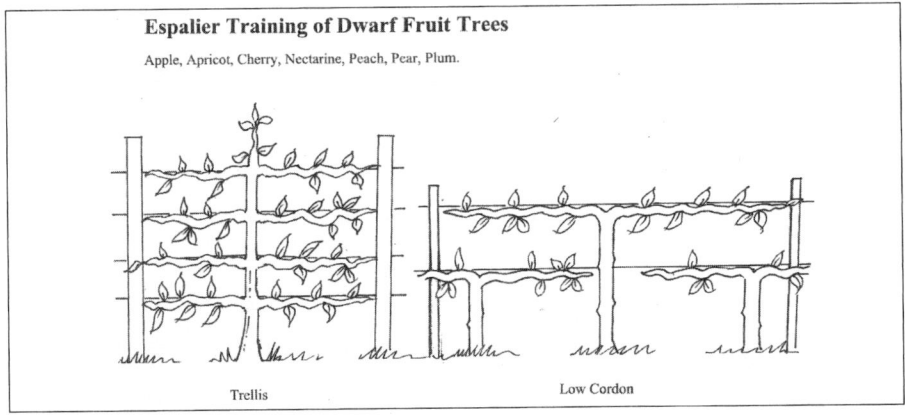

Espalier Training of Dwarf Fruit Trees
Apple, Apricot, Cherry, Nectarine, Peach, Pear, Plum.

Trellis   Low Cordon

Shown here are various designs for growing the above fruit trees. Note that the low-growing design can be used as an edging to a lawn area or vegetable garden. When trained low like this the training is called a Cordon (meaning rope).

TEE-PEE SUPPORTS - There is nothing quite so simple for growing plants skyward than three or more poles arranged in a triangle or circle and secured at the top with string to form a tee-pee. These simple upright structures are ideal for growing pole beans and vining tomatoes.

TENT SUPPORTS - A series of bamboo canes, spaced 18 inches apart, placed parallel along a row of plants can be tilted to the center and secured along its length with a long cross piece to form a rigid tent. This form of support is good for cucumbers, pole beans and tomatoes.

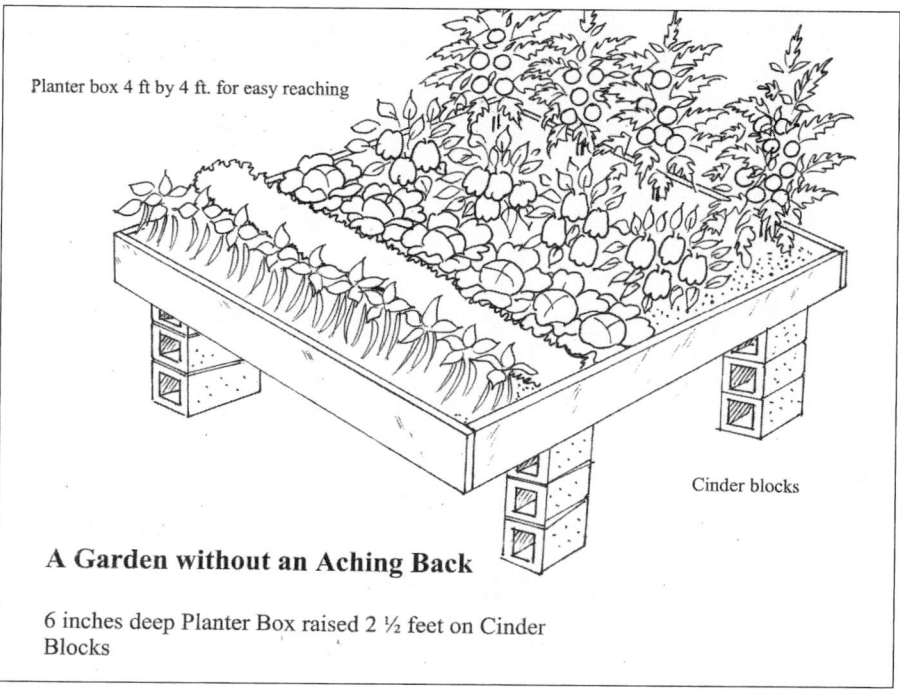

A Garden without an Aching Back

Planter box 4 ft by 4 ft. for easy reaching

Cinder blocks

6 inches deep Planter Box raised 2 ½ feet on Cinder Blocks

TRELLIS - There are numerous commercial trellis units that can be used to grow fruits and vegetables vertically. Mostly they involve either wooden slats in a criss-cross pattern or heavy guage nylon netting. These trellis materials can be used flat against a sunny wall or else secured between posts to make them free-standing. However, quite sturdy supports are possible using straight sections of tree branches (like willow) and also bamboo. Although many varieties of bamboo are tender, there are several hardy varieties that produce long, strong canes. At Cedaridge Farm I have a clump of bamboo positioned close to the vegetable garden for the express purpose of providing canes for support. Also, they are inexpensive when purchased ready-cut from a garden center. I find bamboo trellis especially suitable for growing pea vines.

The simplest bamboo trellis requires a series of uprights hammered into the ground at two foot spacing and more slender, pliable canes used to weave through the uprights to create cross bars, best spaced 12 inches above each other. Although a sturdy trellis is possible simply by weaving the pliable cross pieces through the uprights, you can make the structure more secure by using twist-ties where the canes cross each other.

A single row of upright trellis can also be made from builder's wire stretched between two posts for support. Alternatively, garden netting with 6 inch reach-through mesh is also an inexpensive material for creating a garden trellis.

ARBORS & ARCHES - Some vegetables and fruits are so vigorous they can easily cover an archway or arbor in a single season. Pole beans and edible gourds, for example, are

Tomatoes growing up trellis

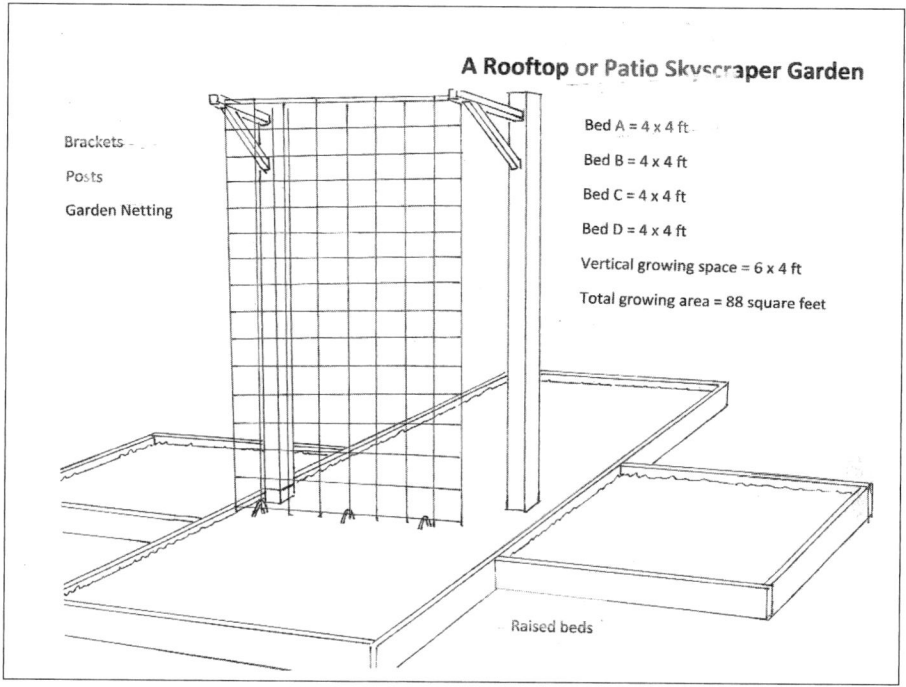

suitable for temporarily covering even a tall, broad span, while grape vines and kiwi vines are ideal as permanent fixtures, since they are hardy perennials. Consider an arbor as a decorative entrance to your vegetable garden.

SKYSCRAPER GARDENS. I have trademarked the name Skyscraper Garden to describe a kit that allows home gardeners to grow plants vertically, since there are many vegetable varieties that will climb. These varieties not only save space by growing UP instead of OUT, they tend to be ever-bearing, as opposed to bush varieties that give a much smaller yield and soon exhaust themselves. Not only is it possible to grow Sugar Snap peas and Blue Lake pole beans up trellis to save space it's possible to grow a variety of climbing spinach that is heat resistant, a climbing zucchini, climbing cucumbers, vining tomatoes, even mini pumpkins and small winter squash. My kit can be used against a wall or it can be made free-standing through the use of a pair of cedar brackets, a 4 x 6 ft. section of nylon netting, a metal cross bar to hang the netting from and three metal pegs to hold the netting taught to the ground. Visit Skyscraper Garden.com for more information.

GARDEN WITHOUT AN ACHING BACK. If you do not like bending in order to care for your garden space, consider raising it up 2 ft. off the ground. This is possible by making a wooden frame 4 ft. by 4 ft. and 6 inches deep, fitting it with a plywood bottom and drilling holes 12 inches apart for drainage. You then raise the entire bed up off the ground on cinder blocks and fill it with soil. This amount of elevation allows you to stand and work at the

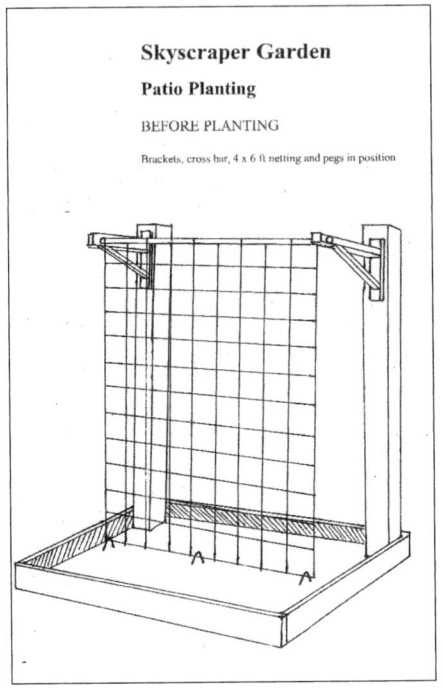 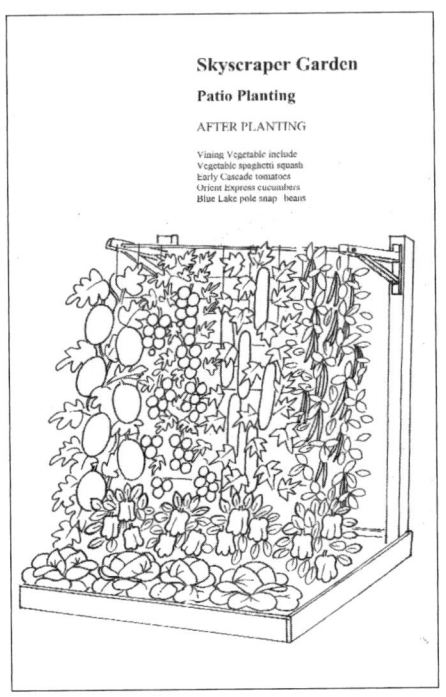

garden or sit at it. Even people confined to a wheelchair will be able to work at the garden, the 4 ft. square shape small enough for arms to reach into the middle. Of course the depth can be more than 6 inches, but 6 inches is considered the minimum for most common vegetables.

FOUNDATION PLANTINGS. The sunny side of a house is a great place to plant a small-space, easy care vegetable garden. Although a foundation planting is usually a narrow strip against a wall, a big return can be expected because:

1. Reflected light and heat from the wall will help plants grow and produce heavy yields earlier than vegetables out in the open.
2. The wall can provide heat from the house for vegetables planted early to escape frost damage.
3. The wall can be used to provide support for a trellis or Skyscraper Garden (see page 27).
4. The apron of soil in front of the trellis can grow low-growing vegetables such as peppers, cabbage and lettuce.
5. It's easy to run a soaker hose along the house foundation to water plantings at the turn of a water faucet.

Avoid planting along a shady wall and on the north side of a house. The south and east are especially good sites as full sun and morning sun are better for plants than afternoon sun.

Just be sure that the soil along the house foundation is not toxic or heavily alkaline since builder's debris is often left to lie along a house foundation. Consider raising the soil level by creating a raised bed with wooden boards up-ended.

If a window is positioned above the foundation, consider placing a window box along the ledge for growing herbs and mini-vegetables like Tom Thumb lettuce.

SEASONAL DIFFERENCES. Over much of North America there are four distinct seasons. Spring and fall can be cool and pleasant with abundant rainfall, suitable for growing cool-season vegetables like lettuce, spinach, peas and broccoli. Summer can be hot and humid with rainfall mostly the result of thunderstorms, and sometimes several weeks with little or no rainfall. Hot, sunny summers are perfect for growing warm season vegetables like tomatoes, peppers and sweet corn. Winter can be cold with snow cover in many areas and the ground frozen solid for a month or more. But even during winter months it's possible to grow some hardy vegetable varieties so that fresh vegetables are possible year round.

WINTER VEGETABLES. Writer Henry van Dyke wrote that "Weather means more when you have a garden. There's nothing like listening to a shower and thinking how it is soaking in around your lettuce and green beans." Fall and winter months usually produce abundant rainfall to drench the soil and encourage crisp, succulent nutritious flavors in hardy vegetable varieties like Brussels sprouts, Swiss chard, kale and parsley. I often wake up in the morning to a fresh fall of snow, pull on some rubber boots and a bathrobe to investigate the vegetable garden. There I will shake off the crisp, cold snow from plastic row covers that provide just enough protection from cold for a wealth of green treasure.

Brussels sprouts are members of the cabbage family that produce hard golf-ball size sprouts along a tall stalk. After frost, pinch out the growing tip to allow the top buds to fatten up. Their flavor improves after a frost.

Carrots can stay in the ground even after frost for harvesting during winter months. To prevent the ground freezing, place straw bales over the row or make a plastic tunnel.

Chard used to come in just two colors (red and white), but today you can purchase mixtures that contain yellow, orange, pink, apricot and bi-colored stalks. The leafy part of the stalk is a tasty substitute for spinach, while the crisp stalk can be braised like celery. It's hardy and will remain healthy even after severe frosts.

Kale is a type of cabbage that doesn't form a head. The leaves are tasty as a cooked green, and several varieties will survive freezing cold, including serrated Russian bronze-leaf, curly Scots blue leaf and Japanese mizuna that displays sweet, green, indented fan-shaped leaves.

Leeks are a hardy onion that grows an elongated white stalk and a cascade of edible green leaves that can serve as a substitute for chives. The stalks are sweet and tender when cooked and the plants can remain in the ground until the ground freezes.

Parsnips are a hardy root vegetable (even hardier than carrots). The long, white tapered roots can stay in the ground over winter. The only problem is pulling them from the soil when it has frozen. To prevent freezing make a plastic tunnel or place straw bales over the row.

I'll Make You a Gardening Wizard Overnight!

Parsley, Curly leaf... Parsley is a hardy biennial that can survive severe freezing.

Spinach is best sown in September to make a mature crown of tasty green leaves before cold weather arrests its growth. The luscious green leaves can survive even severe frosts and snow, especially with a mulch of straw or a clear plastic tunnel.

Rutabaga is a large root vegetable also called swede. It is related to turnips and has a flavor similar to a turnip, but hardier. It can be left in the ground and covered with bales of straw or plastic tunnels to prevent the ground from freezing rock solid.

Watercress At Cedaridge Farm I have a clear running stream where watercress grows year round in a sandy/gravel soil even in mid-winter. Watercress is a tasty, nutritious salad green with a zesty flavor eaten fresh. It also makes a fine soup simply chopped fine and blended with potato and onion.

SUCCESSION PLANTING. To get maximum yield from garden space, consider succession planting. This involves clearing an early crop from the garden, like spinach and planting the space with a different vegetable family, like cucumbers for a summer harvest. Even three crops are possible in the same space since a crop of cucumbers can be cleared after harvesting and space replanted with a fall and winter crop, such as kale and chard. Before each succession planting I like to cultivate the soil with a hoe, add more compost, mix it in and drench the soil with an organic liquid fertilizer like fish emulsion.

INTERCROPPING is the planting of two vegetables (usually an early variety and a late variety) in the same row. For example, a bed of lettuce can be interplanted with tomatoes, the lettuce to be harvested before the tomatoes have started to branch out and form fruit. Intercropping is particularly space-saving for certain herbs. For example a row of chard can be edged with parsley, the parsley not interfering with the growth of the chard even though they are planted shoulder-to-shoulder.

MICROCLIMATES. Walk around your property after snowfall and see where the snow melts first. That will indicate a micro-climate where warm season crops like tomatoes might do better than a cool season crop like lettuce. On frosty mornings observe where the frost lingers longest. Low spots can be frost pockets where the soil will stay cool longer than the surrounding area.

Swiss chard, Bright Lights

A plot that runs parallel to a wall of your house can benefit from the house heat, allowing an earlier planting and frost protection.

Large bodies of water can have a profound effect on first and last frost dates. I am about two miles inland from the Delaware River, while a friend upstream has his garden right next to it. In spring he can plant two weeks earlier than I can, and in fall his first expected frost date is generally two weeks later. Moreover, an early morning mist from the river can provide his garden with moisture, whereas I am beyond the fog belt and will remain high and dry.

Carolyn's Comments:

"I recall helping Derek make a pair of raised beds when we first established our vegetable garden. We realized that certain vegetables, such as Scarlet Nantes carrots, Cylindra beets, radishes and turnips do best in a deep, crumbly soil and so we selected a level site and sifted topsoil through a screen to remove all kinds of debris, from stones and tough weed roots to buried metal horseshoes and broken bottles. We also added sand so carrots could penetrate the soil even more easily and produce perfectly straight roots. We are especially fond of carrots, not only as raw snacks and a cooked vegetable, but for making carrot juice. It's very easy when you have a juicer because after the carrots are peeled and the tops removed, they can go straight into the juicer. No sweetener is needed since organically grown carrots are already sugary-sweet. These raised beds require no digging – simply a blanket of compost in spring and fall raked into the upper soil surface. One spring we received a visit from HGTV and we had the raised beds filled with a special trial planting of many different lettuce varieties for evaluation. In addition to green looseleaf, cos and head lettuces we had red, pink, yellow, speckled, deer tongue, oak leaf and frilly leaf kinds. There wasn't a blemish on any of them, the tapestry of color looked spectacular on television and we have since received visits from other television stations, interviewing us about our success.

Derek's discussion about micro-climates reminds me of a trip we took to the Island of Tresco, in the Scilly Isles, off the south-west coast of England. Tresco has an amazing micro-climate, bathed in sunshine when the mainland is being deluged with rain, and no frost when the rest of Britain is in the deep freeze. There are no cars allowed on the island, and at its heart is a beautiful sub-tropical garden where banana trees, Canary Island date palms and Australian tree ferns flourish outdoors. In late June – the best month to visit – South African daisies and blue agapanthus bloom riotously along the waysides. The island has rental cottages and a fine hotel, the Tresco Island Hotel, with cliff walks to powdery beaches safe for swimming, and meadows of wildflowers. The views from the dining room of rocky islands thronged with seabirds is spectacular and the menu superb, using mostly local food products, including delicious black figs and kiwi fruit gathered from the garden. Derek has written twice about Tresco for Architectural Digest magazine, and we became friends with the Robert Dorrian-Smiths, owners of the fabulous garden. One evening we were invited to dinner at their home, the historic Abbey House and we were picked up at the hotel by a tractor driver pulling a jitney. There was a full moon and a cloudless star-filled night sky, and the two-mile drive along the shore-line to the cobblestone courtyard under the massive arching branches of Monterey cypress trees was unforgettably romantic. Every couple at some time in their lives should visit Tresco for rest and recuperation. Although there is a ferry service from Penzanze, there is a much faster helicopter service that lands at the entrance to the garden, a short walk from the hotel."

CHAPTER 2
The White House Vegetable Gardens

"When the Ford White House wanted to plant a vegetable garden as a means to fight inflation, the USDA resisted the idea. They wanted the farmer feeding America."
– from my article The White House Vegetable Garden, **Nouveau** magazine

The two most recent administrations to announce plans for a vegetable garden at the White House are the Ford Administration and the Obama Administration. They were designed for quite different reasons. The Ford Vegetable Garden was planned as a means to win the war against inflation, and the idea of planting a vegetable garden was delivered in Ford's famous WIN speech. The Obama Vegetable Garden was planned for health reasons. The First Lady, Michelle Obama wanted to have chemical free fresh vegetables to feed her family since she had seen that a diet rich in vegetables helped her children maintain a healthy weight. Jimmy Carter, who followed President Gerald Ford, was urged to plant a vegetable garden because inflation was still a problem, but Carter considered himself a farmer rather than a gardener. He wanted to maintain that 'farmer' image, and so his vice president Walter Mondale agreed to plant a vegetable garden at his residence and thereby set a good example.

THE MICHELLE OBAMA WHITE HOUSE VEGETABLE GARDEN

It was on Friday, March 20 2009 that Michelle Obama called a press conference on the White House lawn and announced she wanted to plant a vegetable garden for health reasons. The previous month, on February 28 2009 I wrote the following letter to Michelle Obama through her social secretary, Desiree Rogers.

Dear Ms. Rogers:
I am a garden writer and author of more than 84 publications on gardening and I published the best-selling "Vegetables – How to Select, Grow & Enjoy" which received a best book award from the Garden Writers Association.
I am sure you have received a large number of requests for you and the President to plant a vegetable garden at the White House as an example of how people can eat healthy and fight the recession
I have designed a vegetable garden that I would like the First Lady to consider for her children to plant . The Park Service – responsible for the White House grounds – could care for the garden as one of their duties, and the children could be involved by

I'll Make You a Gardening Wizard Overnight!

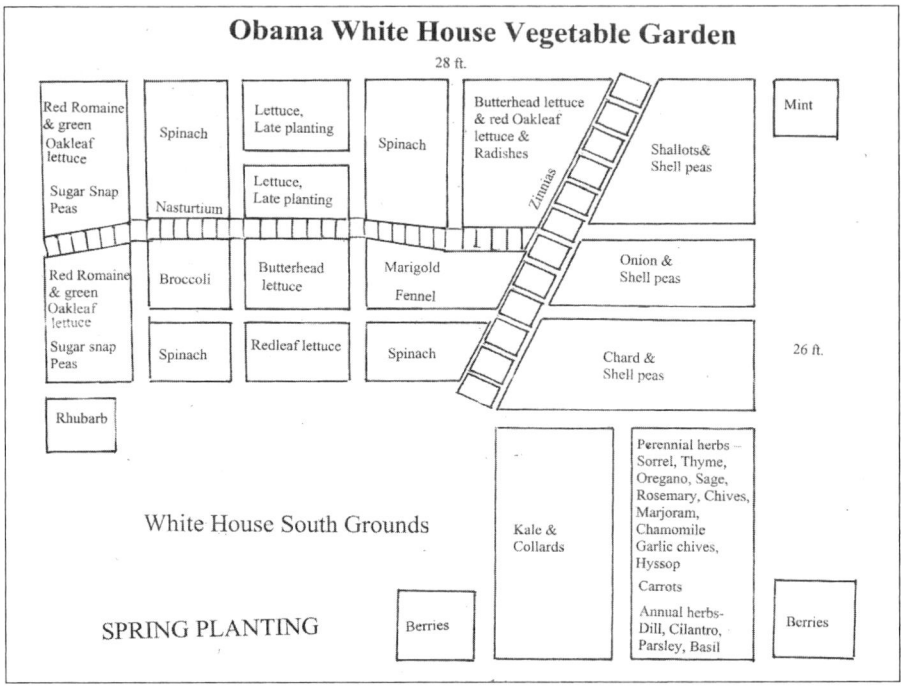

helping to plant seeds in a prepared plot, perhaps watering and nurturing the garden, and then harvesting the results.

It is known that 21% more American households will start a vegetable garden in 2009. Google searches for gardening information have almost doubled. Mental and physical fitness, good nutrition, teaching self-help and many other benefits are attributed to vegetable gardening.

The enclosed plan is capable of nearly $1,000.00 worth of fresh vegetables. It can be modified to suit the children's desires.

Very sincerely, etc.

Three weeks after my letter, the First Lady chose a sunny spot on the Front Lawn and announced that the White House would be planting a vegetable garden, aided by 23 fifth-graders from the local Bancroft Elementary School. Sam Kass, a White House chef was given overall responsibility for the garden, aided by Dale Haney, White House groundskeeper and his crew employed by the National Parks Service. All were on hand to help with the ground breaking, and a planting plan was subsequently released. Occupying 1,100 square feet, to grow 55 vegetable varieties, it is too big for the average beginner gardener to handle, but even so I was surprised to see how the selection of vegetables and planting plan was well thought out. In addition to vegetables (even rhubarb and arugula salad greens) it included herbs, and berry plants such as blueberries, raspberries and strawberries.

Chapter 2 - *The White House Vegetable Gardens*

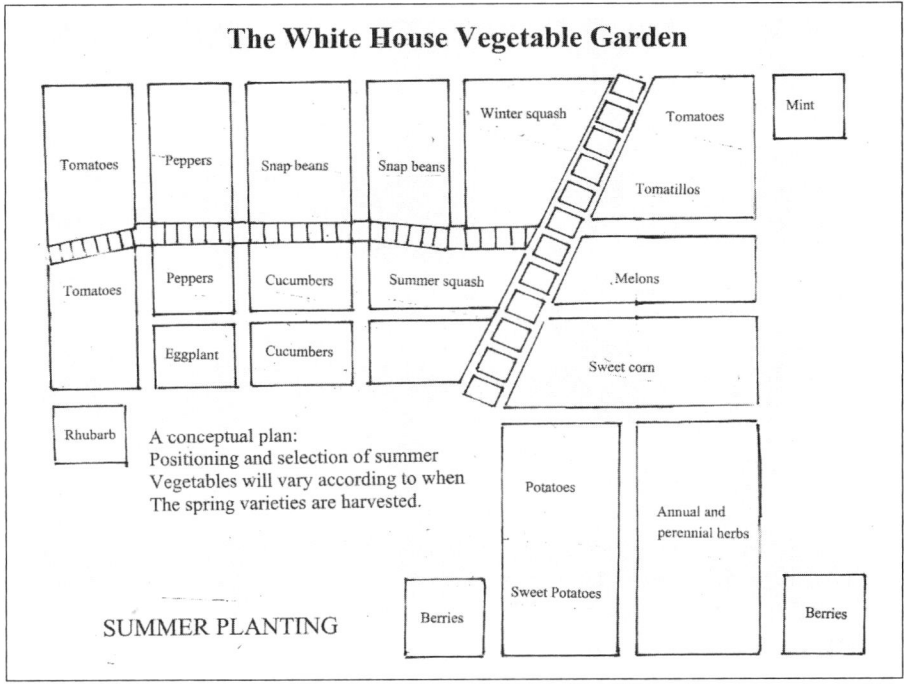

Mrs. Obama announced that her principal reason for approving the vegetable garden was to educate her children about the importance of fresh, flavorful food – key to fighting malnutrition, obesity and diabetes in America. The Obama vegetable plan, shown here, is composed of various plots divided by paths and raised above the indigenous soil surface for extra drainage and soil depth. Varieties shown in the planting plan are cool season crops only. As the cool season crops (like lettuce and sugar snap peas) are harvested they are followed by a succession crop of warm season vegetables, such as tomatoes, peppers and squash.

Ladybugs to control aphids, praying mantis to control Japanese beetles and other insect pests, were used as a means of organic pest control. Compost, crab meal (ricl. in phosphorus) from the Chesapeake Bay, and greensand (high in phosphorus and calcium) were used as organic fertilizers.

At the ground breaking the First Lady announced to the attendant reporters that she had decided to plant a vegetable garden at the White House even before her family moved in. And though my letter was one of many the White House received, encouraging the planting, I think perhaps my advice to make it a children's garden helped make it a reality.

THE PRESIDENT FORD WHITE HOUSE VEGETABLE GARDEN

What especially pleased me about the Obama garden was its similarity to a vegetable garden I designed for the Ford Administration when President Ford wanted a vegetable garden at the White House. That was in 1974 when Ford decided that planting vegetables could help win the fight against inflation.

My planting plan for President Ford was much smaller than the Obama plot, and I was invited to Washington to plant it after my plan appeared in the Sunday edition of the Washington Post. I was subsequently appointed to chair an action committee which met several times at the White House. Once our recommendations were approved I met with several people who would be responsible for the day-to-day maintenance of the garden, and the White House announced its intentions in a letter to me on White House letterhead. Unfortunately, that garden was never planted, because by the time planting time arrived, Ford had his hands full bringing the Vietnam War to a conclusion, and the planting of a vegetable garden was by then seen as a low priority.

Every major initiative considered by the White House – whether it is a decision to go to war or whether to promote home vegetable gardening - requires an authoritative person to write a position paper, looking at the proposal from all angles and reaching a conclusion concerning the merits of the case and potential side effects.

At the time of the Ford Administration – while I was involved in writing a position paper for the White House about the benefits to the country of vegetable gardening - I invited George Gallup Jr. to speak before the American Seed Trade Association at the Fairmont-Roosevelt Hotel, in New Orleans. The president of the Gallup Organization, a national polling company, Gallup revealed that 30,000,000 more people in America would garden if they had the land, and among those 18,000,000 more would garden if the land was available to them in the form of community gardens (for more about starting a community garden, see page 183).

Gallup announced other findings from his National Garden Survey – that there were five main reasons for an increased interest in vegetable gardening. They were (1) - A desire to save energy and spend more time at home; (2) - a desire among Americans to save money by growing their own food; (3) - A desire among many individuals (especially young people) to be closer to nature, see more greenery, and get involved in working the soil.; (4) - Health. "Americans are on a fitness kick," he said. "They are turning to gardening for healthier food and exercise."; (5) - Americans have extra time. That extra time allows them to consider starting a new hobby like gardening.

Carolyn's Comments:

> "I was working in Washington as a congressional aide when Derek began working at the White House as a consultant on vegetable gardening. Our paths didn't cross until twenty years later after I had switched to a career in fashion and had a cutting garden at a farm I owned in upstate New York. We met at a tree trimming party at Christmas so he likes to tell people that he found me under a Christmas tree. We had both been previously married, and after three years of living together we decided to get married. We were both widely travelled, and wanted a quiet wedding somewhere neither of us had been. We totaled our air miles and discovered we could fly to New Zealand. Derek called the New Zealand embassy and they confirmed we could be married there without much fuss, so we traded our old wedding rings for a new ring for me, and after landing at Auckland airport, rented a car and drove straight to the down-town registry office to see when we could be married. We were told to return in three days after the paperwork had been processed. The ceremony took place in a chapel above the registry office, and we

enlisted two students applying for passports to be our witnesses. We had a wedding lunch in the Domain Botanical Garden, feasting on lobster tails. Back at the hotel I called my mother to say we were married and Derek wrote his mother a postcard. A New Zealand garden writer who lived on a sheep farm on the slopes of an extinct volcano gave us some contacts, and we then spent three blissful weeks touring New Zealand gardens. We made many friends among the garden owners and Derek eventually published a beautiful full color book titled The Great Gardens of New Zealand (David Bateman Ltd), for which he won a best book award from the Garden Writers Association."

I'll Make You a Gardening Wizard Overnight!

CHAPTER 3
Getting Started with the Best Deals on Tools

"Good gardeners never die. They just spade away."
– *from my murder mystery novel,* **Dieback**

The right tools can make gardening pure pleasure. In spite of owning 20 acres I don't even own a tractor. A lot of my tools have not been purchased new from stores, but acquired inexpensively from garage sales, goodwill stores and auctions. For years I got by with cultivating my vegetable and flower gardens with basically a spade, a rake and a trowel. Now, with five acres of test gardens to maintain, my arsenal has grown considerably. Here's what I have found valuable:

SPADE. If I could have only one garden tool it would be a spade, especially the kind called a shovel that has a scooped blade and a pointed end for easily penetrating soil. Of course, there are advocates of NO DIG gardening systems (like in-situ composting) that tell you to "Throw away your spade", but for me there is something soul satisfying about biting into soil, turning it over, raking it smooth and using a hand trowel to set seeds or transplants into position. But now one spade is not enough. I have a second spade with a flat blade for edging beds and levering up sod and a manure spade that is fashioned like a large scoop for shoveling not only manure and compost but also sand and piles of mulch material such as wood chips.

RAKE. I use a long handled rake to level newly dug soil. The curved tines are good for breaking up large lumps into smaller lumps, and the back of the rake is then used to break these up into finer particles and to make a level, smooth surface for planting. I use a leaf rake with finer tines and a fan shape to rake up glass clippings and leaves onto a tarp for dumping on my compost pile.

TROWEL. I'm forever losing my trowels so I may have a dozen at one time. With a hand trowel I dig up weeds, make furrows for seeds and set transplants into position. Cheap trowels are a waste of money. They often bend at the neck when prying up a tough weed root or digging up a stone.

WHEELBARROW. I have a metal wheelbarrow with a rubber tire and prefer it to a garden cart. Although a garden cart will hold more than a wheelbarrow, and it is especially good for carting leaves and straw bales in the fall, a wheelbarrow is more maneuverable. There's also a tendency to overload a cart and strain yourself.

BACK-PACK SPRAYER. A 3-4 gallon capacity back-pack sprayer has been a big labor saver. I not only have a preference for organic liquid fertilizer like kelp concentrate, I sometimes use an organic garlic/pepper spray against insects and an organic deer repellent, Liquid Fence, to cover ornamentals and shrubs. With the back-pack sprayer I can cover three acres of my garden in an hour, spraying susceptible plants like garden tulips, garden lilies, day lilies and hostas. Cedaridge Farm adjoins a state park, we have deer in the garden every night, and I couldn't have any flower displays without it.

GARDEN HOSE. A rubber hose with a trigger nozzle are essential to water in plants and provide irrigation during dry spells. The trigger nozzle allows you to go from a powerful jet to a fine spray with fingertip control. I also like to sometimes attach a watering wand to the end of a garden hose in order to probe the end between foliage so vegetables are watered directly at the root zone, especially in containers such as window box planters and hanging baskets.

SPRINKLER. Although I use soaker hoses to water my main vegetable plots, I sometimes need to apply water to areas of the vegetable garden without it (such as my raised beds.) For this purpose I use a common lawn sprinkler with an oscillating head.

SEEDS. There really isn't a better way to grow plants from seed than to buy them in a packet. A packet of lettuce can cost less than a dollar and provides 500 or more seeds with a germination of 95%. For a list of mail order seed companies see the appendix under sources. Many people have tried to improve over the traditional seed packet, but they are mostly gimmicks that seem good at first glance, but prove to be inefficient. Seed tapes, for example, are promoted as a labor saving way to sow seeds, but the tape buckles when you try to apply it, and you still have to bury the tape. Moreover if it gets wet from dew it becomes sticky like flypaper. Nor do I want my seeds pre-spaced because there are bound to be gaps.

Then there are pelleted seeds. I know many growers like to sow pelleted seed for fine seeded vegetables like carrots and lettuce, because it allows them to use a mechanical seed drill. But the average home gardener doesn't use a drill and doesn't mind handling fine seed to save cost. Some seed is coated with a fungicide – like peas, beans and corn – to encourage a higher germination. But again, the home gardener is not likely to plant an acre or more like many farmers. The home gardener can ensure a high germination by pre-germinating the seed in a moist paper towel and planting the sprouted seed for accurate spacing.

There is a good reason to coat some seeds with a nitrogen fixing agent called an innoculant. Legumes like peas and beans need nitrogen to grow their best and the innoculant will help nitrogen fixing bacteria attach themselves to the roots. It's a black powder that looks like soot and you simply ensure that your peas and beans are coated with it before planting.

PLANNING YOUR GARDEN BUDGET

The following list is based on an average price for garden supplies available from home and garden stores such as Lowe's. Look for many of these items at garage sales for substantial savings. Also consider substituting some of the seed starting supplies with discarded containers used for packaging foods (see Chapter 5).

TOOL
Hand trowel 1.99
Hand fork. 3.97
Garden shovel. 14.98
Garden hoe 9.98
Garden rake. 9.48
Garden fork. 24.98

IRRIGATION
Watering can (2 gallon) 5.48
Garden hose (100 ft) 38.97
Spray nozzle 5.97
Sprinkler 14.98
Soaker hose (30 meters). 50.00

SEEDS & TRANSPLANTS
Seed packets. 1.25
Large transplants (per pot). 2.48
Small transplants (6-packs) 2.48
Tubers & sets. 6.98

PLANT POTS
Plastic pot (8 in). 2.94
Plastic pot (10 in). 4.98
Plastic pot (12 in). 8.97
Plastic pot (20 in). 17.98
Window box planter 7.98
Peat starter pots (set of 22) 1.98
Spray bottle. 2.48
22 comp. tray with clear cover 6.97

SOIL
Bag of potting mix. 6.77
Top soil per yard. 30.00
Sphagnum for baskets – 8 qut 3.97
Vermiculite – 8 qut 3.97
Perlite – 8 qut 3.97

SOIL AMENDMENTS
Organic cow manure (40 lbs) 2.45
Organic fertilizer (12-12-12) 17.94
Organic bone meal (26 lbs) 24.98
Peat moss (2 cu ft) 9.47
Lime (6 lbs) 6.98

MULCH
Bag of cedar bark (2 cu ft) 3.20
Straw bales per bale 4.00

MISCELLANEOUS ASSESSORIES
Garden gloves. 2.98
Plant labels 6.77
Wheelbarrow (6 cu ft). 49.98
Bucket (5 gallon) 2.34
Soil test (lab report) 10.00
Twine 2.78
Bamboo stakes (4ft) 1.98
Bamboo stakes (6 ft) 22.46
Outdoor compost bin 50.00

The above list and prices are based on a chart provided by the Green Education Foundation, a non profit group that provides manuals for garden instruction to schools.

HUGE SAVINGS OVER STORE-BOUGHT VEGETABLES. During my last visit to a major supermarket store specializing in fresh vegetables, I recorded these prices for the most common vegetables:

Apple, Granny Smith - $1.69 lb
Artichokes – 2 for $5.00
Arugula - $1.99 a bunch
Green beans - $1.69 lb
Soybeans - $7.98 lb
Golden beets - $2.99 bunch of four roots
Red beets - $1.99 bunch of 5 roots
Bok choy - $2.99 lb
Blueberries - $5.00 for 12 ozs
Broccoli - $1.49 lb
Brussels sprouts - $2.39 lb
Cabbage – 69¢ lb
Cantaloupe – $2.99 each
Carrots – 99¢ lb
Cauliflower – $1.49 lb
Celery - $1.99 a bunch
Cilantro - $1.99 a bunch
Collards - $1.99 a bunch
Cucumbers – 99¢ each
Eggplant - $2.49 lb
Grapes, seedless - $2.49 lb
Fennel - $1.99 lb
Head lettuce - $1.49 each
Romaine lettuce - $1.99 each
Okra - $1.99 lb
Mustard greens - $1.99 a bunch

Parsnips – 2 for $5.00
Pear, Bosc - $1.49 lb
Green peppers - $3.49 for 2
Red peppers - $5.49 for 2
Hot peppers - $3.99 lb
Parsley - $1.99 a bunch
Parsley root - $4.99 for 6 roots
Potato Yukon Gold - $1.29 lb
Pumpkin - $5.00 for two small sugar sizes
Radish - $1.29 bunch of 10 roots
Raspberries - $4.89 for 12 ozs
Radicchio - $3.99 lb
Spinach - $1.69 lb
Squash, Zucchini - $2.49 lb
Strawberries - $3.99 lb
Sugar snap peas - $3.99 lb
Sweet potato - $1.69 lb
Swiss chard - $2.49 bunch
Heirloom tomatoes - $3.99 lb
Beefsteak tomatoes - $2.49 lb
Cluster tomatoes - $3.49 lb
Turnips - 99¢ lb
Turnip greens - $1.99 a bunch
Vegetable spaghetti - $1.99 lb (4 lbs weight)
Watercress - $1.99 a bunch
Watermelon - $3.49 each (ice-box size)

OVER $2,000.00 FROM A 10 X 20 FT PLOT. Using the above figures, compare the production from a 10 by 20 ft plot. Using the plan on page 45, I estimate the following yields from a spring harvest, based on optimum growing conditions:

Row 1 - Sugar Snap peas (10 lbs) - $39.90

Row 2 - Romaine lettuce (15 heads) - $29.85

Row 3 - Head lettuce (20 heads) - $29.80

Row 4 - Early cabbage (10 heads) - $20.70

Row 5 - Arugula (10 bunches) – $19.90

Row 6 - Turnips (80 roots) plus greens (20 bunches) - $59.60

Row 7 - Broccoli (10 heads) – $37.25

Row 8 - Cauliflower (10 heads)- $44.70

Row 9 - Golden beets (80 roots) - $59.80

Row 10 - Parsley (5 plants) and Cilantro (5 plants) - $19.90

TOTAL VALUE: $361.40

Once the spring harvest has been cleared from the garden, by planting a succession crop of warm season vegetables, I estimate the following additional production, based on optimum growing conditions.

Row 1 - Tomatoes (150 lbs from 5 plants)- $523.50

Row 2 - Bell peppers (168 fruits from 10 plants) - $462.00

Row 3 - Cucumbers (300 fruits from 10 plants) – $297.00

Row 4 - Green beans (20 lbs from 20 plants)- $16.90

Row 5 - Soy beans (20 lbs from 20 plants)- $39.90

Row 6 - Carrots (360 roots) – $89.10

Row 7 - Swiss chard (24 bunches from 8 plants)- $59.79

Row 8 - Squash, Zucchini (100 fruits from 5 plants)- $62.25

Row 9 - Potato Yukon Gold (40 lbs from 10 plants,)- $51.60

Row 10 - Vegetable spaghetti (40 fruits from 5 plants, each weighing 4 lbs)- $79.60

TOTAL VALUE: $1,681.64

The total season's value from a spring and summer crop is $2,043.04

Even if conditions are not optimum for these yields (which depend on variety selection - see page 87), the savings over store-bought vegetables are significant.

Carolyn's Comments:

" Cedaridge Farm is quite historic, established in 1791 as a Mennonite dairy farm. We think there may have been a cabin on the property 100 years before that because there is a date stone at an old quarry in the woods that says 1698 – just a few years after William Penn landed in Pennsylvania. When Colonists arrived from Europe they would follow Indian trails up the Delaware River and where a trail forded the river and went inland, the Colonists would explore along it. There is an old Indian trail at the top of our property bordering Tohickon Creek and so this area was settled soon after Penn arrived from England. There are no power lines visible at Cedaridge Farm (they are all underground). We enjoy sharing our garden with others and we enjoy visiting other people's gardens.

One of our favorite garden destinations is Magnolia Plantation, near Charleston, South Carolina. Before I met Derek, he used to go to Magnolia every spring at the invitation of the owner, J. Drayton-Hastie, to photograph the garden for publicity. Derek used to stay in the Plantation House but he liked to rise before dawn to catch the early morning light, and this would wake the dogs, so Mr. Hastie built Derek a cabin in the woods next to a lake. One afternoon Mr. Hastie took Derek out in a canoe so he could take photographs of the gardens from the water, and as they rounded an island they came face to face with an enormous alligator which promptly torpedoed into the water like the crocodiles in an old Tarzan movie. The alligator surfaced three feet away, and then submerged. Derek saw from its bubbles it was swimming right under the canoe and braced for a jolt, expecting the beast to tip them into the water. Instead it swam off to a far corner of the lake. Derek wrote about this incident in Garden Design magazine, and shortly after the article appeared Mr. Hastie was interviewing a horticulturist for the job of Director. Towards the end of the interview the wife said she had read Derek's article about the alligator, and wondered how dangerous they could be. Mr. Hastie laughed, accused Derek of exaggerating the incident and said she could live at Magnolia for ten years and never see one. He then took the couple out to his country club for a meal, and they returned to the Plantation House for a nightcap. There they discovered the same alligator had wedged itself in a swing door used by the dogs. The alligator was firmly stuck with its head inside the kitchen, and Mr. Hastie had to shoot it. Needless to say, the couple never took the job."

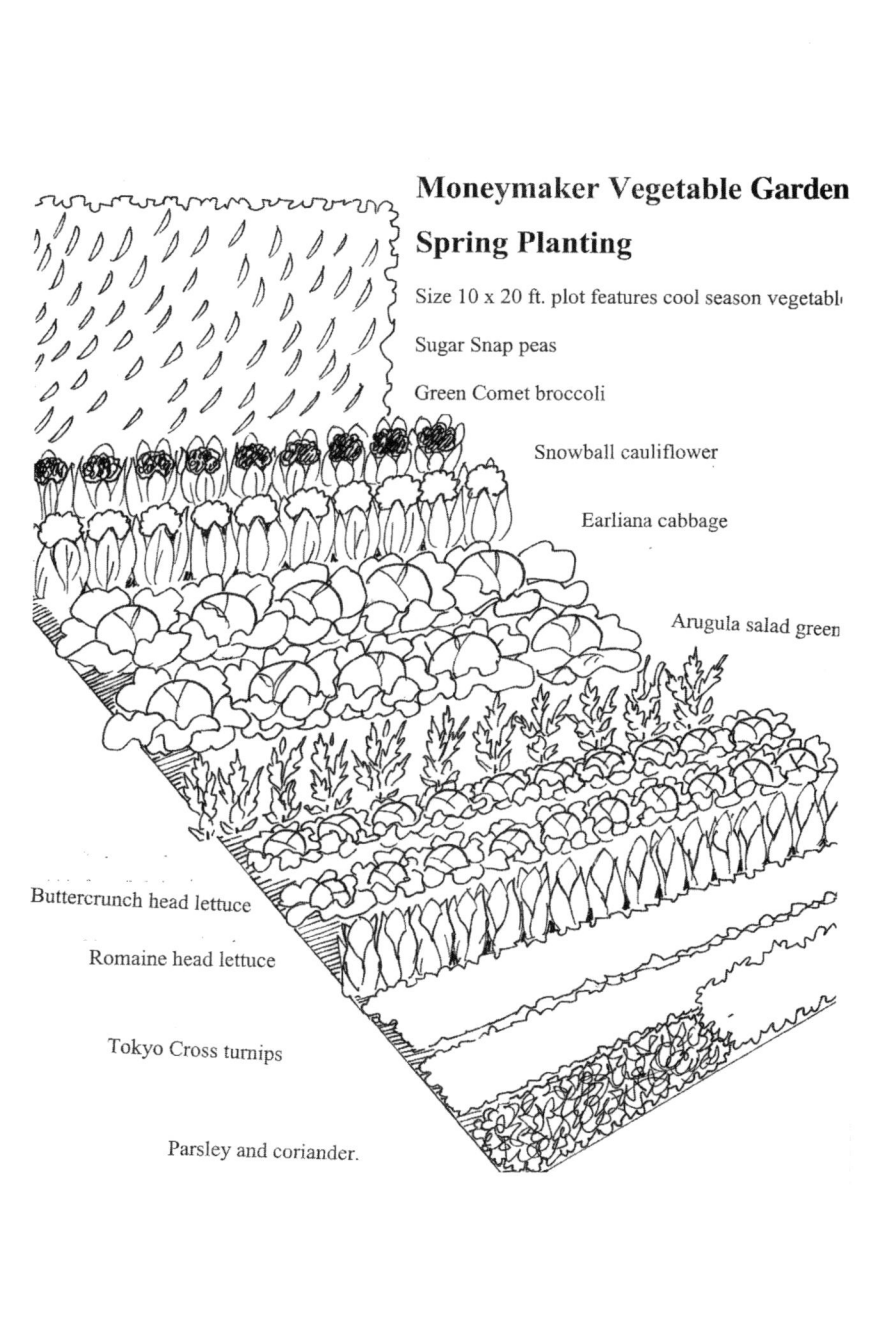

Moneymaker Vegetable Garden Spring Planting

Size 10 x 20 ft. plot features cool season vegetabl

Sugar Snap peas

Green Comet broccoli

Snowball cauliflower

Earliana cabbage

Arugula salad green

Buttercrunch head lettuce

Romaine head lettuce

Tokyo Cross turnips

Parsley and coriander.

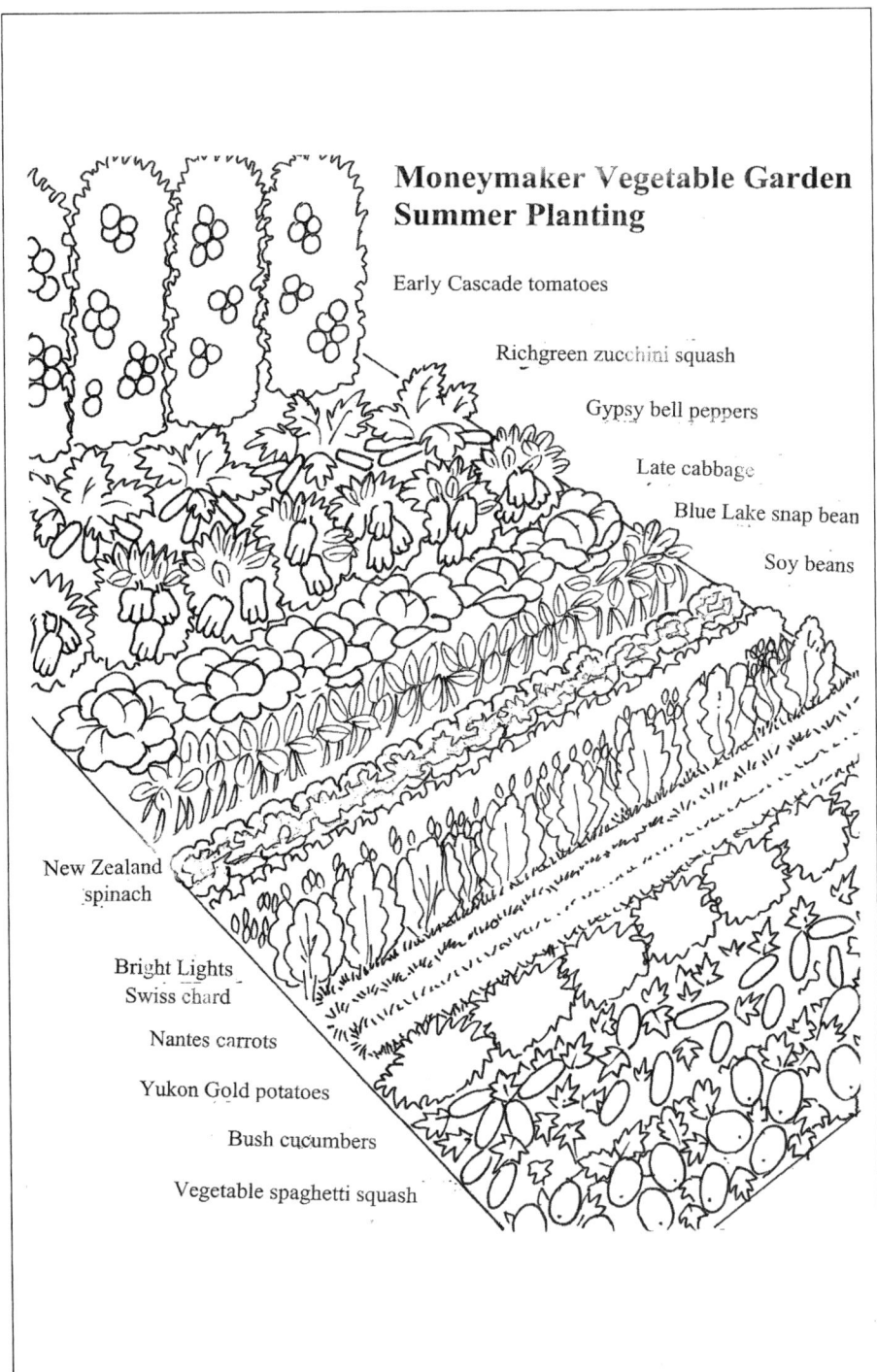

CHAPTER 4
The Wizard's Secret Soil Formula

*"Good soil is the foundation of gardening success.
Almost always the answer to poor results lies in the soil."*
– from my book **Vegetables, How to Select, Grow & Enjoy** (Criabooks.com)

When I first moved to Cedaridge Farm, Pennsylvania to establish my test gardens there was hardly a flower to be seen anywhere, and no vegetable garden. The indigenous soil was hard clay and impoverished. Many areas were poorly drained, and so I chose a flat, high, sunny place to site my vegetable garden, and followed the instructions from a soil test (see page 7). Above all, the site needed lots of compost to improve its health.

I hired a carpenter and gave him a rough design showing a three-compartment compost bin – one to hold finished compost, the second to hold compost in the making, and the third for starting a new pile from kitchen and garden waste and stable manure brought in from local farms. My 'Rolls Royce' of compost bins was published in several magazine articles and books on garden structures, and twenty years later when I visited the historic Chelsea Physic Garden, on the banks of the River Thames, in London I was amazed to discover that THEIR composting system was a design identical to mine.

COMPOSTING – FREE FERTILIZER. One of the most amazing of Vincent van Gogh's paintings – at least in my estimation, and probably his also as he wrote about it a lot – is *The Sower* (1888) where three quarters of the canvas shows a newly plowed field in amazing colors. Although from a distance the soil looks violet, it is actually a mosaic of many bright colors, including yellow, white, blue and pink. The picture is a simple composition showing a peasant broadcasting wheat seed onto bare soil, yet it is a parable of life, for the sower is casting seed onto freshly plowed earth AND onto a ditch where the seed will never reach its full development. Also, there is a flock of black crows stealing some of the grain, representing the criminal elements of life that lead a person astray or prevent one's full development. Across the top of the field is a magnificent band of ripe wheat, glowing orange beneath a rising sun that casts its life giving warmth and light over the field to make the seeds germinate and grow.

When you study the painting you realize that Van Gogh has given the soil a majesty that had never been seen before, and is not likely to be seen again, for the nurturing potential of soil is so forcefully presented it is hard to conceive of any more powerful image to show the power of soil. The painting is a metaphor that should be emblazoned in the mind of every gardener

If the metaphor had been more clearly understood, then the great Dust Bowl of the

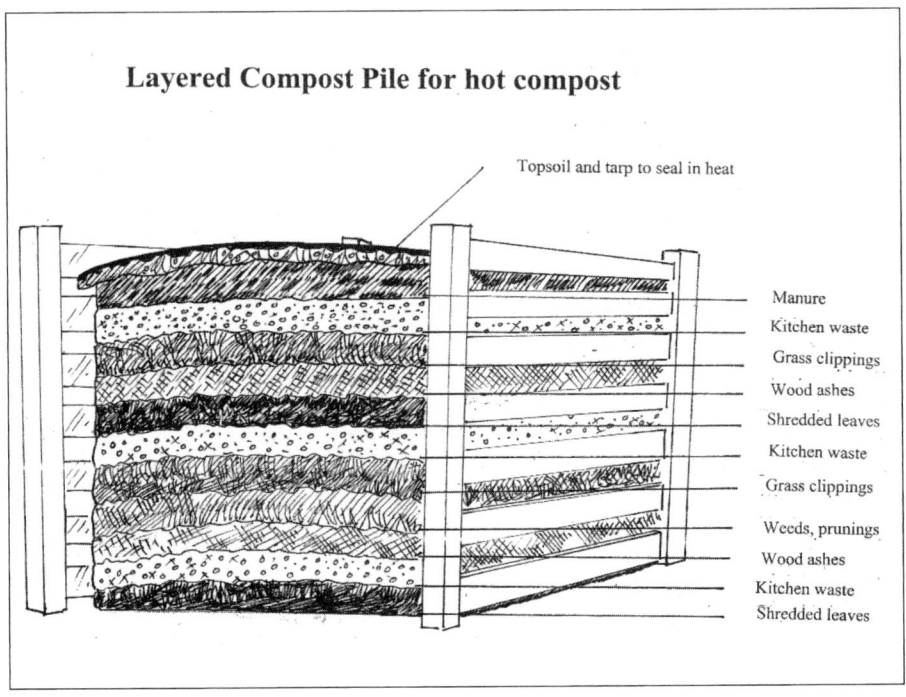

1930's in North America might never have happened. Instead, it caused an estimated 100,000 farmers to be made destitute by soil ruination, from repeatedly plowing the land, a total reliance on chemical fertilizers which create a poisonous build up of salts when used alone, and the burning of stubble that should have been plowed back into the soil to bulk it up and stabilize it. Amish farmers, on the other hand, have a reputation for being the world's best soil stewards, fertilizing their fields with compost and animal manures. The soil is the Amish source of wealth, their reliance on artificial fertilizers is minimal, and as a consequence of their sound soil management their land stays productive, encouraging healthy populations of earthworms and beneficial soil bacteria that continue nature's replenishment cycle.

COMPOST MATERIALS. Few endeavors are more satisfying to me than making good compost. It is truly amazing that in a relatively short time, garden and kitchen waste – even woody hedge trimmings and uprooted weeds – will decompose into a dark brown, fluffy, sweet-smelling substance that looks like soil, and when added to impoverished soil – or clay and sandy soils – can produce bountiful harvests. Here's a list of the prime nutrients in compost and the waste materials I use for best results:

   Nitrogen (denoted by the letter N in a nutrient analysis): Kitchen waste (potato peelings, grapefruit rinds), shredded leaves (fresh or dried); grass clippings (fresh); weeds (fresh), hedge trimmings (fresh), wood chips (fresh or dried), earthworm castings, animal manures, spent legume stems and roots (eg: pea and bean vines), fish scraps and seaweed (washed of salt content), bloodmeal.

Phosphorus (denoted by the letter P): Fish bones (other bones – like chicken and animal bones- should be reduced to ash by burning as they take a long time to decompose), banana skins, cantaloupe rinds, eggshells, shrimp peelings, crab shells, coffee grounds and tea leaves.

Potash (denoted by the letter K): Wood ashes, banana skins, cantaloupe rinds, greensand, weed stems.

A POSITIVE ATTITUDE - The ancient Greeks told of a strong man named Anteus (pronounced an-THEE-us) who lived in a beautiful valley and would not let anyone pass through. Hercules, a strong man, decided to test his strength with Anteus, but each time Hercules threw him to the ground, Anteus jumped up with renewed strength. Close to exhaustion, Hercules realized that the *soil* was the source of his opponent's strength, and so he changed his tactics. He embraced Anteus in a bear hug, lifted him clear of the ground and crushed the life out of him.

When I began gardening I felt like Anteus, for I experienced a similar sense of power whenever my fingers touched soil. You can scarcely realize the miracles which can take hold in this humble and noble product. By planting tiny seeds, and caring for them, you can (with nature's help) produce all kinds of magic – like raising a nearly 2,000 lb pumpkin from a simple seed no bigger than a dime, and germinating tree seeds of varieties capable of lasting a thousand years. Cares and troubles can disappear when working with soil.

MICRO-ORGANISMS. At first glance a handful of soil seems nothing remarkable, but crumble a clump in your hand and you may find earthworms and other tiny creatures. Under a microscope you will find soil populated with microbes and beneficial bacteria that pass soil through their bodies and expel it as waste – a product richer than the original soil particles.

In a healthy soil – one that is crumbly, fluffy, warm (preferably above 50F), and moist these creatures thrive, enriching the soil with essential nutrients and trace elements that plant roots can absorb in liquid form to thrive. Soil also anchors plants. If soil is too light (like sandy soil) plants are easily uprooted and water and nutrients drain away too quickly. In heavy clay soil plant roots have difficulty penetrating to any depth and extracting nutrients from the impervious mass. The best soil is a product called loam, composed of sandy and clay particles, plus lots of humus (a spongy material made from decayed vegetable and animal matter). Humus creates air spaces so soil bacteria can flourish, and it holds moisture.

A well made compost pile can replace chemical fertilizers, especially when it is made up in layers. There are many ways to make the best compost. I sometimes make compost in-situ – where I want to make a planting bed - simply by laying down a blanket of newspapers to kill off the turf and weeds, then piling garden and kitchen waste on top, in layers. But whether you do the composting in-situ or in a bin, the steps are the same. Most in-situ composting is known as cool composting because the amount of materials and the height of the layers are usually insufficient to generate a lot of heat. Hot composting – where the materials form a pile that heats up and decomposes more quickly – is mostly produced in a bin, with a balance of green material (like grass clippings) for nitrogen, and brown material (like dried stems) for carbon to generate the required heat. My own recipe for creating hot compost is as follows:

First, I spread a thick layer of wood chips obtained by either shredding my brush piles with a rented mechanical shredder or asking municipal tree trimming crews to give me a truck load. On top of this I like to pile shredded leaves (up to 12 inches thick). Small leaves like willow and Japanese cut leaf maple do not need shredding, but oak, sycamore, sugar maples and others with large, leathery leaves will rot down more quickly if you run over them with a lawn mower. On top of that I add a layer of kitchen waste such as grapefruit rinds, banana peels, potato peelings, coffee grounds and eggshells to a depth of six inches. Then a layer of green material such as grass clippings or hedge prunings or freshly pulled weeds to a depth of six inches, and then wood ashes from my burn pile or from my three wood-burning fireplaces to a depth of 1 inch. I use manure from a local stable and add a six inch layer. I repeat the layers until the pile is chest height, and top it off with a six inch layer of topsoil. I cover the whole pile with a tarp to seal in the heat and weigh it down at the edges so it does not blow away. Your layers do not need to be this thick, but I have a large garden. Once a week I roll back the tarp and with a pitchfork turn the heap to allow aeration. This speeds decomposition.

After about six months (less in summer) the pile shrinks to about a third its original height and becomes compost - a potent soil amendment full of plant nutrients. The leaf layers convert to leaf mold, rich in plant nutrients and trace elements. The kitchen and garden waste does the same. Eggshells especially add calcium. The wood ashes add mostly potash. The layer of topsoil adds earthworms and soil bacteria that work their way down through the heap, passing all this waste through their bodies and speeding the decomposition process. On occasion I have also purchased bone meal to add extra phosphorus to my compost, and sprayed a seaweed solution over the layers as an extra source of nitrogen to serve as an activator. The extra nitrogen benefits the soil bacteria, speeding decomposition. Compression and decomposition makes the inside of the heap hot and kills most weed seeds.

Avoid dog droppings and used kitty litter as these may harbor intestinal worms that can be transferred to humans. You could make a separate compost pile with these and use them only to improve flower beds.

COMMONLY AVAILABLE COMPOST MATERIALS & NUTRIENT ANALYSIS

In addition to complete organic fertilizers available at garden centers and catalogs, the following generic organic products will stimulate plant growth:

Bat Guano is an odorless, almost black organic fertilizer mined from caves located mostly in Jamaica. Some of the deposits are thousands of years old, offering a nutrient analysis that is 1% nitrogen, 8% phosphorus and 2% potash.

Blood Meal is a natural high nitrogen fertilizer that benefits leafy vegetables like lettuce and cabbage, and stimulates bacterial growth in the soil.

Bone Meal has a nutrient analysis of 5% nitrogen, 12% phosphorus and 0% potash, plus 25% calcium. It stimulates bacterial activity in the soil and especially benefits vegetables that flower and fruit like tomatoes.

Earthworm Castings look like bat guano and can serve as a complete plant food as well as a soil conditioner. Recent university studies have shown that a potting soil of 50% earthworm castings and 50% builder's sand (salt free) is an excellent potting soil for container plantings.

Fish Emulsion is a complete organic plant food and a soil conditioner. It contains the three essential nutrients, N-P-K and also trace elements. Plus it improves the ability of soil microbes to manufacture additional nutrients.

Kelp Meal is a source of nitrogen and potash, produced from renewable forests of seaweed mostly harvested in South Africa.

Soft Rock Phosphate is naturally high in phosphorus (22%) and calcium (25%) and like bone meal stimulates root development, flowers and fruit.

The following table shows a nutrient analysis by percentage. Note that even a small nutrient content can be beneficial when added to a compost heap or used as manure tea. Source: University of Florida, 1994

Ingredient	Nitrogen (N)	Phosphorus (P)	Potash (K)
Banana skins	-	3.25	41.76
Cantaloupe rinds	-	9.77	12.21
Coffee grounds	2.08	.32	.28
Corn stalks	.30	.13	.33
Crabgrass (green)	.66	.19	.71
Eggs (spoiled)	2.25	.19	.15
Feathers	15.30	-	-
Fish scraps (including bones)	2.00-7.50	1.50-6.00	-
Greensand	-	1.00	6.00
Oak leaves	.80	.35	.15
Orange culls	.20	.13	.21
Pine needles	.46	.12	.03
Ragweed	.76	.26	-
Seaweed	1.00	-	4.00-10.00
Tea leaves	4.15	.62	.40
Wood ashes	-	1.00	4.00-10.00

Avoid putting bones or raw meat directly into a compost pile. Rather, add these to a burn pile and turn them into ashes. Bones are a source of phosphorus and when burned they become brittle. They turn into a white powdery ash that can feed plants.

I spread the finished compost over my beds in fall when the garden debris is cleared away, and again in spring before planting. The effect on plant performance is astonishing. Sometimes I even plant winter squashes and pumpkins with large vines directly into the compost pile, no digging needed. The size and quantity of the resulting fruits is even better than growing in enriched garden soil.

COMMERCIAL COMPOST. The word compost can be confusing. Compost you make yourself from a variety of biodegradable ingredients, like kitchen and garden waste, shredded leaves and wood ashes, can supply all the nutrients your plants need. But the word compost can also apply to a single composted ingredient, like cow manure, cottonseed hulls and sawdust. When you use compost from a single source it can often lack an important nutrient (check the label). To provide your plants with a balanced diet you may need to mix several kinds of commercial compost. I have also found that potting mixes can make a good compost substitute. These are usually a blend of soil amendments such as vermiculite and perlite (gritty particles that provide aeration and absorb moisture like a sponge), plus peat and various composted materials. The mixture is loose, dark and fluffy. But even if you need to use these packaged soil amendments because you lack your own finished compost, begin composting as soon as possible so you have a continuous source of home made compost to keep your soil in good heart.

COMPOST TEA. Plants absorb nutrients in soluble form. Whether they take it in through the stomata of their leaves or through their fine feeder roots, it must be liquefied. This fact is what makes fertilizing with compost tea (also called manure tea) so important for high yields or growing giant vegetables to win contests. Of course, individual growers who consistently win at state fairs have their own secret formulas for making manure tea, but basically it requires a rain barrel and dumping in the bottom a two to three feet layer of well decomposed compost. As the rain barrel fills (either from natural rainfall or your garden hose), the water turns a rich, brown color. Once every two weeks I will take a two-gallon watering can or a four gallon backpack sprayer and drench the soil around plants with the compost tea. The basic ingredients of my compost tea are: leaf mold (from rotted leaves); wood ashes; decomposed animal manure (cow or horse or poultry preferred); decomposed kitchen waste including eggshells, banana skins, melon rind and grapefruit rinds; decomposed grass clippings.

COMPOST TEA FORMULA 2. Harvest giant Walla Walla onion 5 inches across; 5 lbs of snap beans from a single plant; tomatoes as big as cantaloupe melons. Those are some of the results reported by gardeners who use a readily available organic product called Spray-N-Grow and Bill's Perfect Fertilizer. The first product is a blend of micro-nutrients that help plants produce more flowers and fruit; the second is a liquid fertilizer made from fish parts with a 6.5-11-5 nutrient analysis. Mix 1 gallon of warm water with 2 tablespoons of Spray-N-Grow and allow the solution to stand for 15 minutes; then add 1 tablespoon of Bill's Perfect Fertilizer. Spray plants once a week to see spectacular results. To make the mixture even more effective, add a 'sticking' agent such as coconut oil. It allows the solution to stay on plant leaves even after heavy rainfall. And it's not expensive. A 16 oz. bottle of Spray-N-Grow concentrate makes 48 quarts – 12 GALLONS. This formula can also be applied as a soil drench at planting time. The slightly fishy aroma deters insect pests. I have also used

Nitron organic fertilizer in both liquid and granular form. The granular form looks and smells like oatmeal that you could tip into a bowl, pour milk on and eat. But please do not do this as it is a powerhouse of nutrients that includes bat guano and rock phosphates and enzymes that have helped me grow two feet wide Simpson Elite lettuce, a three pound Delicious tomato, asparagus as thick as my thumb, and 18 inch wide heads of Premium Crop green broccoli. See the appendix under sources.

EASY TO MAKE COMPOST BINS

Listed here are some easy-to-make compost bins. In addition, there are numerous commercially available compost bins.

Wooden bin. This can be made from 2 x 4" boards available from a lumber yard. Or you can use straight sections of tree trunks such as juniper. Allow gaps between the cross members for aeration. Another readily available, inexpensive compost bin can be made from wooden pallets, often available free from local businesses such as garden centers. Three pallets, up ended can form the sides, with a side left open for access to the pile.

Wire bin. A rectangular section of chicken wire or builder's wire can be easily bent to form a cylinder shape for a roomy compost bin. When you rake leaves in the fall it is often a good policy to create a special bin like this for storing the shredded leaves as unshredded leaves can take up too much room in an all-purpose compost pile. These will turn into a dark brown fluffy product called leaf mold that works miracles as a soil conditioner.

Cinder block bin. Cinder blocks can be costly and unsightly, but they will make a sturdy, rot-resistant enclosure for making compost. To ensure stability for a cinder block bin it is best to build it on a foundation of crushed stone.

Compost Tumbler is an example of a commercial product. Consisting of a barrel-shaped drum on legs, the drum can be rotated by turning a handle. The benefit of tumbling compost is speedy decomposition. Usable compost made in a tumbler can be ready within two weeks during summer. Note that compost to be useful does not need to be completely decomposed and resemble soil. Partially decomposed compost can be applied to improve poor soil. See appendix under sources.

LATERAL GROWTH. Whenever I have been called to a person's garden to witness and photograph extraordinary growth, such as roof high tomato vines loaded with fruit, 22 lb cabbages, 100-lb watermelons and 1,000 lb pumpkins I've noticed that the roots extend out in all directions for a considerable distance just below the surface. Many growers agree that it is this *lateral* surface growth more than deep roots that are responsible for gigantism. So, when adding compost to plants, don't just pile it up against the stem, but spread it out generously for several feet in all directions.

GREEN MANURE – Also called a cover crop. Certain plants – clover and winter rye, for example - attract beneficial bacteria that manufacture nitrogen so when the crop is dug in at the end of the growing season the soil is enriched. That is why many farmers plant a green manure crop over winter for plowing under in early spring prior to sowing a summer crop (especially leaf crops like cabbage and corn that benefit from high nitrogen). Since a green manure crop may deplete the soil of phosphorus and potash, a fertilizer that includes these two nutrients may still be necessary. For home gardens green manuring is not essential providing compost is dug into the soil prior to planting.

CROP ROTATION. Avoid growing the same family of vegetables in the same place two years in succession. Divide your plot into quarters and rotate crops so a particular spot grows the same plant family only once every four years. The major plant families are:

Cabbages (also broccoli, cauliflower, kale, collards)

Tomatoes (also peppers, eggplant, potatoes)

Cucumbers (also summer squash, winter squash, melons)

Root Crops (carrots, parsnips, beets, turnips, radishes, onions)

THE IMPORTANCE OF EARTHWORMS

Earthworms plough the soil by burrowing, digesting organic matter and enriching it as waste. In heavy clay soils their burrowing creates aeration, allowing plant roots to use the tunnels to penetrate deep and wide in search of moisture and nutrients. Earthworms manufacture essential plant nutrients by ingesting all kinds of organic matter such as leaf litter and spent plant parts, passing it through their bodies and expelling it as castings. These castings are richer in nutrients than the original soil. Healthy soils have healthy earthworm populations.

Gardeners generally do not need to purchase earthworms as their microscopic egg clusters can be found in most cultivated soils, but if your indigenous soil is composed of pure sand, gravel or hard clay, a starter population can be obtained by mail order over the internet, and from local places selling fish bait labeled as night crawlers.

MAKE YOUR OWN WORM FARM. Commercial worm farms are made from stackable containers that create a drainage area at the bottom, an area for the finished worm castings to collect, and an area for fresh food supplies. A simple worm farm can be made from an opaque box (such as a picnic cooler) and kept in the basement or a garage for fast results. Drill a hole to one side of the container, at the bottom in order to insert a screw-in drainage spigot (available from hardware stores). Create a drainage area by placing a fine wire screen 2 inches above the base over gravel or supports at the corners. This allows moisture that collects in the bottom to be drained off and prevent the worms from drowning. The drain-off can be used as a manure tea. Also drill a series of tiny holes in the lid and sides to allow air into the box since earthworms must be able to breathe (but small enough to keep the inside of the box dark). Start with a layer of moist shredded newspaper or shredded leaves and place a layer of topsoil over it. Introduce a handful of red worms (either by digging them from the garden or purchasing from an internet source or bait shop) and pile in some kitchen waste such as banana peels, melon rinds, eggshells, coffee grounds, used tea leaves, spoiled vegetables and more shredded newspapers to about 4 inches deep. Replace the lid to make it dark, and earthworms will work ceaselessly, rendering the waste into a black, moist, crumbly soil ingredient. Kept indoors such as a basement or garage, the worms will multiply so fast, after a month you can have the container half filled with black castings. Check the contents at weekly intervals to replenish the waste layer, add moisture from a spray bottle if the mix seems dry, and drain off liquid using the spigot. You can also tip the entire contents onto a compost pile where the earthworms will continue to multiply. Save a handful of worms to start a new batch.

Avoid citrus rinds and members of the onion family (like garlic) as these repel earthworms. Too dry a bedding and the earthworms may have difficulty breathing; too wet and they could drown. You can also create a larger worm farm outdoors, using a trash can or even an old bath-tub providing there is a means of drainage. The outdoor container can be left open or have a closed lid to keep out excess rain.

Carolyn's Comments:

"When we were dating and Derek's birthday came up, I thought for a long time about what to buy him. I was working in New York at the time and as I passed Saks on Fifth Avenue I noticed their window displays were being changed and spotted a beautiful old wooden gate with peeling paint. I talked to the manager and he sold me the gate. It is now used as the entrance to our vegetable garden. Since then we have collected more old gates, antique wheelbarrows, goat carts, a collection of galvanized watering cans and old garden tools from garage sales and antique stores. One day when we had our garden open for charity a lady came up to Derek and said 'I love your imperfections'. What she meant was that she liked the wooden gate with peeling paint and a metal gate with a rusty patina, and the fact that we had allowed weeds like Queen Anne's lace to grow among our perennial borders. The informal appearance is deliberate. It reminds me of Renoir's garden at Cagnes-sur-Mer in Provence. Renoir purchased an old farm to save an orchard of ancient olive trees from being cut down. Rather than demolish the old farmhouse he kept it as a landscape feature and built a new house on a corner of the property that did not intrude with the old orchard. He liked the meadow grasses to grow tall and flash silver and gold in the Mistral wind. One day a gardener approached him and asked permission to cut down the weeds. Renoir answered 'What weeds?' To the gardener the meadow grasses were weeds that should be mowed to look tidy, but for Renoir the tall grasses spangled with wildflowers produced a natural effect that made him feel comfortable and close to nature."

I'll Make You a Gardening Wizard Overnight!

CHAPTER 5
Inside Tips for Free Seed Starting Supplies and More

"Be sure of your seed, otherwise carrots may come up as parsnips."
– from my book, **Vegetable Gardening for Beginners** (Friedman/Fairfax)

Surely, one of the most satisfying gardening experiences is seed starting. Get a jump on nature and save money over the cost of transplants by germinating seed indoors so that at outdoor planting time you can transfer to the garden your own husky seedlings, sometimes with flower buds already showing.

FREE STARTER POTS - It always puzzles me why people buy commercial seed starting supplies when it's unnecessary and expensive. I simply don't like paying $1.50 for a packet of seeds, only to pay another $15.00 or more for commercial starter pots or a seed starting kit, when there are plenty of handy food containers that are as good as commercial pots. Don't toss quart or pint size milk cartons out with the garbage. They make roomy, deep starter pots capable of growing a healthy rooted transplant. The root ball on a plant grown in a quart capacity milk carton can be 8 inches long! Grow tomato, pepper and squash transplants in these 'deep root' containers and you can gain 20 days of earliness over transplants grown in smaller starter pots.

FREE MINI GREENHOUSE - Some leafy vegetables – such as lettuce, basil and spinach – like to be started in a group, and then the seedlings transferred into individual pots when they are large enough to handle. Garden supply stores sell 'seed trays' for this purpose, often with a clear plastic dome to trap heat and humidity and encourage faster germination, like a greenhouse. Again it makes me wonder why people buy these products when there are dozens of food containers that will serve the same purpose if saved after using the contents. For example, clear plastic sandwich trays, and deep aluminum Chinese take-out containers often have a clear plastic lid. Cheesecake and numerous fresh fruits – such as strawberries and blueberries - are also packed in these clear plastic containers. Simply fill these with moist potting soil, scatter the fine seed over the surface and lightly cover, just enough to anchor the seeds, snap the plastic lid shut and you can be assured of rapid, reliable germination, given light and a warm room temperature.

FREE SPRAY BOTTLE - When watering seeds in seed trays do not use a watering can since water pouring from a spout can disturb the seeds and disrupt germination. Rather, use water from a spray bottle. There's no need to buy a fancy copper spray can like garden centers sell. Simply save empty plastic spray bottles used for detergent soap, rinse out the residue, and fill with clean water to apply a gentle, penetrating spray to seedling trays.

FREE POTTING SOIL – As a starter mix to raise seedlings do not use garden topsoil or last season's pots unless the pots are thoroughly cleaned with hot soapy water. That's because unsterilized garden topsoil and aged pots with old soil clinging to them are a haven for damping off, a fungus disease that's a killer of seedlings. Traditionally, the best advice is to use a commercial potting soil or a mix of vermiculite (a brown granular volcanic substance that has good drainage and aeration) and perlite (a white gritty volcanic substance that has good moisture holding ability).

However, to save money there's no need to purchase potting soil at $15.00 or more a bag, or vermiculite and perlite, because it's easy to make your own potting soil to start seeds. Simply visit Starbucks (or any other coffee shop) and ask for a bag of their spent coffee grounds. It is Starbucks policy to provide these FREE for the asking. Then take a deep aluminum tray for roasting turkey and mound it with garden topsoil. Place it in the oven at 450F for 40 minutes and mix it in equal parts with the Starbucks coffee grounds. You will then have the finest, cleanest, sterile potting mix imaginable. I like to mix in a dilute solution of fish or kelp liquid fertilizer, and that's all seedlings need to get them off to a good start. A word of caution however – do not use the coffee grounds alone as they will inhibit germination unless mixed with an equal amount of sterilized topsoil.

Direct seeding spinach seeds

BOTTOM HEAT – The majority of seeds germinate reliably at 70F, especially when the heat source is beneath the seed starting tray. To generate heat for seedlings place your seed starting trays or pots over a house heating duct or a radiator, or position them over a table lamp so the heat from the bulb warms the starter mix from below. You'll save up to $25.00 over buying a commercial heating mat.

DIRECT SEEDING – There are plants that can be sown directly into the garden (known as direct-seeding), such as snap beans and corn; a reason to direct seed is because the seed is large and easy to handle and germination outdoors is reliable or because the plants resent any kind of root disturbance, like radishes and carrots. There are plants that need starting indoors for a variety of reasons: the seed is tiny and subject to poor germination outdoors, usually because of susceptibility to soil diseases like damping off disease. This is a common fungus that attacks many kinds of sprouting seeds at the soil line, making them keel over. Seed starting is also advisable where subsequent growth after germination is slow (such as artichokes), requiring up to 10 weeks to grow a transplant. A lot of tender vegetables are best transplanted, such as tomatoes, even though direct seeding is reliable, in order to get a head start on the season and an earlier crop.

After you direct-seed, alternate wetting and drying may cause the surface to 'crust' and make it difficult for some fine seeds to break through the surface. If your soil is prone to crusting (such as clay soil), cover the seeds with sand or compost which resists crusting.

PRE-GERMINATING SEEDS. Chitting is a term to describe pre-germinating seed. Whenever you have experienced poor germination with a particular seed, try soaking them for an hour and then placing them on a moist paper towel indoors (I like to do this with peas, beans, corn and okra). Then, as soon as the seed coat splits and the root emerges, plant out in the garden, covering the germinated seed with a layer of fine soil.

AVOID STRETCHED SEEDLINGS. When you use a windowsill to start seeds indoors, be sure to elevate the container up to the level of the window and place a panel of aluminum foil at the rear to reflect light onto your seedlings. This will prevent 'stretch' whereby seedlings grow towards a light source. Stretched seedlings become stressed and do not make good transplants. When you grow your own transplants, it is generally best to introduce them to an outdoor environment gradually to avoid transplant shock. This is best accomplished by placing the seedlings in a cold frame – a box with a glass cover can serve as a cold frame – for four or five days. Similarly, with transplants purchased from a garden center, ask if they have been hardened off. Remember to keep windowsill plants adequately watered. The hot sun through a glass window can quickly dry out the potting soil. Sun shining through a lace curtain is often better for seedlings.

AVOID ROOT-BOUND TRANSPLANTS. With commercial plastic or peat containers for transplants tear out the bottom of the pot to give roots freedom to grow. If you buy transplants where the root ball is enclosed with a biodegradable netting, tear the netting to release roots even if the instructions say there is no need to. I recommend this practice because there are occasions when the biodegradable peat pot or netting has failed to decompose fast enough, causing stress and restrictive growth.

When you buy plants from a garden center, avoid transplants that have too much top growth in relation to the size of the pot; or a spindly look from infrequent watering or stretching towards a light source. Yellowing leaves or the lower stem section devoid of leaves is also a sign of stress. A stressed plant can take a long time to recover and delay maturity.

FROST PROTECTION. There are cool season vegetables like cabbage and spinach that can tolerate mild frosts, and warm season vegetables like tomatoes and peppers that are sensitive to frost damage. There is often the temptation to transplant frost-sensitive plants

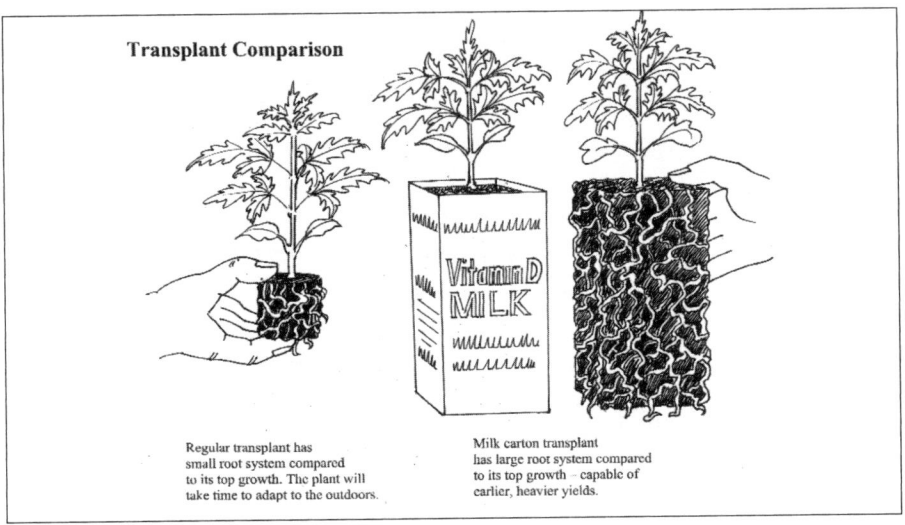

Transplant Comparison

Regular transplant has small root system compared to its top growth. The plant will take time to adapt to the outdoors.

Milk carton transplant has large root system compared to its top growth – capable of earlier, heavier yields.

too early, but even if you can give a plant frost protection by covering it with a glass cloche (a bell jar) or upturned peach basket, a later transplant will usually catch up and yield an earlier crop.

Keep an ear tuned to weather forecasts, and if a frost is predicted and threatens your plants, you can take precautions. In addition to bell jars and peach baskets, consider a covering of horticultural fleece. This is a lightweight fabric that covers a row of plants like a spider's web, and offers sufficient protection to ward off a mild frost.

To protect early planted tomatoes from frost I often plant them against the south facing wall of a house so that the house heat can protect them from a late frost.

New on the market is a product called FreezePruf Protector, a spray that improves a plant's cold tolerance for up to six weeks, and up to 9.5F degrees below its normal cold tolerance. The spray is biodegradable and resists rain.

SAVE MONEY ON SEEDS. Using seed is the least expensive way to grow vegetables and provide the biggest return on your investment! A packet of seeds often will cost less than a single transplant purchased from a garden center. The packet may contain certain symbols: OP meaning Open Pollinated; HY meaning Hybrid; and PVP meaning an open-pollinated variety that has Plant Variety Protection. If there is no symbol then the variety is most likely OP.

OPEN POLLINATED SEEDS tend to be the least expensive seeds to buy. That is because bees do the pollination in open fields and the resulting seed 'breeds true.' Seed from open pollinated varieties can be saved for another season.

HYBRID SEED. A great deal of misinformation has been written about hybrids. For example, it is not true that all hybrids are man-made and therefore un-natural. Thousands of hybrids exist in the wild, both among animals as crosses between horses and zebra and polar bears and grizzly bears, and between plants, especially among different species of oak tree which hybridize readily in nature.

It is also completely untrue that hybrids among plants have been bred only for the commercial market. Numerous hybrid vegetables – especially those that win All-America Awards – are bred specifically for home gardeners. Moreover, the reason plant breeders breed hybrids is NOT to control their sale by knowing the cross-breeding formula that produced the hybrid, but because hybrids can be far superior to open-pollinated varieties in terms of yields, disease resistance and flavor. Hybrid seed tends to be more expensive than open-pollinated varieties because the parents of hybrids need to be isolated and hand pollinated by a labor force. Otherwise the hybridizing process can become contaminated and the resulting seed may be either sterile or of little value. Therefore, it is inadvisable to save seed of hybrid vegetables.

In particular I disagree with the opinion of many writers that hybrids are bred only for mechanical harvesting since that represents a very small percentage of hybrids. Rather, a large number are bred specifically for the home gardener (such as the large, smooth-skinned, high yielding Big Boy hybrid tomato and the cold-tolerant, early-maturing Gypsy Hybrid pepper) with no thought of supermarket sales.

A question often asked about hybrids is why different varieties often look alike if only the breeder knows the parents involved in the cross. That's because when a hybrid makes its appearance, competitive breeders will often make a guess at the parents and by trial and error produce a similar hybrid.

Cross pollination between plants was understood by the Assyrians and the Babylonians more than 5,000 years ago when they realized that by shaking pollen from male date palms onto female flowers they could obtain a heavier crop. Gregor Mendel, an Austrian monk, further shed light on the nuances of cross pollination when he crossed different varieties of peas, and in 1885 published his findings of how plant characteristics are inherited by cross breeding from one generation to the next.

Big Boy hybrid tomato was among the first vegetable hybrids specifically bred for the home gardener. The breeder began its hybridizing on tomatoes in 1937, and the reason for a higher cost than open pollinated seed is that an acre of tomatoes will grow 4,500 plants, each plant averaging 30 blossoms. This means that a crew of hand pollinators must fertilize 135,000 female parts (called stigmas) in order to obtain hybrid seed. To collect male pollen for the cross another group of hand pollinators must hold a cluster of blossoms and use a vibrator to shake the pollen from the flowers onto a glass vial no bigger than an index finger. It requires a day's vibrating to collect one vial full of male pollen to make the cross.

The process of hybridization is easier among some vegetables than others. Hybridizing tomatoes is tedious because the male and female parts are contained in the same flower and the male parts of the female parent must be emasculated (pinched out with tweezers) before the pollen ripens and self-fertilizes. The hybridizing process is easier on cucumbers, squash and melons because male and female flowers are on separate parts of the plant.

PATENTED SEED VARIETIES. Seed varieties with the initials PVP are all open-pollinated because hybrids do not need the protection of a plant patent. You can legally save seed of patented varieties and grow another crop for personal use. However, you would be in violation of the law if you sold the seed.

I asked Glenn Goldsmith, a prominent California plant breeder, why he continued to breed hybrids when he could breed OP varieties at a tenth of the cost, and have plant variety protection. He replied: "Because hybrids produce far better results and growers are willing to pay the extra cost for double and triple yields, a sweeter flavor or disease resistance."

SAVING SEED. There are several ways to obtain seeds. You can save seed from non-hybrids and after drying them place them in labeled envelopes for storage in the crisper section of your refrigerator (cold dry temperatures generally preserve seed, while heat and humidity can kill them). Many vegetables are annuals, meaning that the seed is produced in one season, but others may be biennials – such as parsley and onions which means the seed production is delayed a year.

SEED RACK VERSUS SEED CATALOG. You can more conveniently purchase packets of seeds from a seed rack at your local hardware store or garden center, OR you can purchase seeds from a mail order seed company. Generally, a mail order catalog will provide you with the biggest selection and good growing advice. Also, seed catalogs generally contain good advice on growing different classes of vegetables. Some may even be regional; for example the Territorial Seed catalog specializes in varieties suitable for the Pacific Northwest; while Hastings Seeds specializes in seed varieties for the Southeast.

Cost of seeds can vary considerably. A company like Pinetree Garden Seeds in Maine prides itself in supplying the least expensive seed, and a 95 cent packet of beets, for example, may cost $2.50 from another seed company. Sometimes the higher cost is justified, for example when a seed company uses only organic growing methods to produce its seed, and when a paper packet will not preserve seeds as long as a foil packet that locks out moisture.

The huge selection of varieties offered can be confusing. When I first started gardening I asked neighbors what varieties they grew, especially old timers, and devoured garden magazines. Now that I have gardened for 50 years in the US, written more than 80 garden books and a thousand garden articles, I can confidently pass on my own variety recommendations (see page 87).

A reason not to save seed is that it may be contaminated with a disease you cannot see from your own garden. Lettuce seed from many seed companies, for example, is produced in special valleys out West where a ring of high mountains prevents disease entering the valley and contaminating the crop. A question I am often asked is why seed saved from hybrids will usually produce inferior results. That is because a hybrid needs two parents from plants that don't normally mate in nature (jackass and a mare). The resulting progeny – the mule - may be bigger and stronger than either parent, but the hybrid mule cannot produce viable seed (semen) to perpetuate itself.

Carolyn's Comments:

"I was raised a farmer's daughter in Ohio and my mother always planted a substantial vegetable garden for canning the produce. My favorite crop is sweet corn and it was always a special occasion when the first ears of Golden Bantam were brought in from the garden. In those days it was my job to have the water boiling as the ears were being picked because the sugar changed to starch so quickly. Now there are hybrid varieties that can retain their sweetness for more than a week. One of my favorites today is the bicolor Honey & Pearls, but Derek always plants a patch of the heirloom variety, Golden Bantam, for nostalgic reasons. Another popular heirloom variety we grow is the Lazy Wife bean, introduced by Burpee Seeds in 1888. The first completely stringless pole bean, Derek received a shoe box full of seed from a neighbor, Bill Byrd. After Bill died his widow gave Derek Bill's stock seed and Derek continued to save his own seed until 2008 when he harvested a very small crop. Subsequent germination was poor and heavy rains rotted the plants so he experienced a crop failure. One day he was out in the garden in an old dressing gown and rubber boots, and rummaging around in his pocket he found a single Lazy Wife bean seed. He planted it in a pot and that single seed swelled up, split its seed coat and sprouted. From that single seed he was able to start a new crop."

I'll Make You a Gardening Wizard Overnight!

CHAPTER 6
No Weeding, Sure Feeding & Automatic Irrigation

> *"Plants do not have teeth. They can only absorb nutrients through their roots or leaves in soluble form."*
> – my introduction to selling a water soluble fertilizer on QVC

While weeds can be a curse in many gardens it was only when I visited some pristine islands in the Sub-antarctic, where mostly indigenous plants grew, that I realized nature did not create weeds, for when life evolved every plant had its place, its special niche in the natural order of things. It was only when man changed from being a hunter-gatherer and tried to create monocultures with plants of his choosing, that weeds came into being, for a weed is simply an aggressive plant that invades another's space.

A WEED-FREE SOIL. Weeding is probably responsible for more failures among gardeners than any other single cause. Short of gardening under plastic and growing plants in raised beds filled with a sterile potting soil, it is extremely difficult to keep weeds out of a garden. Weed seeds can blow in from a neighbor's garden, birds will deposit them onto soil when they relieve themselves, and many weed seeds can survive composting. Moreover, seeds of the most pernicious weeds can stay viable for years, so eliminating weeds by uprooting them will not necessarily eradicate them.

In a small space there is an easy way to eliminate weeds and that's by building a raised bed at least 6 inches above the indigenous soil, filled with a sterile soil substitute. For his Square-foot Gardening system Mel Bartholomew advocates a mix of 1/3 peat, 1/3 coarse vermiculite and 1/3 packaged compost, available from garden centers. This may seem a little extravagant since a 2 cubic ft bag of these products can set you back $15.00, and sufficient mix to fill a 4 ft by 4 ft space 6 inches deep could cost $120.00 or more. But also it's possible to create a weed-free growing medium by baking garden topsoil or garden compost. In particular I like the combination of baking garden topsoil and mixing it with an equal amount of Starbucks coffee grounds (which are already sterile from the roasting process). I do the baking of the topsoil in batches in a roasting pan. Never have I experienced such a more desirable planting medium, and the fragrance from the coffee grounds is a tonic for the soul.

For a large area, where the purchase of packaged soil mixes would be exorbitant, and the amount of baking and trips to Starbucks for coffee grounds impractical, a more efficient way to eliminate weeds is to rely on mulches.

MULCHING - Be aware that organic mulches will keep the soil cool, which benefits cool season crops like lettuce and peas, but for warm season crops like tomatoes, peppers and melons, you will be better off planting them through strips of black plastic. The black plastic will warm the soil and keep it warm during cool nights when many warm season crops will stop growing. Both kinds help to retain soil moisture.

Here are some popular mulches and what I think of them. Those with an asterisk are FREE:

Mulches that Cool the Soil:

*Shredded leaves are my favorite as they look good and eventually break down to become part of the soil. They are freely available by simply raking up leaves in the fall, running a lawn mower over them and catching them in a mulch bag attached to the mower.

*Pine needles can be raked up from beneath evergreens, although they are also sold in bales. I like them as a mulch as they are attractive and it's not necessary to make a thick layer to create a weed barrier. I don't agree that pine needles as a mulch will turn the soil highly acidic. I use wheelbarrow-loads of pine needles in my compost piles and soil tests always show the same result – a near neutral reading.

Straw is sold in bales. It is inexpensive and also good looking, although I prefer straw made from rye as it has a golden yellow color that is very attractive. Tear the straw off the bale in slices and use the slices to lay down a dense blanket. If you pull the straw apart it may not make enough of a weed barrier.

*Grass clippings are free although not especially attractive. They are easily accumulated by attaching a mulch bag to your mower. Grass clippings tend to pack down to form a barrier that weeds find hard to penetrate.

*Newspapers are unsightly but make an excellent weed barrier. It is best to lay them down between rows of plants and cover with a more attractive organic mulch like shredded leaves.

Washed sea shells reflect light and can help increase light intensity in a shady area.

White plastic reflects heat and comes in rolls, usually with black on the reverse so you can use the white for cool season crops and black for warm season.

Mulches that Warm the Soil:

Black plastic does more to encourage earliness among warm season crops than any other factor. It warms soil and keeps it warm during cold nights so that vegetables sensitive to cold – like melons – will not be stressed. Black plastic comes in rolls, usually 4 ft. wide and wherever I need to use black plastic I like to make a raised row so the plastic stretches across it and can be anchored along the side with soil. Black plastic is often used in conjunction with horticultural fleece (also called floating row covers). This white, lightweight fabric covers crops like a spider's web, making a barrier against infectious diseases and insect pests. It protects against late frost by keeping the plants warm. The plastic is laid in place and then planting stations cut with scissors for seeds or transplants to be set into the soil.

Chapter 6 - *No Weeding, Sure Feeding & Automatic Irrigation*

Bush snap bean, Blue Lake mulched with straw

Clear plastic has proven to be beneficial for promoting earliness in melons, even better than black plastic, but since light can penetrate through to the soil it encourages weeds around the melons to grow. Also it looks unsightly.

Brown plastic is sold as a more acceptable alternative to black and clear plastic since it is the color of soil.

Sand. The glass particles in sand help to warm soil. Sand makes an especially good mulch for melons such as cantaloupe and watermelons and all kinds of squash. Never use beach sand as it contains too much salt.

FALL & WINTER CLEAN UP. There are some simple ways to prevent weeds, especially in a home garden, and the first step is in the fall by making sure any existing weeds are cleared from the garden before they have a chance to disperse their seeds. Either delegate the weeds to a burn pile or place them in a heap on the compost pile.

It is essential to get the root of a weed since many weeds are hardy perennials, and any piece of root left in the soil can regenerate a new plant. This is particularly true of thistles, dock and dandelions. The best way to tackle a weedy bed, without resorting to a weed-killer like Round-up, is to wait for a rainy day when the soil softens and weeds are easier to pull. Tackle the shallow-rooted weeds first by giving them a good yank. Crabgrass, ragweed and chickweed come up easily. Then take a trowel to uproot the more obstinate ones.

Always wear gloves pulling weeds, as some have prickles, like thistles, and others may have sap that can irritate skin. To weed a recently tilled plot, do not step on the soil. Rather, place a board to step on and cushion your weight. When weeding close to desirable plants, take care that the act of pulling the weed does not uproot the good neighbor. Once you have cleared the site, till the soil and remove any roots that may have broken off. Then lay down a weed blanket or mulch to prevent any dormant seeds from breaking through to the light. In the fall you can lay down sheets of newspaper and weigh them down with boards to kill weeds without digging.

By spring, when you begin planting your weed free plot you may need to replenish the previous season's mulch with another thick layer. Scoop back the new mulch to set into place transplants or sow rows of seed.

FERTILIZER. When you buy a commercial fertilizer the nutrient formula is expressed in three numbers, such as 5-10-5, meaning 5% nitrogen, 10% phosphorus and 5% potash. The rest is 'filler' that acts as a distributor. Therefore, if you find a similar size bag of fertilizer with the higher percentages, such as 10-20-10 for the same price, then the higher percentage bag is a better deal. However, it doesn't quite work that way comparing a chemical fertilizer with an organic formula because the organic formula – even with lower percentages – can be MORE EFFICIENT at feeding plants. Remember, also, that total reliance on a chemical fertilizer can create a salt build up over time, while an organic fertilizer will not.

Whenever you are in doubt about what formula to use, consider a 1-2-1 balance; in other words 5-10-5, 10-20-10 or other combination.

Nitrogen is responsible for healthy leaves. It occurs naturally during thunderstorms, entering the soil during downpours. It is also available in decayed vegetable matter and animal manure, liquid seaweed, fish emulsion and blood meal. Natural nitrogen from these sources is released slowly and there is no risk of 'burning' your plants. In chemical form nitrogen is supplied as fast acting and slow release. Fast release acts quickly but soon drains away from the soil and repeat applications may be need to maintain healthy green color. Fast release nitrogen fertilizers can burn plants if not applied strictly according to label instructions. Slow release nitrogen fertilizers release their nitrogen content gradually over the entire season to avoid burning. Nitrogen especially helps leafy vegetables like cabbage and lettuce. Too much nitrogen applied to a fruiting crop like tomatoes and peppers can inhibit fruit yields.

Phosphorus promotes root development, also flower initiation and fruit formation. It is found naturally in bone meal and rock phosphate. If not used by plants phosphorus stays in the soil a long time. When fruiting crops like tomatoes and peppers lack fruit or take a long time to ripen their fruit, the problem may be too much nitrogen and too little phosphorus.

Potash (also called Potassium) is responsible for overall vigor and disease resistance. The most common natural source of potash is wood ashes.

Trace Elements are required by plants in such minute amounts that they often are not shown in a fertilizer analysis. They include calcium, iron, sulphur, copper, zinc, and magnesium. A well made compost pile will provide these elements. Calcium deficiency is common in highly acid soils, causing tomatoes and peppers to develop blemishes on their fruits. Lime or wood ashes will contribute calcium, also eggshells incorporated into compost piles.

GRANULAR FEED OR LIQUID FEED. Most commercial fertilizers – whether organic or chemical – are sold in granular form, for raking into the upper soil surface. However, since plants absorb nutrients in soluble form it can take time for a granular fertilizer to act. Liquid fertilizer, on the other hand, is generally in concentrated form for mixing with water (according to label directions) and applied either as a soil drench or onto leaf surfaces since leaves have stomata that allow the leaves to absorb nutrients as well as the roots. The advantage of a liquid feed is that plants can immediately absorb its nutrient content.

BACTERIAL FERTILIZERS. Plant nutrients are also manufactured by soil organisms such as microbes and earthworms that pass soil through their bodies and expel it in a richer form than its original composition. Certain fertilizers are formulated to add micro-organisms to the soil and feed them so their populations explode and they become more efficient at enriching impoverished soil. These bacterial fertilizers usually have a low analysis, such as 3-4-4, but this is misleading for once the micro-organisms are added and they increase, they manufacture nutrients much higher than the initial formula stated on the label.

Don't let all this confuse you. Start by making compost since well made compost will manufacture all the nitrogen, phosphorus, potash and trace elements you need. Add compost to the soil at the beginning and end of every season and you may never need to apply a commercial fertilizer. If you do, be sure to identify it as organic, even if the nutrient analysis appears to be low. Personally, I like to apply Bill's Perfect Fertilizer (a kelp concentrate) as a soil drench at the start of the season, and then follow it up with a foliar feed – such as Spray 'N Grow - as a booster application every two weeks during the growing season. See the Appendix for sources.

IRRIGATION

Water at timely intervals is key to healthy growth of all plants. Water dissolves nutrients so roots can absorb them. Since vegetables are composed mainly of water, and sugars move into the fruit from leaves in soluble form, lack of moisture can inhibit growth and cause poor flavor. Of course too much moisture can be as harmful as too little. Too much moisture allowed to puddle around roots will cause rot. Too much moisture on leaves can encourage fungus diseases. The best way to water is in the early morning or late afternoon, applied directly to the root zone.

The best type of water is rainwater collected in a cistern, pond or rain barrel. City water can be contaminated with chlorine and fluoride obnoxious to plants. Well water is good, but can be icily cold and cause shock to warm weather plants like tomatoes and peppers, if not first collected in a receptacle and allowed to warm before application.

WATERING CANS – if you have a small space to water then a 2-gallon capacity watering can may be all you need.

LAWN SPRINKLER. A step up from a watering can is the oscillating type lawn sprinkler that throws a curtain of water across a wide section of garden, back and forth drenching the soil like a shower of rain. Water pressure keeps the sprinkler head oscillating, and the sprinkler can be moved at intervals to water quite a large area.

SOAKER HOSES. There are a number of drip irrigation systems (also called soaker hoses) that can be used to water a vegetable garden at the turn of a faucet. The best consist of plastic or rubber hose that 'sweat' moisture all along its length. Although these can be laid flat on top of soil, they work best when covered with a light layer of organic mulch (such as straw) or with a covering of black plastic.

There is a misconception that a drip irrigation system is too costly for home gardens, and that an oscillating lawn sprinkler is all that's needed, but there are inexpensive drip systems available. My personal favorite (and least expensive) is a home garden kit manufactured by Irrigro. For less than $50.00 you can install 30 meters of soaker hose that allows you to irrigate up to 250 square ft. of vegetable garden. It connects to a water faucet or to a gravity-flow water tank. A typical installation uses four T joints that allow four sections of porous tubing to extend parallel from a 10 ft. wide header. It works entirely on water pressure or gravity flow, can be used in conjunction with an automatic organic fertilizer applicator, and saves 75% water compared to a traditional overhead sprinkler system. A soaker hose irrigation system can operate for a month with no more expenditure of water than a traditional overhead sprinkler system uses in an hour.

For aesthetic reasons I like soaker hoses out of sight. By covering the soaker hose with black plastic or an organic mulch and using the fertilizer applicator, the Irrigro system avoids weeding, hand watering and hand fertilizing. It is truly an automatic, labor saving system, once you have the soaker hose installed. See the Appendix for sources.

Carolyn's Comments:

"Over a period of 50 years Derek has built a library of more than 150,000 images of gardens and plants, some of them slides and many of them digital. Initially, these were to illustrate his articles and books about gardening, but as interest in gardening grew he was called upon to photograph products for numerous seed and nursery companies. This requires his growing them in the garden and so we are often able to evaluate a new variety ahead of introduction to the general public. One of our most memorable trips was through California, visiting vegetable breeders scattered along the coast from Ventura to Salinas, driving miles along dusty tracks to locate a production field of some new cabbage or strain of onions. Many of the images you see on seed packets today were taken by Derek, the vegetables either grown in our garden or from one of our field trips. Derek still shoots photographs for seed packets and also catalog publication. His book How to Photograph Flowers, Plants & Landscapes (HP Books) sold 40,000 copies worldwide and this was revised with a new title, Flower & Garden Photography (Silver Pixel Press), selling another 25,000 copies. Derek learned his garden photography skills from a famous British garden photographer, the late Harry Smith, Derek taking up photography in the early 1960's and continuing to this day. His first sale of images as a professional photographer was to Encyclopedia Britannica; and soon after that he was working on assignment for Architectural Digest magazine, shooting some of the world's most beautiful gardens, including celebrity gardens.

Over the years Derek has published 55 garden features in Architectural Digest, including an underwater garden on Virgin Gorda, established by professional treasure hunter, the late Bert Kilbride. The underwater part featured a shipwreck thronged by colorful fish, a Spanish cannon, and sea walls for corals. The garden was even home to a friendly shark. One of Derek's photographs showed Kilbride's island home and garden through the bleached bones of a humpback whale on a nearby beach. After the article appeared a famous fashion photographer called Derek and asked where he could rent the whale skeleton for a swimsuit photo shoot he was planning in Bermuda. Derek explained that he didn't rent the skeleton from anywhere — he was just lucky enough to find it on the beach.

I'll Make You a Gardening Wizard Overnight!

CHAPTER 7
The Wizard's Top Ten Secrets for Amazing Gardens

> *"The answer lies in the soil."*
> - comedian **Ted Molt**'s answer to every gardening question

Gardening, like farming, has its good years and bad. But if tomatoes experience a poor year from blight disease because of high rainfall, then another crop - like peppers and sweet corn - will experience bumper years. Rarely do all the factors favoring good growth come together for a perfect growing season where EVERYTHING does well. Flooding, periods of intense heat and drought, and unseasonable cold nights are examples of factors beyond our control. Even so, there are still some basic rules to ensure a bountiful harvest and beautiful crops. Here are my top ten tips:

1. Learn the difference between varieties. In particular check the number of days to maturity as harvest times can vary by several weeks. Store seed packets in the refrigerator crisper until ready to use. If you don't use the whole packet at one planting, fold over the packet tightly, and promptly put back in the crisper to prolong germination.
2. If you use a timed release fertilizer that releases nutrients over a protected period, I still advise giving the soil a fast-acting general-purpose liquid feed as it takes time for timed release fertilizers to act.
3. Grow UP rather than OUT. Vines produce more than dwarf varieties, will crop all season, taste better and demand less space.
4. When an early crop is harvested, rake in more compost into the soil surface, add more fertilizer and grow a succession crop; for example cucumbers to follow an early spring planting of peas.
5. Collect rain water from roof run-off in a rain barrel to conserve water. Dump in a bucket or two of compost to make a manure tea. Plants love to be watered with manure tea because the liquefied nutrients are immediately absorbed by roots.
6. Use spent food containers such as deep, quart milk cartons for husky seedlings like tomato and peppers. The bigger the root system, the better the transplant, and the earlier it will produce.
7. For biggest strawberries from a new planting, disbud the flowers until mid-summer as this encourages a stronger root system for subsequent crops and

a longer life for the plant. Grow a large fruited variety like Earliglow for extra-large strawberries.
8. Mulch to maintain weed-free rows, but use an organic mulch on cool season crops and black plastic on warm season crops.
9. Stake tomatoes to avoid rot. Use a wire cylinder so they can be self-supporting.
10. Compost continuously. Add compost in spring before planting and again in fall after the first frost.

FREQUENTLY ASKED QUESTIONS - The most popular radio show in England (and one of the longest running) is called Gardeners Question Time. A panel of four experts and a moderator meet in town halls across the country and take questions from a live audience. I occasionally receive a tape of the show, and I delight in the hour long banter that takes place as questions are answered. I especially enjoy the delightful range of English accents, not only from the audience but from the experts themselves. Usually there is a woman (or two) and almost all the women seem to talk like Emma Thompson in the movie Howard's End (whose garden I thought was the real star of the show).

The men usually represent two extremes. One invariably has an academic Oxford accent and answers most questions with a string of Latin names with perfect diction, like *Dolicos lablab* to describe the hyacinth bean . The other male expert invariably is the head gardener at some large aristocratic estate with an accent you can almost cut with a knife. I envision these down-to-earth "fingers in the dirt" experts as still wearing their rubber gardening boots and sporting sun-tanned fingers as thick as bananas. Usually they talk with a broad Lancashire, Yorkshire or Scottish accent.

It's especially good fun when the no-nonsense head gardener and the Oxford don disagree over an answer, or when one of the peaches-and-cream, so-polite ladies takes issue with a male response and chides him in the most disdainful manner. It's great entertainment, and the moderator usually manages to sort out the right answer. I wish America had something like it to listen to. I'd love to be the moderator, and I know a diverse number of experts who could bring just the right touch of color to the show.

Over the years I have been a guest on radio gardening shows and answered a lot of questions about vegetable gardening, from how to prevent iguanas eating vegetables in a Florida garden (very difficult) to which way up to plant onion sets (pointy side up). Here are some that I am repeatedly asked.

Q: My zucchini squash are flowering but they don't set fruit.

A: Lack of bee activity may be the reason. Take a male flower (the one with a powdery center) and rub it on the female blossoms (the ones with a shiny center). This usually guarantees 100% pollination.

Q: My tomatoes are a healthy, dark green color but the flowers are few and not setting fruit.

A: The reason usually is too much nitrogen (responsible for leafy growth) in the soil and too little phosphorus (responsible for flowers and fruit). Most

Chapter 7 - *The Wizard's Top Ten Secrets for Amazing Gardens*

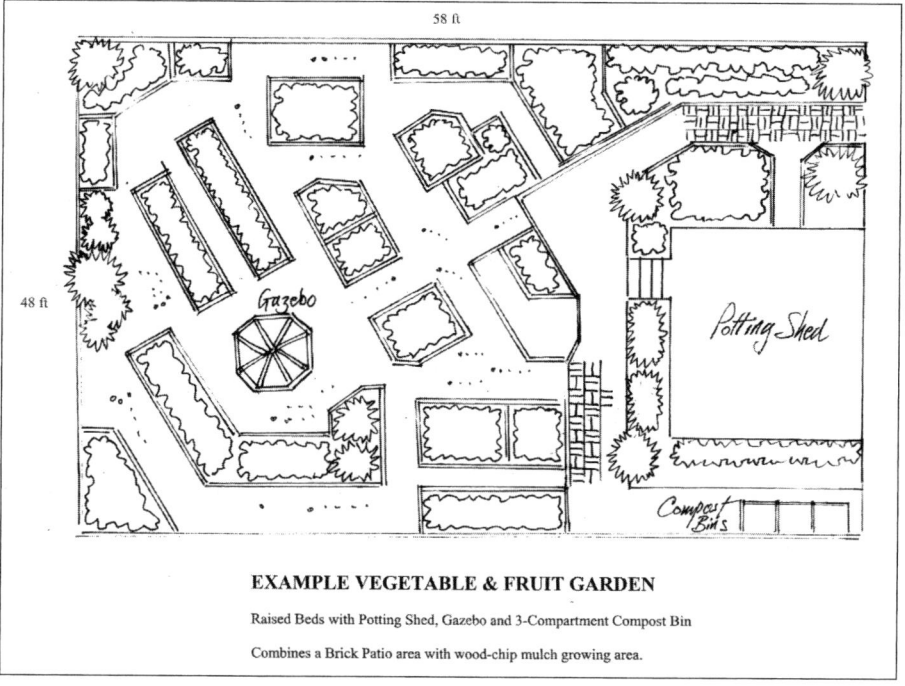

EXAMPLE VEGETABLE & FRUIT GARDEN

Raised Beds with Potting Shed, Gazebo and 3-Compartment Compost Bin

Combines a Brick Patio area with wood-chip mulch growing area.

often the excess nitrogen is caused from using too much stable manure as a soil amendment. Cold temperatures can also prevent tomato flowers from setting fruit.

Q: If my tomatoes are blackened by frost is there any way to save them?

A: Trim away all the black parts, leaving only the green parts and the plants may revive. However, a stressed tomato plant can take a long time to recover, so I'd recommend you use new transplants.

Q: How deep should I plant asparagus roots? Some books tell me to dig a trench 8 inches deep and line it with 2 inches of compost.

A: Tests have shown that shallow planting of asparagus roots encourages higher yields. About 4 inches is considered ideal. Instead of digging a trench you can lay the roots on bare soil and create a raised bed over them.

Q: I read that rhubarb leaves are poisonous. How much of the leaf is poisonous and are there any other poisonous parts of vegetables?

A: The green, ruffled fan-shaped part of a rhubarb leaf is poisonous but the stalk is not when cooked (raw rhubarb will likely give you a stomach ache). Other poisonous vegetable parts are the green shoots of potatoes, and all parts of a tomato plant except the fruit. In general, avoid eating the leaves of any solanaceous plant (such as tomatoes, potatoes, eggplant and

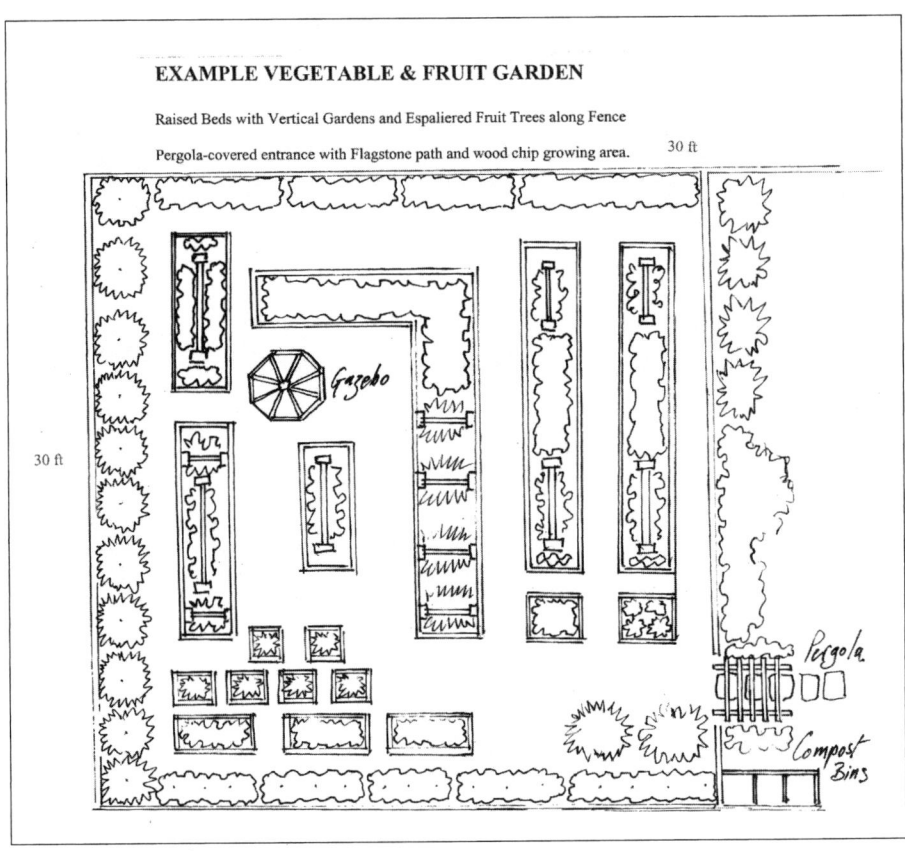

peppers). Some people can experience an allergic reaction to peanuts (a legume) and fava beans (also known as broad beans). The hyacinth bean is edible stir-fried when young and tender, but becomes poisonous with age so I only ever use it decoratively.

Q: I have a black walnut tree close to where I wish to start a vegetable garden. Will the black walnut affect the growth of my vegetables?

A: Most likely it will. The roots of a black walnut contain juglan, a plant poison. Since the roots can extend out well beyond the tree's drip line it could inhibit the growth of your vegetables. If you have no other choice, then create a raised bed so the vegetable roots remain above the walnut roots.

Q: I'm told not to put bones, fat and meat scraps on a compost pile. Why?

A: They attract rats, raccoons and other foraging animals. Bones (except fish bones) take a long time to decompose. These are best added to a burn pile so the heat makes them brittle and powdery.

Q: Why is sawdust not recommended as a mulch?

A: It depletes the soil of nitrogen as it decomposes. However, nitrogen is never a stable nutrient since it leaches from the soil quickly after rains. If you use sawdust to mulch simply ensure you drench the soil with a liquid nitrogen fertilizer according to label directions.

Q: How much topsoil do vegetables need?

A: A minimum of 6 inches since the main feeder roots of vegetables remain in the first 6 inches of soil. However, in impoverished soils, or heavy clay soils I recommend a minimum of 10 inches.

Q: Is it really necessary to remove excess fruit if my fruit trees set a large amount of fruit?

A: Yes. Fruit trees like apples, pears, peaches and nectarines sometimes alternate between a lean crop one year and an abundant crop the next. Too many fruit may stress the tree and cause it to drop all its fruit or cause the fruit to be small. It is generally not necessary to thin fruit on cherries or plums.

Carolyn's Comments:

"For six years Derek hosted the Step-by-Step gardening show on QVC, the television shopping channel, and I was hired to work as his stylist. We made television history by giving QVC its first successful garden show selling live plants. Derek still cherishes a letter from the president of QVC complimenting him on his achievement. The studio is only an hour drive from our farm, and we would load up our pick-up truck with flowers and vegetables to display on the set for we found that it was difficult to sell a product without actually having a sample of it to show. I recall one time when a variety of strawberry sold out so fast Derek gave the hostess a gentle hug and she hugged him back so tightly their belt buckles locked. Derek especially enjoyed the part of the show where viewers could call in to ask a question because he liked to test his knowledge. The shows were always live, unscripted and completely spontaneous - sometimes two hours in length - and he enjoyed it, but after six years he decided it was preventing him from doing other things he wanted to do, like writing more books. I have continued my relationship with QVC as a set designer. They keep me busy from the end of January to the end of May with their garden shows."

I'll Make You a Gardening Wizard Overnight!

CHAPTER 8
How to Make Pests & Diseases Disappear

"The best protection any living thing has against disease is to avoid stress." -
Charles H. Wilbur, *How to Grow World Record Tomatoes (Acres USA).*

First, I should say that in the past twenty years I have never used a commercial insecticide - organic or chemical - to protect my crops. I rely on a healthy soil to make my plants pest and disease resistant and if I do spot a potential problem - like a colony of aphids on my fava beans or Brussels sprouts - I blast them with a jet of water and rub the bare stems with a dishcloth. If they persist I spray with a home-made brew of garlic and hot pepper juice (see page 79). If I see slug damage I hunt them in the morning and remove them by hand. If an infestation of bean beetles occurs I cut off the parts that are colonized and burn them. If the damage is so bad the leaves of an entire plant turn brown, I will uproot it and burn it.

FLOATING ROW COVERS. I do not grow my vegetables and fruits to sell. They are all for personal consumption, so a few slug bites on my cabbages or lettuce doesn't concern me. If it did, rather than use any kind of pesticide - organic or inorganic - I would use horticultural fleece, also known as floating row covers. This lightweight white fabric protects plants like a spider's web, allowing in sunlight but blocking out insect pests and disease organisms.

I have always admired the poetry of Robert Burns, the Scottish ploughman poet. He had a close affinity to nature, and wrote some fine poetry about some strange topics: Ode to a Flea, Ode to a Mouse and Ode to a Haggis (a traditional Scottish dish that tastes like scrapple). He wrote in a Scottish dialect that is sometimes difficult for people to understand, but since I lived in Scotland for two years, I have no difficulty with it. To help more people understand the genius of Burns's poetry I re-wrote his Ode to a Flea and made it an Ode to a Slug:

THE GARDEN SLUG
Hey, where're you going you creepy crawly?
Your ugliness protects you, surely.
I can't bear to even touch you, munching slowly
Over every succulent leaf and petal.
Though faith! I fear you dine too grandly
In such a hallowed place.

You slimy, crawling, boneless wonder;
Detested, shunned by child and gardener,
How dare you set to scrounge and plunder
In so fine a garden!
Go somewhere else and seek your dinner
In some wild dominion.

Begone! In someone else's plot go ramble;
There you may creep and crawl and scramble
With other kindred, slithering beasties,
And eat heartily on less precious fare,
Bereft of lettuce, beets and cabbage
To feed your appetite.

If I stoop to pick, you drop out of sight,
Below the stems, snug and tight.
But still you'll stir at the approach of night,
to the very towering topmost height
Of every tasty plant.

Good grief! How bold your eyes and nose stand out.
As plump and gray as any grapelet.
Oh, for some nasty powder or lethal poison -
I'd give you such a dose o' it
To snuff your life out
And save my plants from your bitter bite.

I would not be surprised to discover
You under a stone after every shower,
But on my precious salad greens, why
How dare you trespass
And steal what's mine.

Good riddance to your sticky trails!
Never more to hide beneath straw bales
To forage more and make me rail.
For I have a hefty boot to stop your evil ends.
One stomp is all it takes.
And a hungry toad to rid me of your friends.

DEER CONTROLS. My biggest problem pest is deer. I live next to a nature preserve that exceeds 600 acres, and I have deer in the garden every night. I have tried every product that is supposed to repel deer and none that I know of are approved for use on vegetables. No vegetable garden book I have ever read explains that deer are NEOPHOBIC - they have a natural fear of anything new. Even a new planting they will tend to avoid, sometimes for several years; then POW that planting of peppers or tomatoes you were told had deer resistance, is wiped out. So when you attached pouches of human hair to poles around your vegetable garden, or bars of shiny soap it's not necessarily the hair or the soap that deters them, it's the oddity that raises their fear instinct, but you can be sure that eventually they will overcome that fear and no amount of hair or soap will stop them raiding your garden. In my experience, nothing works better against the depredations of deer than a high fence or a garlic/hot pepper liquid spray.

GARLIC SPRAYS. Not all household remedies are useless. When I visited the late organic gardening expert, Dr. Shewell Cooper of the Good Gardeners Association, at his immaculate garden and research facility north of London I could find hardly a blemish on any of his vegetables and fruits. I asked him what he used as a control and he showed me a bottle containing a garlic concentrate. For myself I like to use a garlic and hot pepper mix (see page 195) which has proven especially effective on mite and aphid concentrations, and available commercially as a concentrate to dilute with water.

INSECTICIDAL SOAPS can be purchased commercially and also home-made to control soft-bodied insects. Here's a recipe I can recommend: Select any liquid dishwashing soap that does not contain a degreaser. Mix 2 tablespoons of the liquid soap with one gallon of water. Pour into a spray bottle and spray the stems and leaves on both sides for protection. Apply either early or late in the day. Commercial insecticidal soaps usually contain a 'sticking agent' (usually coconut oil) so the spray doesn't wash off immediately after rain.

INSECTICIDAL OILS can also be purchased commercially or home made. These cause many potential pests and their eggs to suffocate before they can form colonies. Insecticidal oils are effective on apples in the bud stage and on corn silks to deter the earworm that burrows into the kernels from the top of the cob. Here's a home recipe for an insecticidal oil: Use a light cooking oil such as sunflower, corn, or soybean. Mix 2 teaspoons of oil with 1 gallon of water and spray on plants either early or late in the day.

Here are some organically approved insecticides available commercially:

BT (also known as *Bacillus thuringiensis*), is a bacterium that attacks caterpillars. It is available as a powder or liquid for spraying on plants, killing caterpillars soon after they emerge from their eggs. Another biological control, *Bacillus papillae* (also called milky spore), is sold as a powder specifically to control Japanese beetle grubs that overwinter in soil. In addition to cultivated soils, apply it over lawn areas, as the grubs like to hide under turf as well as bare soil. The best method of protection is to treat the ground in spring, dropping one level teaspoon of the powder every two or three steps. The biological control can remain effective for 20 years.

DIATOMACEOUS EARTH is a powdery substance mined in areas where tiny marine creatures eons ago died and built up limestone-like deposits sometimes hundreds of feet thick. The dust is composed of tiny needles that tear apart the breathing systems of numerous insect pests, including slugs. Be sure to choose 'natural grade' or 'agricultural grade' and not 'swimming pool grade.'

PYRETHRINS are an extract from a perennial African daisy called painted daisy or pyrethrum daisy. It is effective against a wide range of insect pests, especially when combined with another natural insecticide, *Rotenone*, derived from the roots of the Derris tree. Use it against aphids, flea beetles, Japanese beetles, caterpillars and mealy-bugs.

INSECT TRAPS use colors or odors to attract target pests, such as Japanese beetles and aphids. The Japanese beetle trap attracts beetles through a pheromone lure - a sexual attractant. Avoid placing these traps in the middle of your vegetable garden, but rather to one side so that the lure empties your garden space rather than drawing beetles in from other areas.

BENEFICIAL INSECTS - An important part of organic pest control is to encourage insect predators like songbirds, toads and beneficial insects. Top of my list of beneficial insects is the preying (or praying) mantis. It's an odd looking creature - a kind of miniature version of the monster in the fright movie, Aliens. It has a long, slender body with bug eyes and a pair of horny front legs that extend a long way forward in a praying posture. These are used to grab harmful pests like Japanese beetles, Colorado potato beetles and bean beetles. They lay eggs inside a bee-hive shaped brown case attached to grass stalks and bushes. After mating, the female eats the male, and when the babies hatch in spring on a hot, sunny day, as many as a hundred may emerge from the frothing, melting egg case, perfect miniatures of their parents.

Another beneficial insect is the ladybug, easily recognized by its VW Beetle shape, red coloring and pair of black spots on its back. It devours aphids.

To attract beneficial insects, plant flowering annuals around your plot or among your vegetables, especially cosmos, strawflowers, zinnias and pincushion flower.

COMMON INSECT PESTS. Here are some ways I have controlled insect pests:

Aphids - These tiny soft-bodied, pear-shaped insects form colonies along tender plant parts such as the tips of Brussels sprouts and fava beans, sucking their juices. When I see them I blast the colonies with a strong jet of water, and rub the infected part of the stem with a gloved hand or dishcloth. Several more treatments may be needed before they do not re-appear. Also, insecticidal soap, neem and rotenone/pyrethum spray controls them.

Borers - When a vine such as a cucumber or squash vine suddenly wilts it is the sign of a borer inside the stem. The borer is a caterpillar stage of a night flying moth that lays its eggs on the vine. The eggs hatch and the caterpillar bores a hole into the hollow center, tunneling its way some distance until the vine becomes stressed and dies. A hole and pile of sawdust indicates where the borer entered. Garlic spray is effective in confusing and repelling the parent moth.

Cabbage Worms - These are the caterpillar of the cabbage white butterfly that can often be seen flitting around cabbage crops such as broccoli and cauliflower. In the early spring I used to spend time in the garden catching the butterfly but I found that it is easier to inspect the underside of leaves of susceptible plants for egg colonies and crush them with a gloved hand. Diatomaceous dust is also effective.

Corn Earworm - This caterpillar stage of a night flying moth burrows into the silks of sweet corn and enters the cob. There it feasts on the kernels, gradually working its way down the cob. Most home gardeners (like me) don't mind sacrificing the topmost rows of kernels to the pest, and organic growers who sell sweet corn often will cut off the topmost rows where the worm generally resides. Some sweet corn varieties are more susceptible than others, depending on how well the wrap leaves protect the cob from entry. An organic oil placed on the silks with an eye dropper can prevent entry of the corn earworm.

Cutworms spend daylight hours curled up in the soil and emerge at night to eat transplants at the soil line, particularly tomatoes, peppers and beans. I save the cardboard cylinder of toilet rolls to use as cutworm collars. As you place a transplant in the soil simply bury an inch of the collar so the tender stem and leaves of the transplant is out of reach of the worm. Drenching the soil with neem and applying Milky spore bacterial powder also control cutworms.

Flea Beetles. These tiny hard bodied beetles are hardly bigger than a pin head, yet they can infest eggplant and other broad leafed vegetables, punching holes in the leaves so they look as if someone hit them with a shotgun blast. If you are fond of eggplant, use a floating row cover to form a barrier. Diatomacious earth is also effective.

Japanese Beetles are a scourge in most gardens, and the best control is to apply Milky Spore powder according to label directions.

A second effective control I discovered by accident. I captured a handful of the adult beetles and tossed them onto the surface of my pond. When my young children saw how the fish quickly snapped them up in a feeding frenzy, they immediately dashed about the garden collecting as many beetles as possible to feed the fish. And each morning they would race out into the garden to collect more for a repeat performance.

Nematodes are tiny eel-like worms that are mostly prevalent in sandy, warm soils. They invade plant roots and are responsible for a lackluster appearance. If you suspect nematodes are the cause of poor growth then you can obtain a special soil test through local garden centers to positively identify them. Planting the area with marigolds has a repellent effect. Dig the marigolds into the soil prior to planting as a preventative measure. Do not use 'odorless' marigolds like Hawaii. You can also buy beneficial nematodes that will attack and kill the bad ones. For really bad infestations create raised beds filled with a sterile potting soil or plant your vegetables in sunken containers filled with a sterilized (steam-treated) potting soil.

SYMPTOMS OF INSECT PESTS. Here's a quick reference to diagnosing problems that can occur in a vegetable garden:

Symptoms	Diagnosis	Control
Leaves are riddled with holes as if hit by a shotgun blast.	Flea beetles.	Insecticidal soap
Leaves are skeletonized	Japanese beetles	Pheromone trap
Leaves have holes and silvery slime	Slugs and snails	Organic bait/hand pick
Corn kernels are eaten from the tip	Corn earworm	Insecticidal oil
Curled leaves, lackluster appearance	Aphids	Insecticidal soap
Curled leaves, fine webbing	Mites	Insecticidal soap
Seedlings disappear overnight	Cut worm	Use collars/Milky spore
Cabbage heads have holes and brown patches	Cabbage worm	Rotenone/Pyrethrum
Bean leaves shrivel and die	Bean beetles	Rotenone/Pyrethrum
Cucumber, melon and squash leaves shrivel and die	Cucumber beetle	Rotenone/Pyrethrum
Cucumber, melon and squash vine wilts and dies	Borer	Rotenone/pyrethrum
Plant has lackluster appearance and colonies of white flies	White flies	Insecticidal soap
Root crops have tunnels inside and out	Root maggots	Rotenone/pyrethrum

DISEASE CONTROL. It's difficult to take precautions against fungus and virus diseases by using a fungicide because there are so many that can cause potential harm. But even if you do see a disease, like powdery mildew (a white powdery fuzz on cucumber vines, for example), the affliction often isn't enough to kill the plant. Also, be aware that diseases affecting vegetables are most often caused by insects (like leafhoppers and cucumber beetles) spreading the disease, so if you can keep the insect population under control, it often follows that disease problems will be lessened.

The very best protection against the spread of diseases, or a disease re-appearing the next season is to clean up the garden thoroughly in fall and winter. After the first fall frost start to delegate dead stems to the compost heap or burn pile since many disease organisms will overwinter in leaf litter. I like to turn over the soil to expose any soil diseases, and lay down a thick layer of compost so beneficial bacteria can feed on disease colonies.

There are basically two kinds of plant disease - a group called parasitic because the culprit causing the disease is generally a microscopic organism that lives off plant tissue, causing stress and sometimes killing the host. These harmful organisms can be fungi, bacteria, viruses, mycoplasmas and nematodes. The effect of these parasites on a host plant shows itself as a disease - sometimes by leaf curl, by leaf spots, sudden wilting, blistered leaves, discoloration of leaves or fruit, and rot. These are the most difficult to anticipate and eradicate as many atmospheric and environment factors can play a part, like excessive rainfall in the case of fungus diseases.

Non-parasitic diseases are the result of some physical, nutritional or atmospheric condition. A good deal of preventative control can be taken to avoid them - for example sunscald (a pale patch that occurs on peppers, eggplants and tomatoes) is caused as a result of too much exposure to sun. Avoid pruning too many side branches on the sunny side of the plant, or stake plants so the upper foliage can cascade over the fruit. Blossom-end rot (where the bottom half of the fruit turns black) can be caused by irregular watering and/or lack of calcium. For more on these physiological diseases specific to growing tomatoes see page 153.

There are varieties of vegetables that have been bred to resistant common diseases. For example anthracnose shows itself as sunken black spots on fruit. Bacterial wilt is suspect when the tips of vines like cucumber and squash wilt, while black rot turns cabbage heads mushy and black. Fusarium and verticillium wilts turn the leaves of tomatoes, potatoes and eggplant brown, while rust causes brown or red pustules on leaves and an early death. Though farmers may spray against these problems to protect their livelihood, it makes no sense for the homeowner to do so. Rather, keep a watchful eye for early signs and burn infected parts, or use floating row covers to form a barrier against the disease being blown onto the plants, or introduced by insects.

Also, if you feel that diseases might be a problem you can choose disease-resistant plants. Read the seed packet or seed catalog information which will tell you whether a particular variety has good resistance to a disease or group of diseases.

With fruit, diseases can be regional, and so it is best to check with a local authority like the USDA Extension Service, for advice on problem diseases in your area, and how to cope with them. The Extension Service will also provide information on varieties that are most susceptible to a particular disease, and varieties that have some tolerance to it.

Carolyn's Comments:

"Derek was in his vegetable garden one day, harvesting cabbage and pleased with a new 8 ft. high deer fence when he heard the telephone ring at the house and went indoors to answer it. He returned to find a doe had wandered through the open gate and was eating the cabbages. As soon as she saw him, she bolted and bounced off the deer netting. She ran the other way, her hooves causing terrible damage to heads of lettuce and rows of bush beans, and bounced off it at the other end. So she stopped, looked to see how high the fence was, and in two clips she soared skywards and cleared the fence. Moreover, she came back in the evening and finding the gate closed, tried to cut the netting with her sharp hooves. She made a slash about three feet long for her fawn to get through and it finished off the cabbage. Since that incident I'm pleased to see that most manufacturers have increased the gauge of their deer netting because of complaints, but I'm sure some of the old flimsy netting is still around. There is a commercial product called Liquid Fence that we use on ornamentals to repel the deer. It has a rather powerful odor of rotten eggs when first applied, but as soon as it dries the odor is not detectable by humans. Moreover, we have found it tolerant to 1 inch of rainfall. Without fencing out the deer from our vegetable garden, and spraying ornamentals with Liquid Fence once a month, we couldn't have a garden, the deer damage would be so great. Derek has been so pleased with the product he allowed them to film their television commercial at Cedaridge Farm."

I'll Make You a Gardening Wizard Overnight!

CHAPTER 9
Variety Selections for Huge Garden Yields

"Selection is the beginning and end of plant breeding."
– Luther Burbank

The internet is a remarkable tool when you wish to find a source for any vegetable variety. Although I do give sources for seeds and other supplies in the Appendix, the easiest way to source any kind of garden equipment, seeds or plants is to enter the tool or variety name as a search.

A word of caution, however, about buying seeds or plants on Ebay: For years I had been trying to find a source for a rare flower I had seen in the Organ Mountains of Brazil, the blue amaryllis (*Worsleya rayneri*). I saw on Ebay that a lady in the Midwest was offering ten bulbs. The highest bid was $30.00. I would gladly have paid $50.00 and was about to enter a bid when I decided to click on the 'more information' button. Up came a color photo that did indeed look like the blue amaryllis, with its large trumpet shaped blooms, but as I read the fine print I realized this was not a photo of the blue amaryllis but an extreme close-up of a wayside weed from China with tiny blue flowers, not even closely related to the true blue amaryllis. I looked in a bulb catalog and saw that ten bulbs for this Chinese wayside weed were available for $3.00! Buyer beware.

As executive director of All-America Selections for several years I was responsible for administering test plots throughout the USA, recommending the appointment of judges, and visiting plant breeders worldwide to inspect their new introductions and advise them on which varieties might be worth entering for an award. The main purpose of the organization is to bring to the American public varieties worthy of home-garden cultivation. An award winner would ensure the breeder of sales far greater than he could expect without an award because the organization has the support of the entire American seed industry and had the respect of the press. I am therefore, acutely aware of the importance of variety selection in achieving a successful result. Many of the vegetable varieties I helped to introduce in the 1970's are still popular among home gardeners.

Shortly after I left the All America Selections to write garden books I was appointed a consultant on gardening to *Woman's Day* magazine. My first article for *Woman's Day* was about a brand new strawberry, Brighton, the first of a race of day neutral varieties that were truly everbearing and could crop all season. The editor wanted to make it easy for her readers to acquire the plants so she included a coupon at the end of the article offering plants to her readers from a mail order nursery. The response was phenomenal, and for twenty years I continued to write for *Woman's Day* and ensure that at the end of each article the reader could acquire plants, usually at a savings over store or catalog prices.

Other magazines saw these offers and followed suit. For a time I even worked with *Parade* magazine on similar horticultural offers. It was a very effective way to bring worthy new varieties to the attention of the American public.

Vegetable varieties can be highly variable in their performance, depending on many environmental factors, such as rainfall, soil fertility and light. A homeowner in Arkansas made news when he grew 342 lbs. of tomatoes from a single vine of Better Boy hybrid. A news release showed him standing on a stepladder - the vine packed top to toe with clusters of large fruited tomatoes - picking fruit above the roof line of his house. At today's market prices for organic tomatoes that single tomato plant was worth more than $1000.00! Of course, Arkansas has perfect growing conditions for tomatoes – a long, warm season that undoubtedly helped the vine to set a record.

Very few garden experts who write garden books know VARIETIES as well as they should because it requires a lot of travel and research to keep up with the many new introductions and evaluate them over a number of years. Rather, the authors present a laundry list of recommended varieties, with descriptions that read like a seed catalog, but they rarely give SPECIFICS or SUBSTANTIATION for why a particular variety might be worth growing. A recent vegetable gardening book listed six pepper varieties recommended for northern gardens, supposedly because they stand cool nights. Gypsy Hybrid was not among those listed, yet in more than 30 years of testing peppers for cold tolerance and visiting numerous test plots I have seen it outperform every other variety, bearing fruit under cold conditions when other peppers do not. That's why it won an All-America Award.

GIANT VEGETABLES. The world record for a giant pumpkin when I began writing about vegetables was about 300 lbs. Today it is 1,470lbs and the Ohio grower expects to someday produce one exceeding 2,000 lbs. World records for most cool season crops like cabbage and rutabaga are generally achieved in Alaska and judged at the Alaska State Fair. Although the growing season is short, Alaska has long daylight hours in summer. There is always a light on the horizon and it is this phenomenon – plus some home-made fertilizer concoctions each grower keeps secret (see my own formula, page 52) – that allows certain cool season vegetables to grow to enormous weights in Alaska.

There is a British seed company, W. Robinson & Son, that sells seed of giant vegetables suitable for winning contests. Their most famous variety is the Mammoth Improved Onion that can grow to 6 lbs in weight and measure 22 inches around. Other famous Robinson selections include the Mammoth Blanch leek, Exhibition Long parsnip, St. Valery long carrot, and Mammoth White celery. See the Appendix for more information.

EARLINESS. When you look at unfamiliar vegetable varieties on a seed rack or in a mail order catalog, look at the number of days to maturity. Earliana cabbage, for example, can mature within 60 days, whereas Premium Late Flat Dutch will require 100 days, some varieties even more. Similarly the jumbo tomato Ponderosa may take 90 days to ripen, whereas a billiard-ball size variety like Early Cascade can yield in 50 days from transplanting.

Chapter 9 - *Variety Selections for Huge Garden Yields*

Tomato, Better Boy hybrid

Zucchini squash, Richgreen hybrid

Rhubarb, Canada Red

Remember, vegetables can be classified as COOL SEASON and WARM SEASON crops. Examples of cool season vegetables include lettuce, peas, and spinach. Examples of warm season vegetables are tomatoes, peppers and eggplant. Don't rush transplanting warm season crops until after your last expected frost date in spring and keep an ear tuned to weather forecasts in case a late frost is predicted so you can cover susceptible plants with upturned buckets, floating row covers or peach baskets.

HEIRLOOM VARIETIES. Three of the most satisfying vegetable varieties I have ever grown are heirloom varieties – considered by most gardeners as vegetables grown before World War 2, and others to be vegetables introduced 50 years ago or more. Another definition, proposed by author Amy Goldman during a lecture at Google headquarters, California, is any vegetable variety that will grow true from seed, and therefore can be saved. In her tomato book some of the 'heirlooms' featured were bred as recently as 1990. It's an interesting point for debate, but I wouldn't consider a vegetable variety an heirloom until it was at least 50 years old.

Of course, not all heirlooms are worth growing. Most fell out of favor because of poor sales, and for good reason - something better came along, such as a disease resistant variety, one that is heavier yielding, or earlier, or more flavorful, or more widely adapted to adverse growing conditions, such as cool weather, or better looks such as a deeper color or even a different color. Moon and Stars watermelon fell out of favor because its pink-flesh has an insipid flavor compared to many newer red varieties. It has come back into favor through the efforts of the Seed Saver's Exchange. This watermelon has a dark green, almost black skin color, with a big yellow disk representing the moon, and yellow speckles representing stars in a constellation. It is today a popular melon variety among organic gardeners, largely for its novelty value in my opinion. Similarly, Country Gentleman sweet corn has come back into favor as an heirloom. The small, white kernels are irregularly spaced on the cob and the flavor not nearly as sweet as Silver Queen and other newer varieties. Still, it's good to have genetic diversity, so no matter how poorly a variety may perform today, it could have value for plant breeders in the future as germ plasm, which is why we now have seed banks to perpetuate non hybrid germ-plasm (any plant material – seeds or cuttings, for example - that can be used for breeding.)

The three heirloom vegetable varieties I grow every year are Lazy Wife pole bean, Trombone climbing zucchini and Big Rainbow tomato which seems to have a number of other names such as Striped German, Pineapple, Flame and Gold Medal since they are indistinguishable from one another. Fruits of Big Rainbow (and its look-alikes) are yellow with red stripes and a red and yellow marbled meaty interior. Individual fruits are smooth and can weigh up to 2 lbs each, and they are delicious. A mid-season variety, Big Rainbow produces non-stop until fall frost.

BRAND NAMES. Today, the USDA discourages seed companies from calling seed varieties by different names. But in fact there is a legal loophole some seed companies use to get around that – by giving their invented name in big letters and calling it a 'brand' name for the real name printed in small type. Greenbud broccoli, for example, is a brand name for

De Cicco broccoli. The tight-budded De Cicco wouldn't sell as successfully under its registered name, so an enterprising seedsman gave it the different, more salesworthy name Greenbud and trademarked the new name. There's another way around the rule – it applies only to seed, not transplants, such as seedlings sold in six packs. Why? Because the nursery industry lobbied for plants to be excluded from the regulation. There is a simple solution to every political problem. It's just the politicians that make it difficult.

PLANT PATENTS. For many years the government allowed plants grown from roots and cuttings to be patented but not seeds. In order to encourage plant breeders to develop more non hybrid seeds, the government finally established patents for seeds of open-pollinated varieties. This allows the breeder of a superior new variety to earn royalties from his invention, like any other inventor can earn royalties on sales. Just think of it – if Luther Burbank, who bred the Russet Burbank potato or Alexander Livingstone, who bred the world's first commercially successful tomato, Paragon, had been able to patent their varieties you might not have chemical companies among the world's wealthiest, but *seed companies*.

Some seed companies have built a reputation by refusing to supply hybrids, GMO (genetically modified) and patented seed varieties. I can see the rationale in not offering hybrids because they tend to be more expensive and can't become an heirloom. I can also see why they would not offer GMO (known as Frankenstein seed) because of fears of unknown side effects from breeding toxins into vegetables to control insect pests, but why eliminate patented seed varieties if the royalty goes to rewarding a hard working plant breeder struggling to earn an honest living? I suppose the fear is that all non hybrid patented varieties may end up in the hands of conglomerates but I don't believe that could ever happen because there are too many breeders. No-one objects to an author earning royalties from a book, so why object to a plant breeder earning a royalty from his creation?

GMO SEED. The initials GMO stand for gene modified seed. There is a big difference between hybrids and seed of GMO varieties. The use of hybrids is an organically approved way to gain higher yields and better disease resistance than open pollinated varieties. But GMO seed often produces a natural insect toxin for specific insect control. For example, the natural insecticide BT that kills caterpillars, and the natural insect toxin rotenone which comes from the derris plant, can be bred into soybeans, potatoes and corn. However, rotenone is poisonous to fish, and though it is considered harmless to humans, do you really want your rotenone bred into the plant? I don't and a lot of other gardeners don't either. In fact, they have coined a name for GMO plants – 'Frankenstein food.' Because of the controversy surrounding GMO seed, some seed companies have pledged not to sell GMO seed and have joined an organization called the Safe Seed Initiative (visit www.gene-watch.org for more information.)

RAINBOW VEGETABLES. When I visited a community garden in a rough neighborhood of Chicago, I heard complaints about the participants losing their vegetables – especially tomatoes and melons - to thieves. But I met one enterprising youngster who had figured out an original way to avoid theft. He grew vegetables with unusual colors – purple asparagus, white eggplant, black tomatoes, yellow beets, yellow heads of broccoli, yellow chard, black radishes, speckled lettuce that looks like it might be diseased, red Brussels sprouts, lemon cucumbers, purple-podded pole beans, red okra and purple carrots. These colors are so bright they can look painted, or grown for strictly ornamental purposes, and to the thieves - unfamiliar with vegetable varieties - they looked suspicious, even poisonous. And so these off-color vegetables were left alone. In fact, many of these colorful varieties have other reasons to be grown besides a unique color. They can be more flavorful (like Yellow Baby watermelon) and more tender (like Bright Lights Swiss chard and Purple Passion asparagus). If they were not they would not stay around very long. A vegetable must have a better reason for being grown other than an unusual color.

There are thousands of healthy nutrients found in plants, and to get as many as possible into your system it's important to eat a wide range of different colored vegetables – orange/yellow from carrots and crookneck squash; red/green from red and green cabbage; white/black from radishes and eggplant; blue/purple from potatoes and purple-podded snap beans. By putting something of every color on your plate you are more likely to eat the right amount of nutrients to keep you healthy .

ANTI-OXIDANTS. Vegetables are the primary source of anti-oxidants: blood purifiers that ward off disease, such as cancer and diabetes. Since vegetables begin to lose their nutritional value soon after they are picked, it is vital to harvest as close to meal times as possible. Also, much nutritional value is contained in the skin of vegetables like potatoes, carrots, and turnips, so rather than peel, simply scrape the surface clean with a brush or plastic scrubber.

VARIETY RECOMMENDATIONS. The following is a list of vegetable varieties I have found worth growing, having tested them consistently at my research farm, Cedaridge Farm, in Bucks County, Pennsylvania and also judged them at trial gardens across the country. It's an unbiased listing. I make no distinction between non hybrids (open pollinated), hybrid or heirloom. The criteria for recommending these is performance.

Artichoke – An edible thistle.

I always enjoy the drive from San Francisco airport south to Carmel where I like to stay while attending the California seed trials in April. On the approach to Watsonville, along the coast road there are hundreds of acres of artichokes grown for market. The soil is sandy, almost black from heavy applications of compost, and the coastal mists are perfect for warding off frost and ensuring cool growing conditions. In Europe, Britanny is the principle artichoke region, especially around the historic port city of Roskoff where artichoke fields extend for miles right to the cliff tops.

Generally speaking artichokes require two seasons to produce the large, thistle-like edible buds. They are tender perennials and the first season plants normally produce silvery, spiky leaves. They require three feet spacing and normally are not practical for small gardens.

Plants require full sun and a sandy soil that drains well. When the edible buds form they are composed of triangular shaped scales and must be harvested prior to opening out into a purple thistle-like flower. Harvest by cutting the globe with 1 inch of stem attached as this is also edible. The globes are best steamed or boiled until tender (usually 40 minutes). They are eaten by pulling off the scales and scraping the tender base with one's teeth. The closer to the center, the more tender the scales become. Do not eat the choke – the heart of the artichoke, as it is fibrous, but do eat the base and the tender part surrounding the choke, which are the tastiest parts.

Each year an artichoke's roots will spread, and attempt to send up multiple sprouts in spring. Prune away all but four sprouts to obtain the best production. They are heavy feeders, and generally respond well to a high phosphorus fertilizer.

Globe artichokes are not high on my list of worthwhile vegetables to grow since store-bought kinds can cost as little as $1.00 to $2.00, but they are a delicacy and often grown in flower beds for their ornamental leaves, with the edible globes as a bonus. Freshly harvested globes will keep for several weeks in the refrigerator crisper.

ARTICHOKE GREEN GLOBE – Globes the first season.

The variety Green Globe is an open-pollinated variety that reliably grows edible globes the first season from seeds started indoors 10 weeks before outdoor planting after frost danger. A larger number of globes is possible by planting the more vigorous hybrid, Imperial Star. In zones 7 and colder it can produce eight to ten globes the first season and then the plant will rest over winter. South of zone 7 the plants can be left in the ground to come back year after year.

Arugula – Fastest maturing salad green

Also known as roquette, arugula is a tasty salad green best grown from seed sown directly into the garden as soon as the soil can be worked in spring. Choose a sunny site with good drainage. The plants are hardy and will survive mild frosts. Germination occurs within in a few days, and the plants grow quickly, looking like dandelion leaves. They have a pleasant 'nutty' flavor, prized for salads and they will tolerate crowding. Although many seed catalogs give the maturity time as 30-40 days, the leaves can be harvested much earlier, within two weeks of germinating. The more green leaves you pick the more the plant will grow replacements until it finally bolts to seed with a display of dainty white flowers. Sow seed directly into the garden in a broad row, spacing seed at least 1 inch apart. The seed is small and needs covering with just enough soil to anchor it – not more than 1/4 inch. There is a big difference in appearance among varieties. Some have slender serrated leaves, others have large lobed leaves. Personally I prefer the slender serrated leaves for salads, the larger leaves for cooking like spinach.

Several sowings can be made before the hot days of summer inhibit growth. Renew sowings after cool weather occurs in late August and September. Since arugula can cost up to $3.00 a bunch in stores, even a 15 ft row will repay the cost of seed many times over. A packet of arugula usually contains 500 seeds or more, and so with a 90% germination rate there's no need to sow the entire packet at one time, but save some for succession plantings.

ASPARAGUS JERSEY GIANT – All-male hybrid.

I remember in spring of 1980 meeting Dr. Howard Ellison, breeder of Jersey Giant hybrid asparagus, at a New Jersey diner near Burlington and travelling with him by car to his test plots near the Jersey Shore. I had grown a Dutch all-male asparagus called Franklim (sold as Ben Franklin in the US), and wanted to compare the quality of Jersey Giant with Ben Franklin in order to write an authoritative article for *Woman's Day* magazine, who also planned to offer their readers one year old roots.

Dr. Howard was apologetic because he had discovered that his production facility in Puerto Rico had failed to grow his Jersey Giant seed crop properly, and 20% of the crop was coming up female. For a man who had spent 35 years breeding asparagus hybrids to improve yields for New Jersey's asparagus growers, it was a crushing blow, since it would take another year to fix the problem and restore his reputation and he badly wanted the publicity my article could provide. On the way home to my car, parked at the diner, he began to feel better about the prospect of cleaning up the seed and my recommending his variety, and from the glove compartment he produced a Bible. He spoke of a recent spiritual experience that affirmed his belief in God and asked me to read certain passages from the scriptures. In my best Richard Burton accent I obliged, and Dr. Ellison's prayers were answered, for Jersey Giant has become the most popular asparagus in America among home gardeners.

Forget older asparagus varieties, like Martha and Mary Washington, which is a selection of Martha and earlier. They are no longer worth growing compared to the super yielding all-male hybrids like Jersey Giant. That's because in these older varieties there are two kinds of asparagus plants – male and female. You can tell the females because they produce red berries in the fall. Amish farmers used to grow extremely thick asparagus spears by growing asparagus from seed and weeding out the females. That's because the females need to put a lot of energy into seed bearing and so do not produce such thick or succulent spears as the males. Also, male plants live longer, they bear earlier, they outyield females and since they cannot bear seed, inferior volunteer seedlings cannot spring up in the bed like weeds. Jersey Giant is highly resistant to rust disease and tolerant of fusarium crown and root rot. Today, some catalogs sell only year old asparagus roots, but others do sell the seed. With a hybrid like Jersey Giant if you are planning a big bed, it might pay to begin with seed because the growth is more vigorous than a regular asparagus variety, and a modest cutting is possible the next season after planting, which is not the case with non hybrids.

Since asparagus is a hardy perennial you should choose a permanent position for it, preferably in full sun and a well-drained, sandy soil. Start the seed indoors 10 weeks before outdoor planting after frost danger in spring. If you purchase year-old roots you will see that they are fleshy and will spread out like the arms of an octopus. To plant roots, some books advise digging a trench six inches deep and lay the roots in the bottom spaced 12 inches apart. Then fill above them with a mixture of compost and topsoil. However, tests in the UK and Holland have shown that shallow planting of 4 inches promotes the highest yields, and so an easier planting method is to simply lay the roots splayed out over cultivated soil and mound the soil to a height of 4-inches over them.

Mulch heavily over the bed with any organic material, such as shredded leaves or grass clippings, to deter weeds.

Asparagus shoots are among the first vegetables to be harvested from the garden in spring. The roots send up shoots called spears that start to break the soil surface in late April (as soon as a spring warming trend sets in). They will continue sending up edible shoots all season until spring frost, but it is best to stop cutting the spears at the end of June in order for the root to rejuvenate itself. Harvest the thickest spears and leave the thin spears to create foliage to feed the root system.

Harvest the spears by cutting on a diagonal at the soil line with a sharp knife, or simply grasp a spear with thumb and forefinger and allow the spear to snap at the base. Asparagus foliage can be sprayed with a dilute liquid fertilizer, or use a soil drench over the roots to provide nutrients. A fertilizer high in phosphorus is best. Freshly harvested asparagus spears can keep for several weeks in the refrigerator crisper. For longer storage, they may be frozen. Asparagus beetles can skeletonize the foliage. Control them with a garlic/pepper spray or organic pyrethrum insecticide.

ASPARAGUS PURPLE PASSION - Spears as thick as a man's arm.

This high yielding non-hybrid variety was discovered in the alpine village of Albenga in Northern Italy. Its sweetness gives it a mild, nutty flavor, and its unique color makes a distinctive salad garnish when the tender tips are eaten raw. It has become so highly rated for its tenderness and flavor that Rutgers University is using it as a parent for breeding a new race of purple asparagus hybrids. I have seen spears of Purple Passion in French markets as thick as a man's arm and have myself grown them as thick as two thumbs, even thicker than Jersey Giant (though not as many spears per plant). The purple color disappears on cooking. Some catalogs claim that the purple variety does not produce a malodorous aroma in human urine like green asparagus, but this is false.

Asparagus is high on my list of profitable crops, even grown from roots, since they are perennial and store bought kinds can cost up to $3.00 a pound.

Lima Beans – also called Butterbeans

There are two kinds of lima beans – pole and bush varieties. The earliest bush variety was found growing beside a country road and sold as Wood's Prolific Bush in 1885. It was later acquired by the Peter Henderson Seed Company and the name changed to Henderson's Bush. The pods are small compared to pole limas and the seeds less than half the size of a pole lima.

In 1905 Burpee Seeds received a letter from a California grower saying that he had discovered two lima bean plants that were much larger seeded than Henderson's Bush Lima and had decided to auction them off to the highest bidder. Burpee was willing to pay up to $5,000.00 for each variety and obtained them for $1,000.00 each. By 1907 Burpee had enough seed to introduce one variety as Fordhook Bush Lima after his research farm in Doylestown, Pennsylvania, and limited sales to 5 beans per customer. He advised his customers NOT TO EAT THE BEANS, but to save the seed for the next year's crop as he thought it would take him a long time to build up sufficient stock seed to bring the price down.

POLE LIMA BEAN KING OF THE GARDEN – Ten times more beans than bush varieties.

Fordhook Bush Lima was a sell-out because gardeners liked the idea of growing large seeded lima beans on low bushy plants without poles for support. But think of it – a pole variety like King of the Garden – will produce a tower of foliage and ten times more yield in the same space occupied by a dwarf bushy lima bean. A pole lima is everbearing until fall frost, whereas a dwarf bush lima will exhaust itself after several weeks. There's also flavor to consider.

A plump pole lima is a far more satisfying meal than bush limas with their smaller seeds. The pole lima simply needs a sturdy support to grow up to 15 ft. high, loaded from top to toe with large flat pods containing up to six pale green beans that turn ivory white when dried. Introduced in 1883 King of the Garden requires full sun and fertile soil with good drainage. The biggest mistake is to plant the seed too early, for the seed is susceptible to rot during cold weather. Wait until well after frost danger. Since excessive rainfall can also rot the seed, I like to start about a dozen plants indoors five weeks before outdoor planting, or else pre-germinate the seed in a moist paper towel.

For support I like to grow my pole limas up tall bamboo canes, grouped like a tripod or teepee, one plant to grow up each pole. The plants are self climbing by wrapping their lead shoots in a spiral around the canes.

When harvesting pole limas, press the pod between your fingers before picking to determine if the seeds are fully developed inside. An immature pod will feel flat, not lumpy. Expect to begin harvesting in 85 days from sowing the seed. Pole lima beans are very high on my list of profitable vegetables because the dried seed can be stored for a long period in glass jars. The shelled beans also freeze well for long storage.

If you prefer to grow a bush variety of lima bean, choose the disease resistant variety, Fordhook 242.

POLE SNAP BEAN BLUE LAKE – Gourmet flavor

There are two kinds of Blue Lake green snap bean: a dwarf bush variety and a pole variety. Although the pods look alike in appearance the pole variety yields many times more beans than the dwarf, AND it bears all season, long after the bush variety has stopped bearing. The pods are slim, straight, six inches long, extremely tender, with an exceptional flavor. The white seeds remain small even when the pods are mature, unlike the heirloom Kentucky Wonder that quickly grows lumpy and fibrous unless picked young.

POLE ROMANO BEAN – The wide, long, tender flat pods of this Italian bean can grow to eight inches long and taste exquisite, especially served with bacon bits. The vines are remarkably productive, yielding up to 10 pounds of beans from a single vine. At $3.00 a pound, that's $30.00 worth of beans from one plant, $300.00 worth from a short row of just 10 plants. Although there are dwarf versions of the Romano, including Jumbo and Roma II, it is the pole variety that produces bumper crops in small space. Romanos resemble the British runner bean, but for North American conditions the Romanos are more flavorful since runner beans turn tough and fibrous in hot weather.

Both regular snap beans and pole Romanos can be direct-sown into the garden as soon as frost danger is past. Provide full sun in a well drained fertile soil. All pole beans respond well to foliar feeding and frequent watering during dry spells to keep them bearing generously.

BUSH BEAN ROMA II – No staking needed. If you'd like a bush variety of Romano bean make it Roma II. Ready to harvest in 55 days from direct-seeding, the smooth, flat, melt-in-your mouth pods grow to 7 inches long. The bush variety Jumbo is less productive though larger podded.

LAZY WIFE POLE BEAN – high yields and tenderness.

Pole snap beans used to be called string beans because a fibrous suture running the length of the bean had to be removed by hand before cooking. This was done by taking the stem and giving it a sharp pull. Lazy Wife was the first stringless snap bean. Introduced by the Amish into Pennsylvania in the early 1800's and first sold to the general public through the 1888 Burpee catalog, the curious name comes from the fact that it required no stringing and very little cooking to make the beans tender, with a melt-in-the-mouth quality.

Be wary of substitutions when ordering Lazy Wife from catalogs. The true Lazy Wife has a round white seed, not oval like other bean varieties. I received my first seed from a farmer friend, the late Bill Byrd. He had been saving his own seed crop of Lazy Wife beans every year for thirty years after they disappeared from catalogs; and when he passed away his wife Esther presented me with a shoebox full of seeds, saying Bill wanted me to have them. I have perpetuated the variety ever since. One year I wrote an article for a magazine called *Family Food Garden* which has since ceased publication, and in the article mentioned my Lazy Wife beans. I could not find a commercial source so I offered to send seeds to anyone who sent me a stamped, self-addressed envelope and a dollar. A thousand people sent me a dollar. One young lady from Lake Tahoe, who worked in a massage parlor, was so pleased to receive the seeds she wrote offering me a free massage if ever I was in town. It's amazing what you can barter for precious seeds. A couple arrived at my doorstep later that summer and handed me a carrier bag full of home cured bacon, pork chops from their own pigs, home-made sausage and two dozen brown eggs, to thank me for the Lazy Wife beans.

Lazy Wife will grow to 10 ft. high, loaded with clusters of green pods filled with plump, shiny white seeds. Do not plant too early after frost danger, as a cool wet soil can rot the seed. Better to pre-germinate the seed on a paper towel and transplant to the garden, spacing plants at least 12 inches apart. After the growing season, even after harvesting beans every day for meals, you are likely to have hundreds of pods dry on the vine. Shell these and save the seed for next season's planting, and any excess will make the finest baked beans you have ever tasted.

The main reason Lazy Wife fell from favor is its lateness and susceptibility to disease, but in my experience this occurs after a decent crop has been harvested and does not hinder a delectable harvest.

Artichoke, Green Globe

Asparagus, Purple Passion

Arugula

Bush snap bean, Roma II

Chapter 9 - *Variety Selections for Huge Garden Yields*

Lima bean, King of the Garden

Beans, Black eyed

Chapter 9 - *Variety Selections for Huge Garden Yields*

Soy beans, Fiskeby

Beet, Burpee's Golden

Beet, Cylindra

Broccoli Premium Crop

Brussels sprouts, Jade Cross

Cabbage, Stonehead

Cabbage, Savoy Ace

Collard greens

Chapter 9 - *Variety Selections for Huge Garden Yields*

Romanesco broccoli

Edible Soy Beans – super nutritious snacks

Edible soy beans are an excellent source of vegetable protein, also calcium and vitamins A and B; but order a side dish of edible soy beans in a Japanese restaurant and you can pay up to $10.00 for a small serving in a bowl. Grow your own and you will discover that a single plant of the edible soy bean can produce up to three hundred pods, with three or four green beans per pod. When I visited the internationally famous seedsman, Takeo Sakata (now deceased), in Yokohama, Japan, he invited me to his home for dinner and he served one of his edible soy bean varieties as a snack. His wife had simply boiled the pods in salt water to make the beans tender and we sat watching sumo wrestling on television, picking up pods and squirting the beans into our mouths.

Soy beans demand full sun and good drainage, each plant spaced at least 12 inches apart. The plants grow rapidly, do not need support, and will be ready to harvest in 70 days. The beans mostly mature all at one time, so I generally uproot an entire plant at harvest time and strip it clean of pods. Any plants with pods that have turned dry can be shelled and the beans stored for long periods over winter. I don't like edible soy beans with Japanese names as they can be highly regional in their performance. The American bred variety Envy is a good choice, developed by Professor Elwyn Meader at the University of New Hampshire.

FISKEBY SOY BEAN is a special high protein soy bean developed in Sweden by Sven Holmberg. I had a hand in introducing Fiskeby soy bean into the United States. In 1971, as executive director of All-America Selections, I was in London visiting British seedsmen, and Ms Xenia Field, garden columnist for the Daily Mirror newspaper, gave a reception in my honor at the Daily Mirror offices. Christopher Lloyd was there and also the youthful owners of Thompson & Morgan Seeds, Keith Sangster and his younger brother Bruce. Never have I met a more passionate pair of seedsmen. Afterwards the brothers invited me and an editor from Practical Gardening magazine for a drink at a local pub, and we debated trends in vegetable gardening. I mentioned an interest in high nutrition vegetables and the editor agreed, saying he had just interviewed Swen Holmberg about his new high protein edible soy bean. Keith immediately contacted Holmberg and arranged for world wide introduction of Fiskeby through his catalog. It was a sell-out and I'm happy to see it still available in the US through the Seed Saver's Exchange and other catalogs.

YARD LONG BEANS – Also known as Asparagus bean, this is a vigorous pole bean that is often seen in Asian markets. Plants grow quickly from seed direct sown after the last frost date. The long, green slender pods can measure up to 35 inches long, more tender than many snap beans when sliced into 1 inch segments and steamed or stir-fried. As the pods mature, they become soft and are easily shelled to release the shiny black seeds. In addition to green there are purple-podded varieties, but the green kinds are more appealing to most tastes.

BLACK-EYED PEAS - There are a number of bean varieties that are primarily grown for shelling, such as white navy beans, red kidney beans and speckled wren's egg beans. They are low-growing and compact, the pods turning brittle when the beans are ready to harvest. A special family of dwarf, compact beans called cowpeas or crowder beans are extremely heat resistant and grown primarily in Southern states. Chief among these is the famous black-eyed pea, available as a green podded variety or purple podded. Plants grow just 24 inches high, tolerate crowding, but prefer spacing at least 8 inches apart. Direct sow seed after frost danger in spring. Allow 90 days for maturity.

Beets – Red, orange and white

I'm sure everyone must be familiar with cooked beets and how sweet and delicious they can be, or pickled baby beets to eat with a fresh salad; but have you ever tried the famous Russian beet soup called borscht, or delicious crunchy beet chips as a substitute for potato chips? I add a little orange peel to my home made beet borscht and beet chips are easily sliced wafer thin and cooked in a deep fryer.

The trick to growing succulent beets is to ensure the soil does not dry out since they do not like any pause in their growth. Beet seed is a curiosity, rather lumpy and corky and composed of several seeds joined in a cluster, so no matter how carefully you space the seeds to get a spacing of 2 inches apart and 1/4 inch deep, your rows will always need thinning. Since pulling up individual seedlings is tedious and can disrupt the root system of its neighbor, take a pair of pointed scissors and clip away the unwanted seedlings at the soil line. It's quicker and safer than hand thinning. Be aware that eating red beets will turn human urine red.

Beets are a blood purifier and high in nutritional fiber. Like most other root crops they will store for long periods in the crisper section of a refrigerator, especially if the tops are removed. They will store even longer if stored in moist peat in a cool, dark frost-free place like a basement, again with the tops removed.

BEET BURPEE'S GOLDEN – A two purpose vegetable.

I was catalog manager for Burpee Seeds when the company introduced their remarkable Golden Beet. Similar in size and shape to a regular red beet, it has a golden yellow color that doesn't bleed like a red beet, and its leafy crown is more tender than regular red beet greens. They are comparable to spinach in flavor. Baby beets the size of a ping-pong ball can be ready to pick in 45 days from a direct seeding. Allow 60 days to reach slicing size.

BEET CYLINDRA – Space saving; more slices per beet.

This dark red beet is shaped like a torpedo, best harvested up to 8 inches long and 2 inches in diameter. One root will produce thirty 1/4 inch thick slices, compared to 10 from a regular round beet. A single row of elongated Cylindra beets, therefore, is like planting two and a half rows of a regular round red beet, like Red Ball. Cylindra is ready to pick in 58 days from direct-seeding.

BEET CHIOGGA – Colored like a bull's eye.

This oddity among beets is beautiful. The skin color is an intense scarlet-red – brighter than any other beet - while the interior when sliced across shows unusual purple and white rings in concentric circles like a target. The tops are a bright green, tender and a good substitute for spinach. An heirloom variety from Italy, Chioggia is ready to pick in 55 days. It is often a component of beet mixtures that can include red, orange and white varieties. Impress dinner guests by serving up a bowl of beet chips as an appetizer – using red, golden and Chiogga. I find the flavor better than potato chips, and the colors appealing.

Broccoli – Cancer fighting properties.

The anti-oxidant, cancer fighting properties of broccoli are well known, but it amuses me when a list of nutrients is given for broccoli since it invariable includes protein. I asked a broccoli breeder if that was true and he laughed, and explained that the protein comes from tiny green worms that hide beneath the buds and unknowingly get cooked with the broccoli heads when a nutritional analysis is made. The worms are harmless but if you feel a bit squeamish after that nugget of advice, then wash your broccoli thoroughly, breaking up the 'florets' into small clusters in order to remove the worms.

In addition to the heading broccoli, there is sprouting broccoli valued for its numerous small heads no bigger than a golf ball. These are popular for stir fries. There are both green and purple sprouting kinds.

Broccoli is best started indoors 5-6 weeks before outdoor planting. The plants will tolerate mild frosts. The earliest varieties require 60 days to maturity and prefer cool weather. As well as a spring crop, broccoli is good to plant in late August to mature as a fall crop. The heads can be broken up into small golf-ball size pieces and frozen for storage.

Control aphid infestations with insecticidal soap; control cabbage worms with organic BT (Milky Spore powder). Floating row covers will protect crops from flea beetles.

BROCCOLI PREMIUM CROP – You are not likely to find a larger broccoli head than this. The jumbo heads can measure 12 inches across, and mature in just 58 days after transplanting. The Japanese breeder, Takii is one of the world's biggest. They are specialists in breeding vegetables – particularly cabbage crops - and in the 1970's I visited their extensive test gardens in Tokyo to obtain information about this All America Award-winning variety.

BROCCOLI GREEN COMET – Extra earliness

From the same breeder as Premium Crop, Green Comet is the variety to plant for extra earliness. Maturing in just 48 days from transplanting, after the main head is harvested, smaller heads are formed on side shoots, to give you an extended harvest.

BROCCOLI ROMANESCO - Sensational cool weather crop

What an incredibly beautiful, bizarre example of nature's engineering Romanesco broccoli really is. Whereas regular broccoli produces its edible bud clusters in a smooth dome shape, colored blue-green, Romanesco is chartreuse and the tight bud clusters look like minarettes, or a type of exotic sea coral. The head has a spiraled pattern and each floret can be snapped off to eat raw as a snack. Eaten raw, the flavor is mild and crunchy, more like a cauliflower for flavor. First cultivated in Europe in the 16th century, it was reintroduced to British gardeners by the Scottish Horticultural Research Center, and to the US through seedsmen Thompson & Morgan. Do not overcook. To keep its crisp, clean flavor just lightly steam or briefly sauté. Start seed indoors 6-8 weeks before outdoor planting. Although hardy and withstanding mild frosts it sometimes does not have an opportunity to produce tight heads from a spring planting, but transplanted after the end of August in most northern states, it will make strong growth and large heads during cool fall weather.

Brussels Sprouts - Most flavorful after frost.

This member of the cabbage family requires a long growing season to mature (100-110 days). People seem to either love the tight green buds that grow along the erect stem, or hate them. They are one of my favorite vegetables to steam, though they are a magnet for aphids that like to colonize the topmost part of the stalk, sucking the life out of the plant. These can be controlled by blasting them with a strong jet of water and rubbing the stems with a cloth; alternatively spray with an insecticidal soap.

Seed can be direct sown in spring six weeks before the last frost date since they are hardy, or started indoors eight weeks before outdoor planting 24 inches apart. Wait until after the first fall frost to harvest them, as this improves their flavor. When the plants start to mature pinch out the top and this will encourage uniformity in size for the sprouts. By leaving the sprouts on the stem, cutting at soil level vendors at Farmer's Markets sell the stalks for up to $5.00 a stem.

BRUSSELS SPROUTS JADE CROSS. At age 19, I started to work for Hurst Seeds, Europe's biggest wholesale seed house and the only one in Britain that still conducted a breeding program for new flowers and vegetables. Their vegetable breeder was Lawrence Bevin who we called George. He was a big man with a deep, gravelly voice, and strong arms. The company had started in business in Pudding Lane, London before Shakespeare was born, and its first premises were destroyed in the Great Fire of London.

I worked with Hurst to improve their seed catalog and frequently visited their test gardens at Kelvedon in Essex. I used to interview the breeders whenever they developed a new plant variety, and I would photograph it for introduction to the world. Among flowers I introduced for Hurst was the first nigella (commonly called love in a mist) in mixed colors, called Persian Jewels. Ralph Gould, the breeder found a pale pink in a field of blue and from it developed the mixture of deep blue, pale blue, red, pink and white. He was also a judge for the Royal Horticultural Society's annuals award program.

Every Christmas Hurst had a Christmas party in their East London offices, and I remember Bevin making a grand entrance with his arms full of Jade Cross Brussels sprouts. He had not bred it, but he wished he had because he predicted it was destined for the Vegetable Hall of Fame, and he was right. Bevin liked the way the stem developed firm, round sprouts all of the same size to the top of the stem, and the fact he could still harvest a crop from the cold frosty fields of Kelvedon at Christmas was proof of its hardiness. He had to scrape snow from around the plants in order to harvest them. For the breeder, Takii it had won an All-America Award, the judges liking its earliness (90 days from transplanting), quality sprouts and high yield. Little did I realize that ten years later I would find myself inspecting Takii's vegetable trials as head of All America Selections, the national seed trials.

Cabbage – Why Alaska grows the biggest.

I am sure most people are familiar with the enormous cabbages grown in Alaska and wonder what it is that makes them so big. Is it the variety selection or some secret fertilizer like caribou dung that's responsible, or simply the skill of Alaskans to grow big cabbages? Mostly it is a question of light. During summer the sun never sets in Alaska and summers are cool, but it is this light duration that is mostly responsible for growing monster cabbages, although variety selection is also critical since you need a cabbage capable of growing big. Also, parts of Alaska have a cool, sunny growing season and that combination of variety selection, long daylight hours and cool summer temperatures is a winner.

Wasilla grower Steve Hubacek set a new world record in 2009 at the Alaska State Fair with a 127 lb monster he called The Beast, winning $2,000.00. Another champion grower in Alaska is John Evans of Palmer. Born in Ireland, over a period of seven years entering vegetables in the Alaska State Fair, he and his wife have won over 180 first places, and set 18 State and 7 world records. His record beaters include a 45 lb red cabbage, a 19 lb carrot, a 28 lb kale, a 59 lb zucchini, a 39 lb kohl rabi, a 42 lb beet, 50 potatoes from one plant, a 35 lb broccoli, a 31 lb cauliflower, a 53 lb rutabaga, and a 71 lb Swiss chard. He attributes his success not only to Alaska's long summer daylight hours, but also a home made 'tea' he makes from steeping compost with secret ingredients (probably fish fertilizer) in a bucket of water and squeezing it through cheesecloth. Since his well water is cold from glacier runoff he heats it to avoid shocking the plants.

Cabbage can be direct-sown, but I prefer to start seed indoors 6 weeks before outdoor planting. Since cabbages are hardy they can be set out into the garden several weeks before the last frost date. They prefer a fertile clay soil and spacing at least 12 inches apart.

CABBAGE STONEHEAD - Tight heads and extra earliness

Developed by the Japanese breeder, Sakata, this small size, early, smooth headed cabbage grows heads as hard as a rock. While a large cabbage might need two feet spacing, Stonehead needs 12 inches. It has a white, crisp interior good for shredding to add to salads. Plants mature in 60 days, hold their heads a long time in the garden, and store for a month in the crisper section of your refrigerator. It also has the distinction of an All-America Award.

CABBAGE OS CROSS – Jumbo Heads

This is the variety that is mostly used by contestants in the Alaska State Fair giant cabbage growing contest. Developed by Takii, the Japanese breeder, you'll need to give this monster at least three feet of space. Although OS has topped the scales at over a hundred pounds, 20 lbs is more the norm in a fertile, nitrogen rich soil. Even so, a 20 lb

Chapter 9 - *Variety Selections for Huge Garden Yields*

Cabbage OS Cross

Mammoth onion (left)

Chapter 9 - *Variety Selections for Huge Garden Yields*

Turnip, Tokyo Cross - early, cool season vegetable

Mustard, Osaka Purple - early cool-season vegetable

Chapter 9 - *Variety Selections for Huge Garden Yields*

Tomato heirloom, Big Rainbow

cabbage will get your name in the local newspaper. The leaves are a dark green, while the flattened globe shaped head tends to be a lighter color.

CABBAGE SAVOY ACE – A Dutch master

Although bred by Takii Seeds, of Kyoto, this large-headed cabbage always reminds me of the savoy cabbages painted by Dutch masters in their still life arrangements. They adored the savoy cabbage for its rich dark green color and appealing texture – prominent light green ribs and blistered (savoyed) leaves. The center is a buttercup yellow. Winner of an All America Award, plants mature in 80 days.

CABBAGE RED HEAD – All America winner. When I was head of the All-America Selections, two red cabbages won awards the same year for tight heads and extra earliness. They were Red Acre and Red Head. It was difficult to tell them apart without peeling back the wrap leaves that protect the head. Then, the difference was plain to see as Red Head had the most amazing dark red color. I love pickled red cabbage and for handsome looks alone I never fail to plant a row of Red Head cabbage.

CABBAGE GREENS – Collards, Kale & Mustard.

I group collards, kale and mustard together because they are hardy – ideal for winter gardens – and hard to tell apart. They are cool season crops that require identical growing conditions. The cooked leaves are essential to a healthy body, offering a powerhouse of nutrients to fight disease. The flavor of all improves after a light frost.

Among collards Hi-Crop is a vigorous hybrid with slightly savoyed, ruffled green leaves.

Among kale Redbor is an early (55 days) frilly-leafed dark red variety that's decorative enough to grow in a flower garden, although Blue Scotch Curled is the more traditional kale color.

Among mustards Osaka Purple has dark purple, almost black, leaves that are decorative enough to plant in a flower garden, but the blue-green variety Mizuna is the best for flavor. It's blue-green leaves are deeply cut and tasty used fresh in salads, or cooked as a side dish. Light cuttings can be taken within 40 days of direct seeding. There are other colorful mustards, including bronze and green, but Blue Scotch Curled grows just 16 inches high and is ready to harvest within 60 days of direct-seeding.

Carrot – Lots of sizes, different colors

Carrots come in all shapes and sizes, from long tapered kinds shaped like an icicle, to short stumpy varieties that look more like a baby beet. Decide which root length you want by the nature and depth of your soil: in deep, sandy soils you can grow a variety with a long root like Imperator, but in heavy clay soil the nearly round carrot, Parmex may be more suitable.

Carrot seed is tiny and will blow away if you even breathe on it. I like to sow the seed in a broad row and cover lightly with sandy soil – just enough to anchor the seeds. They will come up like hairs on a dog's back and should be thinned to 1 inch apart. Don't try pulling up the seedlings. Rather, take a pair of pointy scissors and snip the unwanted seedlings off at the soil line. Begin to harvest baby carrots in 45-50 days, mature carrots in 70-80 days depending on variety. Carrots can remain in the ground a long time and even remain edible up to the time the ground freezes.

CARROT SCARLET WONDER – Red, red, red!

Sometimes I fail to understand the American seed industry. Scarlet Wonder was developed by Takii Seeds, of Kyoto and when I first tested it I could not believe my eyes. It was the deepest red of any carrot I had seen, yet very few seed catalogs feature it – or any truly red carrot. They are mostly orange. I generally plant a 5 by 5 ft area of Scarlet Wonders in a special sandy soil mix for the express purpose of having enough of these beautiful carrots to make carrot juice. Perhaps after this glowing report more seed companies will be tempted to add Scarlet Wonder to their catalogs. In a farmers' market display it will outsell those French orange carrots like Nantes and Chantenay Red Cored every time.

CARROT KALEIDOSCOPE – All colors mixed

If you are undecided about what color carrot to grow, try this formula mixture. It includes purple, red, orange, and yellow. The 8-inch tapered roots grow to a similar size, and look sensational sliced into a salad. Incidentally, a formula mixture means the different colors have been grown separately and mixed in equal amounts to ensure a balance of all colors. With simple mixtures one color may predominate.

Cauliflower – Edible white, purple, orange and chatreuse bud clusters.

A close relative of broccoli, but later maturing, cauliflower is a cool season crop that is prized for edible, tightly formed bud clusters. The Dutch and Japanese are masters of cauliflower breeding, especially the Japanese breeder, Takii who also pioneered the development of other colors including orange curd, purple and chartreuse. I love to see the three colors displayed together at farm stands and farmers' markets. Plants mature 60-70 days after transplanting depending on variety. Since cauliflower is hardy, space plants at least eighteen inches apart, transplanting to the garden several weeks before the last frost date. Allow six weeks from starting seed indoors prior to outdoor planting. To obtain blemish-free, pure white heads it is best to gather the long leaves surrounding the head and tie them up over it with an elastic band. This excludes light and blanches the head. The blanching is not needed for the orange, purple and chartreuse varieties. There is a small-headed cauliflower called Stovepipe that wraps its leaves over the head automatically. The heads are delicious eaten raw, or steamed.

CAULIFLOWER SNOW CROWN – jumbo heads.

This extraordinarily large size cauliflower came from the breeding program of Takii Seeds, Japan. I was responsible for its introduction through the All-America Selections in the 1970's.

Celeriac - ugly on the outside.

This root vegetable is a type of celery that's much easier to grow than regular celery since it is grown for its large, knobbly, celery-flavored root mass, half of which grows above ground. Start seed at least 8 weeks before outdoor planting after the last frost date, spacing transplants at least 8 inches apart. Plants are slow growing and need 110 days to maturity. Outward appearances are deceiving, since once the tough outer skin is peeled, the white interior can be cooked like mashed potatoes as a delicious side dish. The root can also be shredded to eat raw in salads, or cubed for soups and stews. The variety President is an extra large strain that was selected in Europe. Lift the roots from the garden before or shortly after fall frost and store indoors in a cool, dark place to keep for several months.

Celery – a long growing season.

Seed of celery is best started 8-10 weeks ahead of outdoor planting to obtain husky transplants that can be set into the garden several weeks before the last frost date, planted at least 18 inches apart. It then requires at least 100 days for the plants to develop a cluster of crisp, erect stalks that are sweet and crunchy, with an anise flavor, eaten raw or steamed. Soil for celery should be black with compost, and fertile, with adequate watering during dry spells. Since the upright stalks are more flavorful when blanched, it is customary to heap soil up against the stems or exclude light by wrapping the stalks with a newspaper collar. Although regular celery is green on the outside, towards the center where light is excluded it turns progressively white or buttery yellow. Green celery has more nutritional value, but the white or yellow stalks are more flavorful and sweet.

CELERY GOLDEN SELF BLANCHING – Crisp, yellow stalks without blanching.

This unusual celery variety is amazing, for it produces a bunch of edible stalks without the customary green color of regular celery. The tops usually are green, but the lower part of the stem is yellow or creamy white.

Chayote – Productive vine.

This vigorous warm season, climbing vine produces dozens of pear-shaped fruit the size of an avocado pear, with a flavor like a sweet turnip. To propagate, purchase a fruit from the grocery section of your supermarket and plant the entire fruit, pointed side up, or on its side after frost danger in spring. A green shoot will sprout and grow quickly skywards if given garden netting or trellis for support. The vines fruit late in the season and will remain productive until fall frost. The fruit can also be started indoors by planting in a deep pot 6-8 weeks before outdoor planting.

Corn Salad – also known as Lamb's Lettuce and Mache.

This sweet-tasting salad green is fast growing, creating a rosette of watercress-like leaves within 40 days of sowing seeds directly into the garden. Sow a broad row, at least 12 inches wide, and thin to at least 3 inches apart. The rosettes will make an attractive, dense green groundcover that prevents weeds from coming through. The more you harvest the succulent leaves, the more new leaves will replace them, from spring until after fall frost. It is often an ingredient in mesclun mixes.

CORN SALAD BISTRO - cup-shaped round leaves.

There are several varieties of corn salad offered in seed catalogs, mostly differing in leaf shape, from rounded to strap-shaped leaves. For sheer looks and hearty flavor, Bistro is my favorite. It displays a tight rosette of cupped-shaped or spoon-shaped leaves that extend in a starburst like the spokes of a wheel. They are unusually sweet, nutty and tender. Makes a delicious salad all by itself or blended with lettuce, with just a touch of lemon or vinegar and oil dressing to enhance the flavor. Also use as a garnish for decorating side dishes of beets and potatoes.

Cucumber – slicers and picklers, American, European and Asian.

These warm season vegetables relish the heat of summer and are killed by frost. They respond well to planting through black plastic, maturing earlier and bearing heavier yields. The seed can be directly sown or started indoors four weeks before outdoor planting to get healthy transplants. Although the most prolific varieties develop wide spreading vines up to four feet wide and can occupy a lot of space, I plant mine 12 inches apart and allow them to knit into each other to create a weed suffocating ground cover. I also like to grow them up garden netting for they have tendrils that allow the vines to climb naturally. A higher percentage of fruit is possible by giving the vines support. I have never had problems growing cucumbers, but I do know friends who have been troubled by cucumber beetles that sting the vines and introduce disease. The best organic remedy is to grow your cucumber vines under floating row covers or repel insects with a garlic/pepper spray.

The most widely grown cucumber is the American slicer, like Burpee Hybrid – a hefty oblong-shaped dark green fruit that can weigh 4 lbs apiece and grow to 14 inches long. The fruits are best peeled and eaten raw or sliced into salads. A dash of vinegar and pepper enhances their flavor. At the other extreme are smaller pickle cucumbers. They vary in size and the larger ones can be used for slicing into salads. Another class of cucumber is the European slicing kind, like Tall Telegraph. These are more slender than the American and they are ribbed. A third class – the Asian cucumber – is similar to the European but even more slender and a new class, called Burpless – has a tender, bitter-free skin that doesn't need peeling. Asian cucumbers also include some extremely long varieties, such as Yard Long and the Snake Cucumber, which is not really a cucumber but an edible gourd that is best staked to keep the fruit from curling.

Some cucumbers are seedless and will produce fruit without pollination. Another group is classified as all-female, meaning that they set only female flowers. Some are self-fertile requiring no cross pollination with a male flower. The all-females can yield double the amount of fruit as a regular cucumber. Sometimes in seed catalogs cucumbers are described as white spine and black spine, referring to the color of tiny thorns along the surface of the fruit. Here are several cucumber varieties I can recommend:

LEMON CUCUMBER - a short vine type that grows yellow skinned fruit as round as a tennis ball. It's an heirloom variety ready to harvest in 60 days. It normally sets a dozen fruit quickly and then exhausts itself, allowing the space to be replanted by a succession crop.

There are a number of other cucumber oddities, such as a white skinned slicing cucumber and a yellow skinned slicing cucumber, but the lemon cucumber is the most popular of cucumber oddities.

ORIENT EXPRESS - an Asian burpless cucumber developed in Japan. Maturing in 64 days, it produces long, dark green, blistered fruit with tender, edible, bitter-free skin. Grown up netting to keep the fruit from curling, one plant can yield up to 50 fruits 14 inches long. I have known growers who produced up to 3 lbs of cucumbers PER WEEK from Orient Express.

SALAD BUSH HYBRID - an All-America winner, one of several 'bush' cucumbers that grow such short vines they are good for planting in containers, even hanging baskets. Plants start to yield 8-inch long American-type cucumbers in 55 days. It won its award not only for the compactness of its vines but also for powdery mildew and mosaic disease resistance.

Eggplant – Beware of pesky flea beetles.

Eggplants are closely related to tomatoes and peppers and require similar growing conditions. They like to be grown through black plastic as a mulch. The most popular type is pear shaped and black, though there are green, white, and purple skinned varieties in all shapes and sizes, from small and finger shaped to big and round. Flea beetles are the curse of eggplants. More than any other vegetable they will swarm all over the leaves, eat tiny holes as if the plant has been riddled with buckshot, and turn a healthy plant into a shriveled brown mess almost overnight. You can try controlling them with pyrethrin or rotenone organic sprays, or your own home-made pepper/garlic spray, but they are so persistent, I resort to floating row covers, making sure the plants are covered soon after transplanting. The fruits are susceptible to sunscald where light brown patches will appear on the skin surface, infecting the whole fruit. Grow your eggplant under a floating row cover and it will provide sufficient shade to prevent sunscald .

EGGPLANT DUSKY HYBRID – None better.

The late Ted Torrey was responsible for some of America's most popular vegetable breeding achievements, including the famously sweet Ambrosia melon and the giant-fruited Supersteak tomato. He devoted many years breeding towards an earlier, more productive successor to Black Beauty eggplant. As we toured his test plots l asking him his opinion on a variety called Dusky hybrid that he had in the trials as a comparison. "Dusky is the best eggplant I've ever seen," he said; "When I saw its performance last season it made me want to give up breeding eggplant. I cannot see how it can be improved."

Dusky is not as big as Black Magic, which it resembles, but it is a similar beautiful black color and allows you to cut large slices as big as a slice of muffin. I really don't care for those long, skinny eggplants like Millionaire and Slim Jim because I don't see any advantage to them. I want an eggplant that gives me a big, meaty round slice for roasting or layering in lasagna. Also, Dusky is earlier and more prolific.

Fennel - Anise flavored stalks.

There are actually two types of fennel – Florence fennel which produces a bulbous grouping of swollen stalks at the soil line, and a non-bulbous kind used mainly for its aromatic leaves. The bulbous kind is more difficult to grow since the mass of stalks is temperamental, often failing to form a bulb in warm weather, through lack of adequate moisture and poor soil. Seeds can be direct-sown several weeks before the last frost date in spring, or started indoors 6 weeks before outdoor planting. Space plants at least 8 inches apart. Harvest when the bulbs are 4-6 inches wide after 80-90 days. They can be sliced thin to eat raw in salads, or roasted. The feathery leaves can be chopped fine to use in salads and flavor soups. The seeds are also useful as a flavoring for curry dishes. The variety Orion is a hybrid that grows extra large bulbs preferred by French chefs.

Kohl-rabi - Turnip-like flavor.

This fast-growing member of the cabbage family resembles a turnip that has been pushed up out of the ground on a slender stalk. It also tastes like a turnip. Sow seed directly into the garden several weeks before the last expected frost date as the plants are hardy. Thin to stand at least 4 inches apart. Since kohl-rabi relishes cool weather, after the spring harvest, sow a succession crop in late summer to mature in fall. There are basically two kinds – white fleshed varieties and purple. The skin is tough and requires peeling, but the crisp, tangy interior requires just a short period of steaming to render it tender and delicious.

KOHL RABI GRAND DUKE — All-America Winner.

This extra large hybrid kohl-rabi, developed by Takii Seeds of Japan, won an All America Award for its size and earliness. Harvest the bulbs when the size of a golf-ball within 45 days or allow to grow to the size of a baseball.

Leeks – Extremely hardy

An elongated member of the onion family with a mild, sweet flavor, leeks can grow white stalks as thick as a man's wrist. They are slow growing and require 100 days or more to mature. Seed is best started indoors eight to ten weeks before outdoor planting in early spring. In parts of Scotland and Wales, special contests are held each fall to determine who can grow the biggest leeks. The secret to good growth is a fertile, sandy soil and regular irrigation at all stages of development. Leeks are especially sweet and tender when steamed to make a side dish. They are the principle ingredient in cock-a-leekie soup, a combination of leeks and potatoes. Titan is a variety capable of growing extra large stalks. The plants tolerate fall frosts and mild winter freezes.

Lettuce & Mesclun Mixes – The ultimate health food.

It was a Vermont farmer, Shepherd Ogden, who founded The Cook's Garden, a mail order seed catalog that today is published by Burpee Seeds. Shep and I have appeared together as lecturers on the same program, and I remember grilling him about his business when we found ourselves sitting next to each other on the same flight from

Philadelphia to Charlotte, North Carolina. One of Shep's ideas to make his catalog distinctive was to specialize in salad greens, particularly varieties of lettuce and mesclun which are mixtures of salad greens that contain an assortment of lettuce varieties. Even today the catalog features eighty-five varieties of salad greens, and I have grown every one. Among the lettuce offerings are Crispheads like Green Ice, Butterheads like Bibb, Romaine (or Cos) like Forellenschluss (German for speckled trout) and Looseleaf types like Black-seeded Simpson.

The Crispheads don't have quite as tight a wrap of leaves as Butterheads, but still possess a crispy, sweet flavor. The Butterheads have softer textured leaves in a tight bundle and a buttery yellow center. The leaves of Romaines stand up stiff and erect and are crunchy at the base, the kind most often used in a Caesar salad. Looseleafs mature earlier than the rest and do not form a head, but splay out their leaves in a rosette. They take crowding and can be sown close together. As you pick the outer leaves more new leaves will form in the middle.

Lettuce tolerates mild frost and prefers to be direct-seeded, but can be transplanted from seed sown 6 weeks before outdoor planting. They all like cool weather and when days turn hot the centers elongate and go to seed. I have often had fifteen varieties of lettuce in my garden, and nothing impresses a guest more than to be served a head of lettuce for dinner that they earlier admired in the garden, or to be given a freshly picked lettuce to take home.

Lettuce wilts quickly after being picked, and so I like to pull up the entire plant by the root, preserve a ball of soil and steep the root in a cup of water. This way the lettuce can stay fresh for several days before it starts to wilt.

In recent years the colors and leaf shapes of lettuce have expanded enormously. In addition to all colors of green, there are now pink, red, bronze and speckled lettuce for each of the main categories. In addition to broad, smooth leaves like Deer Tongue, there are feathery, slender leaves like Lollo Rossa, a red looseleaf variety that forms a frilly beautiful mounded cushion and a crispy heart of gold.

LETTUCE BUTTERCRUNCH – a gourmet treat.

In my opinion Buttercrunch is the best flavored head lettuce by far. Developed by George Raleigh, professor of vegetable crops at Cornell Univeristy, I first encountered Buttercrunch the year of its introduction as an All-America award winner, in 1963 while touring the trial garden at Hurst Seeds, near Kelvedon, England. I was in the company of Hurst's vegetable breeder, Lawrence Bevin. When we came to the lettuce trials –perhaps 50 varieties in neat 15 ft. regimented rows – I asked rhetorically "How can there be so many? Don't they all taste the same?" He walked over to a row of head lettuces that were dark green and as uniform as peas in a pod, pulled one up with a snap of his wrist, and broke the head in half with a loud snap. He showed me the buttery yellow interior, took a bite out of one half with a crunchy sound that seemed to echo around the field, and handed me the other. It was delectable – tastier than any lettuce I ever ate – and since that day I have never missed a year of growing it in my garden. It was Buttercrunch!

Years later at the Drake Hotel, in Chicago, while attending the Chicago Flower Show, I noticed the most expensive salad on the menu was Kentucky Limestone lettuce with a blue cheese dressing, and I ordered it. I had never heard of Kentucky Limestone and asked the waiter to inquire from the chef where such a delectable lettuce came from. Back came the answer: "It's another name for Buttercrunch."

The main point to remember about any butterhead lettuce is they will not tolerate crowding. If grown too tightly they may fail to form a head. Rather, start the seed indoors in a seed tray about four weeks before outdoor planting, transfer to individual pots as soon as they are big enough to handle, and set husky young transplants at least 8 inches apart. Rather than growing them in rows between other vegetables, create a block of plants, staggered to make a square or rectangular bed.

SIMPSON ELITE LETTUCE - Better than Black-seeded Simpson.

Black-seeded Simpson is an heirloom lettuce that enjoys wide popularity as a looseleaf lettuce. It produces a rosette of light green, ruffled leaves that mature earlier than heading lettuce (in 40 days). When Simpson Elite came along I was skeptical that it could be any improvement over the original Black Seeded Simpson, but when I saw the extraordinary growth of Elite I was sold. It has impressed visitors to my garden with heads two feet across.

Melons – Fruit of the Gods.

"Entering the melon patch is like walking into the candy store. It's the dessert course, only better." – Amy Goldman, author of *Melons for the Passionate Grower* (Artisan).

Although melon vines take up a lot of garden space if allowed to sprawl over the ground, they can be grown up trellis, the fruits best supported by a sling of cheesecloth so the melon doesn't detach from its stem when ripe and smash itself onto the ground. In the 1960's I worked with Burpee Seeds as their catalog manager and my office was in the top of a carriage house overlooking the melon fields. In August when the muskmelons (or cantaloupes) were ripening, the aroma permeated through the skin and filled the air with a honey fragrance.

To ensure extra-earliness consider starting melon seed indoors 6 weeks before outdoor planting after frost danger is past. Avoid organic mulches such as straw because they keep the soil cool, but rather mulch with black plastic which will heat up the soil and retain the heat during cool nights. Many melons will stop growing when the soil temperature dips below 70F.

CANTELOUPE AMBROSIA - I remember the day the late David Burpee called me to his office at Fordhook Farm, Pennsylvania, and invited me to taste a slice of a new melon from his breeder, Ted Torrey. It didn't look anything special on the outside – no pronounced ribbing like Burpee Hybrid, nor any heavy netting, and not as big. But the interior deep orange flesh was what I described in my catalog copy as chin-dripping sweet. The variety instantly caught on with farm stand owners across the country, and I noticed that in many cases if you asked the farmer for the variety name, he would either keep its name a secret or invent some fictitious name to ensure you would not grow your own, and you would keep coming back for more.

Cauliflower Snow Crown

Carrot, Scarlet Nantes

Celeriac

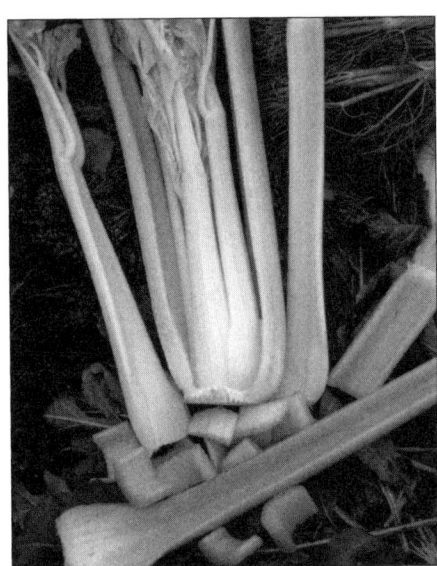
Golden self-blanching celery

Chapter 9 - *Variety Selections for Huge Garden Yields*

Cucumber, Lemon

Corn salad, Bistro

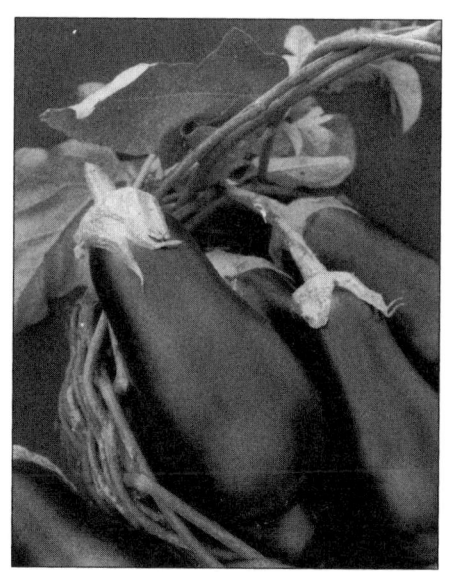

Eggplant, Dusky

Florence Fennel

Leeks, Titan

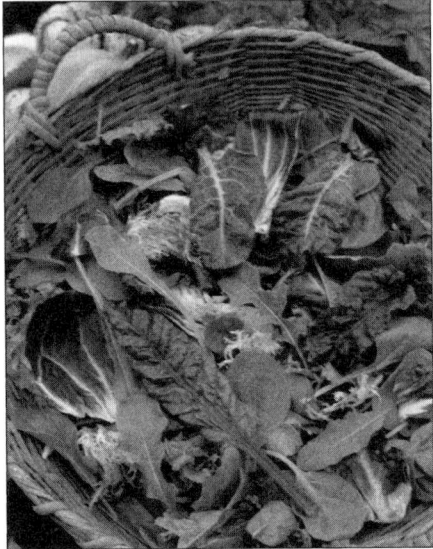
Mesclun mix

Lettuce, Buttercrunch

Cantaloupe, Ambrosia

Chapter 9 - *Variety Selections for Huge Garden Yields*

Melon, Ha'ogen

Okra, Clemson Spineless

Onion, Texas Supersweets

Onion, Walla Walla

Peanuts, Jumbo Virginia

Chapter 9 - *Variety Selections for Huge Garden Yields*

Sugar snap peas

Pepper, Gypsy

Big Bertha bell pepper (right)

Potato, Yukon Gold

MELON EARLY CRENSHAW – Oliver Crane was a melon grower in Santa Rosa, Sonoma County, California, where the plant breeding wizard Luther Burbank did a lot of his breeding work on flowers, fruits and vegetables (ie: the Burbank Russett potato). Crane developed a remarkable melon by crossing several melon types (possibly a Japanese melon, Persian and Casaba) to produce a large fruited late ripening, super sweet melon called a Craneshaw, later shortened to Crenshaw. Lightly netted and pear-shaped, the new melon showed its ripeness by turning from green to yellow. Its major drawback was late ripening, and so it was rarely grown outside Sonoma County with its long growing season, but that was rectified when Burpee Seeds introduced a big, beautiful, lusciously sweet early-ripening, oval variety called Early Crenshaw. In gourmet restaurants I have seen slices of Crenshaw melon on the menu for $10.00 a slice, served with wafer thin slices of proschiutto. The mingling of flavors from the delicate salty Italian ham and the creamy sweet orange flesh of the Crenshaw is surely one of the world's greatest dessert taste combinations.

MELON CHARENTAIS - Sweet and perfumed.

Although you will often see the name Charentais in seed catalogs as a variety name, this highly perfumed, sweetly flavored French melon has many offspring, one of which is the disease resistant Savor. It's the melon you are most likely to be served for dessert all over Europe, especially gourmet Paris, London and Rome restaurants. Its outward appearance is alluring, the size and shape similar to a Ruby Red grapefruit and yellow when ripe, but deeply ribbed. For perfect ripeness the rib divisions must still be green. The interior sweet, juicy, fragrant flesh is deep orange with a small seed cavity that the French often fill with a crumbly goat cheese or creamy Gorgonzolla, and on other occasions with a fruity port wine. I prefer it best with slivers of proschiutto. If certain foods can be described as seductive (boullabaise seafood soup, poached pears in a blackberry brandy sauce, and ginger flavored ice cream with slices of fresh mango come to mind), then a Charentais melon is at the top of the list. Introduced in the 1920's from the Poitou-Charentes region of France, the small size and light weight of the fruit make it ideal for growing up trellis to save space.

MELON HA'OGEN – From Israel with love.

This small melon is very similar in outward appearance to the Charentais melon, except its interior flesh is green tinged with orange. Even the flavor is similar. Although the origin of Ha'Ogen is believed to be Hungary, the melon came to the attention of seedsmen Thompson & Morgan through contact with the Ha'Ogen Kibbutz, in Israel, where it was grown for market and bought up like hot cakes. A favorite way to enjoy its heavenly sweet flavor is with a dash of cinnamon.

Okra – Tender green or red pods

Okra has several other names, including lady's fingers and gumbo. A relative of tropical hibiscus, it is a tender annual that produces slender stalks and white hibiscus-like flowers. The flowers last a day and develop a cone-shaped tender green pod best picked within two or three days before it grows long and fibrous. Do not allow the pods to reach full size as the more you pick the pods, the more the plant will produce until fall frosts.

The tender young pods are delicious cooked in soups and as a component of Indian curry dishes. The plants relish the heat and grow quickly from seed direct sown 1/2 inch deep into the garden. Since the seeds are hard and need a combination of high heat and moisture to germinate, I like to pre-germinate the seeds by soaking in warm water until the seed coats split. Space plants at least 6 inches apart.

OKRA CLEMSON SPINELESS - All America Award.

Although several newer varieties of okra are available from seed sources, including a dwarf variety, Annie Oakley, and a purple-podded kind, the green-podded Clemson Spineless is still my favorite. The stems are without prickles that can snag skin in some other varieties, and it starts to bear early – within 56 days.

Onions – The term "Know your onions", meaning be knowledgeable about a particular subject, comes from the fact that onions can be highly regional and variable in their performance. In particular, there are short day, intermediate day and long day varieties and – thankfully – onion varieties that are not affected by day length and will grow everywhere.

Long day onions are grown mostly in the North (above Washington DC) for they begin to form a bulb when there are 14-16 hours of daylight. They include Sweet Spanish and Giant Walla Walla.

Short day onions are grown mostly in the South, (below Atlanta) and they bulb up when there are 12-14 hours of daylight. Granex onions and Texas Supersweet are examples.

Intermediate day onions are grown roughly in a band that extends across the US from Washington DC to Atlanta, Georgia. Yellow Candy, Red Candy and white Super Star are examples, although these particular varieties can be grown anywhere with good results.

There are also red, white and yellow onions, globe shaped, flattened globe (such as the Italian Cippolini used mostly for pickles) and sausage shaped (such as Red Torpedo). There are bunching onions, also called scallions, that tolerate crowding and need sowing tightly. Other useful members of the onion family are leeks and chives.

Moreover, onions can be grown from seeds, seedlings and sets (immature onion bulbs). Since onions are biennial, meaning they form flowers and go to seed the second season after flowering, the biggest bulbs are generally grown from planting seed or seedlings. That is because the plant can put all its energy into growing a big bulb rather than wasting energy of producing a flower stalk. Growing from seeds takes longest. For earliness, sow seed in seed trays 6-8 weeks before outdoor planting. Onions are hardy and will tolerate mild frosts. Transplant 3-4 inches apart in double rows spaced 6-10 inches apart.

Perhaps the most famous onion in America is the Vidalia, a large, crisp, sweet flavored onion, but you cannot grow Vidalias from seed because Vidalia is a trademark name that applies to several varieties of Granex onion grown in only two counties of Georgia, close to the town of Vidalia. The first Vidalias were grown by an onion grower, Mose Coleman in 1931. Today, state and federal law allows the Vidalia name to be used only on onions grown in the two Georgia counties where a special soil – lacking sulphur (sulphur accounts for the pungency in many onions) – contributes to the Vidalia's pleasant sweet flavor, mostly using seed from the varieties Yellow Granex and Texas Granex.

ONION GIANT WALLA WALLA - Up to 6 inches diameter

This is the onion to beat the Vidalia. Over a century ago on the island of Corsica off the west coast of Italy, a French soldier, Peter Pieri found a jumbo-size (up to 6 inch diameter) Italian sweet onion he liked and brought the seed to the Walla Walla Valley, Washington state, where he and Italian immigrant farmers grew it as a commercial crop and thought it special enough to make selections from each generation for large size, round shape and sweetness. Its fame spread throughout the United States and Washington state adopted it as their state vegetable. A Walla Walla Sweet Onion festival is held each year in Walla Walla, where taste contests are conducted to vote whether the Vidalia or Walla Walla is that year's winner for flavor.

Ailsa Craig, named for an island off the West Coast of Scotland, is similar in size and appearance to Walla Walla. Introduced in 1887 by David Murray, head gardener to the Marquis of Ailsa, it has become a favorite for winning prizes at exhibition. Weighing 2 lbs apiece, the bulbs take 100 days to mature. There is actually another very large onion, Mammoth Improved, only available from the British mail order seed company of Robertson's near Preston. I visited their farm in a cold, wet part of Lancashire and was amazed at the size of the bulbs – more than four times bigger than a regular sweet Spanish onion.

Yellow Texas Supersweets are for Short day regions, but can be grown in Intermediate day length areas. A large, yellow globe shaped sweet onion, it will store for up to 3 months.

Candy is a yellow globe shaped onion that matures in 90 days, and although classified as an Intermediate day length onion, it grows everywhere as a large, mild onion that keeps well.

SHALLOTS - a type of small onion that creates a cluster of tear-drop shaped bulbs. In French cuisine a dish of chopped shallots in vinegar is served at almost every meal to help flavor meat and potatoes, also salads and side dishes of snap beans, beets, kale and cabbage. The British are famous for their pickled onions, and often use shallots, rather than true onions. Plant from seeds or sets, spaced 4 inches apart.

EGYPTIAN WALKING ONION - an interesting onion oddity, ideal for small space gardens since the plant forms a colony of onion bulbs below ground, and leek-like leaves with a strong, erect stalk topped by a cluster of four to six small onion bulbs that can substitute for shallots. The leaves are edible and can be used as a substitute for chives, chopped fine and added to salads and egg dishes. The name walking onion refers to plant's unusual method of propagation. As the aerial bulbs form, their weight bends the stem over and spills the bulbs onto bare soil where they will root. This continual bending (or 'walking') process from season to season can result in a large colony. To propagate simply take a cluster of the aerial onions, divide them and plant where they can perennialize.

Parsnips – Hardy root crop

Before the French developed carrots from the wild Queen Anne's lace and the potato was introduced to Europe from South America, the white-rooted, carrot-shaped parsnip was an important food staple in medieval times. Similar in shape to a carrot, but with a sweeter, celery-like flavor, the plants are hardy and will store for several months kept cool and dark. Today, British seed catalogs will still offer several varieties, whereas American catalogs are apt to feature only one. The variety Gladiator is the first hybrid parsnip, early maturing, broad-shouldered and extra sweet. The tapered root can extend 12 inches and more into the ground. The fine grained texture is sweet when cooked like carrots, a flavor that is improved after frost. Allow up to 180 days to harvest, although baby parsnips can be harvested after 100 days.

Peanut – not a pea and not a nut.

Peanut plants are a strange vegetable, a legume closely related to clover. The bushy, spreading plants grow to three feet high and three feet wide from seeds sown directly into the garden. Usually the seeds are supplied in their shells since the seeds are easily damaged, splitting apart with rough handling. It really doesn't matter whether you shell the seeds before planting or leave them in their shells, except by shelling the seeds you will have more to plant. Space at least 2 ft. apart in sandy soil since the yellow pea-like flowers send out a probe that looks like an aerial root, arching out and burying itself in the soil. Once in contact with soil, the nuts are formed underground inside a brittle shell that can contain two to four oval brown nuts. Virginia Jumbo is a large seeded variety that requires 100 days to harvest. Uncover the nuts by inserting a garden fork next to the plant and leveraging up the roots.

Peas, English – Shelled peas and edible podded.

English peas are different from Southern crowder peas, such as Black-eyed peas. English peas like cool weather whereas crowder peas are really a type of bean and like warm weather. There are three kinds of cool season peas (1) the traditional shelled pea that grows in an inedible pod and must be shelled for eating out of your hand or cooking; (2) the snow pea or sugar pod pea popular in Chinese cooking. The snow pea is best eaten young, before the peas swell the pod because once the peas grow plump, the pod becomes fibrous; (3) then there is the sugar pod pea where the peas are allowed to swell the pod because both the mature pod and plump peas are edible. This doubles the amount of edible product from a vine since you do not have to discard the pods. Although there are dwarf varieties of all three, peas are best grown up trellis for support.

Peas can be direct seeded and should be planted at least I inch deep, spaced at least 4 inches apart. They are hardy and will tolerate mild frosts. Alternatively, start indoors on a moist paper towel to pre-germinate the seeds. This reduces the risk of rotting.

SUGAR SNAP PEAS – Double the edible bulk.

I remember attending a seedsmen's convention in New Orleans as executive director of All-America Selections, when a plant breeder, Calvin Lamborn from Idaho, invited me to dinner to discuss the possibility of entering a new pea he had bred called a Sugar Snap Pea. It was different from any other kind of pea because the peas AND the mature pod were edible. This was not a snow pea used in Chinese cooking, where the edible pods are flat, but a pea that has edible FAT pods and plump sweet peas. The pea was duly entered and it won an All-America gold medal award. The publicity releases were written ready for a launch, and the entire seed industry across the globe readied their catalogs to introduce sensational Sugar Snap pea, when suddenly one late summer afternoon I received a distressing call from the breeder – the introduction would have to be delayed another year because the entire seed crop in Idaho was a failure. There would be no seed available since a devastating disease had started at one corner of the field and swept through the crop like a forest fire.

It was shortly after this news that I resigned from All-America Selections to work with a publisher on a series of garden books, and act as an independent consultant to mail order seed and nursery companies. The telephone rang and it was Keith Sangster, then president of Thompson & Morgan, the old established British seed company that had sold seed to Claude Monet and Charles Darwin. He was extremely disappointed by the delay in introducing the Sugar Snap pea, and now that I was no longer with the All-America Selections, he asked if it might be possible for me to find a replacement. I explained that the Sugar Snap pea was unique and the likelihood of finding another like it with enough seed to make an introduction was unlikely. Sangster replied: "Derek, we've learned that in the seed industry there's nothing new under the sun. We believe there must be another snap pea somewhere. If you can find it we'll pay you a commission of 20% of sales."

Within 20 minutes of hanging up I did indeed find another pea just like the Sugar Snap. The breeder was at a USDA research farm in Oregon, and he explained that he had sampled the new pea to the US seed trade the year before the sugar snap won the All-America award, but because of Sugar Snap's award status nobody wanted his pea. When I explained that Thompson & Morgan wanted it, he said he would be happy to release it to them but he only had about a pound of stock seed available. I called Sangster and he was elated. He wanted the pound of seed over-nighted to his US representative in New Jersey for them to prepare documentation in order to get the shipment through British customs. Sangster then planned to have two seed crops grown – one on the Island of Jersey in the British Channel Islands, and a back-up crop in New Zealand, so he could introduce this new snap pea look-alike on the cover of his catalog. "If I receive the shipment within ten days," Sangster said, "There is just enough time to increase the seed for an immediate introduction."

The shipment was duly sent. But before the shipment arrived in Britain I received a telephone call from the head of seed research at the USDA, in Washington DC. He had heard that a shipment of the USDA snap pea was on its way to Thompson & Morgan, and he wanted it stopped. "It would cause my department acute embarrassment if that American bred pea is introduced by a British seed company," he said.

"But the breeder sampled it to all the American seed companies and nobody wanted it," I explained. "He fulfilled his obligation to the department. He's delighted his new pea will see the light of day."

"Are you refusing to stop the shipment?" he asked.

"No," I replied. "If I could stop it I would. But as far as I know it has already been shipped and may already have cleared British customs. There's nothing I can do."

Hardly had I hung up the phone when Jim Wilson, my replacement at All-America Selections called me and also asked me to stop the shipment as it would scoop the introduction of the All-America winner and steal its thunder. Again, I had to explain there was nothing I could do, that the stock seed was in transit to England. And anyway, the Sugar Snap pea could face the possibility of another crop failure the following year.

Thompson & Morgan never received the stock seed and they missed the planting deadline for offering that spring. I believe that the shipment was apprehended somewhere in transit, returned to the US and deep sixed to avoid embarrassment to the USDA. Calvin's Sugar Snap pea went on to become the vegetable sensation of the century. Time magazine wrote about it using a photograph from my image library, Associated Press syndicated an article to every daily newspaper in America, and even the Burpee Seed catalog – which had never featured a vegetable on its cover other than one from their own breeding program - gave it their front cover and sold a record amount of seed.

PEA GREEN ARROW – more peas to the pod.

Even though I grow lots of Sugar Snap peas, I still like to grow a few rows of regular shell peas to eat like popcorn or steam for more tenderness. The late Lawrence Beavin, vegetable breeder at the British seed firm of Hurst, developed a number of pea varieties, but none as good as his Green Arrow shell pea (known in Britain as Green Shaft). The peas are amazingly long and straight and yield up to 12 peas to the pod.

Peppers - Sweet and Hot.

The first time I visited Japan a big misconception was dispelled immediately – that the Japanese have no sense of humor. I spoke no Japanese and as head of the All-American Selections, the purpose of my trip was to inspect the breeding establishments of several Japanese breeders and evaluate new varieties in the pipeline for possible entry in the All America Selections award system. A Japanese breeder kindly offered to meet me at the airport. We had never met so I sent him a photograph of myself . But when I disembarked at Tokyo Airport nobody came forward at the gate to identify themselves. I went to the information desk and discovered a note that simply said: "Mr. Fell – Go to hotel by yourself." I spotted a bus that said Downtown Tokyo and at the Imperial Hotel disembarked, to be greeted by an apologetic gentleman. He said whenever an American came through the gate he would ask if he was Mr. Fell, and when a businessman said yes he took him to the Imperial Hotel, except the man's name was Farrell, and he wanted to go to a hotel in Yokohama. "But I sent you a photograph," I said. He shrugged and retorted. "All American look alike."

At the trial grounds of Sakata Seed Company I was shown some new ornamental pepper plants suitable for hanging baskets, and asked if I thought there might be any market for them in America. I asked if they were sweet or hot. The breeder picked a cone shaped red pepper and put it to his mouth. "Sweeeet, very sweet," he replied, and offered one for me to taste. "You try."

I popped it in my mouth and gagged. The pepper was so hot it nearly blew my head off. The breeder and his entourage laughed heartily, and that was my first experience of Japanese humor – a almost childish fondness for practical jokes. At another seed house with a garden center, I saw for sale some large stepping stones. I asked if they were popular and was told by my host they were. "But aren't they very heavy," I asked my dour host who wore a dark suit, polka dot tie and a black bowler hat. "Oh, yes," he replied and bent down to try to lift one. "You try."

I bent down and gripped the stone firmly, expecting it to weigh a ton and did a back flip with it in my hands. It was lightweight, made of glass fiber. My host laughed heartily, and as we drove through the outskirts of Tokyo to his company's research farm on the slopes of Mt. Fuji, his normally serious, stoic expression would break out with laughter, recalling how I had fallen for his practical joke.

Peppers, of course, are classified as sweet and hot. Some classified as hot are very mild and others can be so hot they will burn your tongue if you try to eat them raw. Both kinds come in a multitude of colors. Most start off green and then turn to red, but some varieties turn orange, yellow, purple, white and even black, depending on variety. Several hot peppers will display all these colors on one plant. One bell pepper – Islander (also known as Rainbow) will also display a multitude of colors on one plant (see below). Peppers are closely related to tomatoes and their cultural requirements are similar. The sweet bell peppers are the most popular since they can be eaten raw like an apple, stuffed with chopped meat or cheese to make a tasty hot dish, and roasted on a grill at barbecues to bring out their best flavor.

Pepper seed is best started indoors 8 weeks before outdoor planting, and the transplants set into the garden after frost danger. A mulch of black plastic will considerably increase earliness and yields since peppers like a warm soil. Lateness of ripening or poor yields can also be attributed to variety selection and cool weather. The stems of pepper plants are brittle, unlike tomatoes which are pliable, and the weight of fruit can often bend and break the side-branches, even splitting the main stem. So I like to give pepper plants some support, such as a bamboo cane or a cylinder of chicken wire about 3 ft. high.

PEPPER BIG BERTHA – As big as they get.

I love stuffed peppers, but normally you need two bell peppers to fill you up. Not with Big Bertha. Its broad-shouldered, deeply lobed, 10 inch long fruits not only have thick, crunchy, tasty walls, but the seeds are clustered right up against the stem, so the inside is cavernous, with plenty of room for a chopped meat or cheese filling. The fruits turn from dark green to crimson when ripe. Another jumbo pepper I enjoy growing is Golden Goliath, its bright yellow fruits also turning red when fully ripe.

PEPPER GYPSY – Yields when other bell peppers stop growing.

I remember inspecting a field of pepper trials at the Ball Seed Company, near Chicago, after a particularly cool spring and cloudy early summer, with lots of cold rain. Row after row of sweet bell peppers showed not a single ripe fruit, except one – Gypsy hybrid. It was loaded with mature fruit. Moreover, the fruit displayed three colors on one plant – yellow, orange and red. Grow it wherever the pepper season is short or unreliable or you want a generous extra early yield. You will be harvesting sweet, crunchy bell peppers within 65 days when other varieties are still waiting to flower.

This 'foolproof' pepper was developed by a California plant breeder, Dr. Elbert T. T.

Yu, at the former Petoseed Company on its research farm at Woodland, California. The company is now a part of Seminis Seeds. Gypsy is tasty, good for eating raw like an apple, and its flavor improves when it turns red. Up to 70 fruit on a single plant can be harvested over a summer growing season.

PEPPER ISLANDER – Remarkable color change.

It's not unusual to have different colored peppers on a hot pepper variety, but very unusual on a sweet bell pepper. Many seed companies offer seed packets containing a collection of different colored bell peppers to grow individually in your garden, but the sweet bell pepper known as Islander produces an array of colors all on the same plant, including yellow, orange, red and purple. Pinot Noir (70 days) is a similar sweet bell pepper.

BIG JIM CHILI PEPPER is not the hottest of hot peppers, but the one I prefer to grow because of its long, tapered fruit that grow to nearly 12 inches. It has just enough bite to pleasantly flavor salads, soups and stews, and it's excellent for stuffing. There are hundreds of hot peppers to choose from, ranging in hotness from mild to fiery hot. Cone shaped green Jalapenos, long, slender bright red Cayenne, and wrinkled orange Habernero are all hot. They are the kind to use if you wish to make your own garlic/pepper spray to ward off unwanted insects.

Potatoes – The Irish potato versus the sweet potato.

Irish potatoes actually come from the Andes but it is the Irish who made the potato famous as a food staple, as important as bread in their diet. Indeed, plantations of potatoes warded off hunger among Irish families until the turn of the century when a series of blights struck the potato crops and caused such widespread famine it forced many families to immigrate to the United States. On the remote Snares Islands south of New Zealand, three escaped convicts were marooned after the captain discovered them as stowaways. Running dangerously short of supplies himself, he gave the desperate men some moldy potatoes and told them to plant them. They subsisted on crayfish and seabirds eggs until the potatoes yielded a crop. Those potatoes helped keep them alive for three years until an American whaler bound for Philadelphia rescued them.

One of the most interesting experiments I conducted with potatoes was to grow as many different colors I could find and test them for flavor. Although there are varieties of potatoes you can grow from seed, it's quicker and more reliable to grow them from small tubers called seed potatoes. These tubers have 'eyes' that can produce a growing tip, or several growing tips. You plant these after danger of frost to a depth of 1 inch above the tuber, and they quickly produce a crop in the soil, usually within sixty days.

Potatoes can be grown from spoiled potatoes from the supermarket. Some supermarket potatoes have been sprayed with a chemical to retard sprouting, but many have not and if you keep a potato for any length of time chances are it will start sprouting from its numerous eyes on top, at the sides and underneath the potato. You can take a sprouted potato and cut it into sections, making sure each section has one or two sprouts. Then plant these three inches deep, at least 12 inches apart into a loose, sandy soil. The sprouts are tender so do not plant into the garden until after frost danger.

POTATO YUKON GOLD – Golden buttery flavor

The result of crossing a North American white potato with a wild South American yellow fleshed variety, Yukon Gold was developed by plant scientists at the University of Guelph, near Toronto, Canada. Introduced in 1981, it is the first Canadian-bred potato to become a commercial success. Plants average 2 lbs. of oval, light gold, thin skinned tubers with a light yellow flesh. The shallow eyes have a rosy pink tint. Good for baking, roasting and French fries, Yukon Gold also makes excellent potato chips. The plants mature early and make extremely tasty new potatoes after just 40 days by scratching the soil surface and plucking them from the soil like gold nuggets.

FRENCH FINGERLING LA RATTE – Prized by gourmet chefs.

If I want a big red potato that can make 50 French fries from a single tuber then I will choose Red Pontiac, capable of 2-5 lbs yield from a single plant. A white fleshed variety it originated as a mutation in a field of potatoes grown in Florida., and released in 1945, but if I want a more delicate flavor with a flesh that seems to melt in my mouth after baking or sautéeing, then I choose the French Fingerling variety, La Ratte. The long, slender, sausage shaped tubers are yellow with yellow flesh, sensational in a potato salad. The skin is so tender it doesn't need peeling even when harvested at the mature stage.

Pumpkin – 2,000 lbs weight anyone?

In 1971, seven years after I first settled in Pennsylvania I attended a giant pumpkin contest that was the forerunner of the now famous Churchville Giant Pumpkin contest, held the first Sunday in October at the Churchville Nature Center. Today, the event attracts hundreds of adults and children to see entrants as far afield as Texas haul their monster pumpkins on a scale for weighing. In 1971, however, it was a much more intimate affair that attracted mostly local entrants, held at the historic Cornell Farm, in Newtown in the late John Cornell's old barn, immortalized in one of artist John Hicks's 'Peacable Kingdom' paintings. It was a great place to meet local farmers and their wives, and meet some expert pumpkin growers. The late Dick Bailey, county agent, was the weighmaster and sat beside a handsome set of heavy cast-iron scales with the women sitting around in folding chairs arranged theater-style, knitting, and the men standing around the room swapping pumpkin lore and gossip. Spiced hot cider flowed freely, and prizes were awarded to supporting classes, such as the heaviest watermelon, the heaviest Nigerian calabash gourd, and so on.

I attended the contest because the Today show had invited me to find a giant pumpkin for the show's Thanksgiving special, to give a carving demonstration and to tell people how to grow a giant pumpkin.

At the Cornell Farm I learned there is intense rivalry among pumpkin growers, and as the growing season progresses the contestants try to find out how their competitors are doing. Not only must a grower contend with mice chewing through a stem and borers entering the vine, but sabotage. A New Jersey farmer complained that he had been spied on by a competitive grower who worked at the local fire company with access to a helicopter. When he saw the helicopter hovering menacingly over his pumpkin patch he rushed out, brandishing a shotgun, and the helicopter took off.

To grow a contest winner it is important to use seed from the previous year's winner (the winner is honor-bound to share his seeds with the losers). Pumpkin seed can be direct-seeded after frost danger, planting seeds 1 inch deep and 6 feet apart, but I prefer to start seeds six weeks before outdoor plantings to get plants off to a good head start. The transplants prefer a sandy, humus-rich soil (especially one supplemented with well-decomposed stable or cow manure). A deeply spaded, well-drained soil in full sun works best, or one can grow a pumpkin vine in a compost pile. Frequent watering is essential since it is moisture absorption that swells the fruit. The most important nutrient is nitrogen since it promotes healthy leaf growth and the bigger the vine the bigger the pumpkin can grow. Phosphorus is also essential because it promotes early flowering and fruit formation.

Pumpkins set two kinds of flowers – male and female. Only the females set fruit (they have a baby pumpkin already formed beneath the flower), but this flower must receive pollen from the male. To get an early fruit set you must play the part of a bee and examine the flowers as they start to form until you find a female (the males appear first), then pick a male blossom and rub the powdery 'nose' of the male on the shiny nose of the female. This ensures pollination, otherwise the embryo pumpkin will shrivel and die.

Hand pollinate as many females as possible, and allow them to set fruit, but when they reach the size of a grapefruit, examine them for the thickest stem since pumpkins take nourishment through the stem. After selecting the best pumpkin, remove all the rest to allow all the plant's energy to be concentrated into one fruit.

As the congregation at the Cornell weigh-in watched the pumpkins being weighed one at a time, the contestant's name would be announced. Twice the weigh-master had to report that the contestant had passed away between planting time and harvest, and so he would ask for a moment of silence.

Since the winning pumpkin had to be split open in order to distribute the seeds, I took the next largest in size to the Today show's studios at Rockefeller Plaza in the heart of Manhattan. It required five union men to carry it from my pick-up truck to the set, and as we unloaded we were spotted by an Associated Press photographer who took pictures of me with the pumpkin and syndicated it to newspapers world-wide.

At that time the world record was a little over 300 lbs.; today it is 1,725 lbs, set at the Ohio Valley Giant Pumpkin Contest, and a 2,000 lb. gorilla might be just around the corner – a feat possible by keeping a wary eye open for pumpkin rustlers with helicopters!

PUMPKIN PRIZEWINNER - Big and Beautiful.

If you are not interested in winning a giant pumpkin contest, but simply want a giant pumpkin, say 100 lbs. in weight, the variety to grow used to be Big Max. But in my experience the newer variety Prizewinner is a similar size but a deeper reddish-orange color than Big Max. Carving Prizewinner is easy. Faces can be painted onto the skin, or the pumpkin can be carved. Simply cut the pumpkin from the vine with a good four to six inches of stem attached. The stem must be kept hard and dry for if it is allowed to rot the rot can quickly spread to the entire pumpkin. Outline the face on the skin with a felt tipped pen and use a sharp, serrated carving knife, to cut into the flesh. The pumpkin

I'll Make You a Gardening Wizard Overnight!

Pumpkin, Prizewinner

Chapter 9 - *Variety Selections for Huge Garden Yields*

Pumpkin Rouge Vif d'Etampes

Radish, Cherry Belle

Rhubarb, Canada Red

Spinach, Tyee

will be hollow and the shell may be about 4 inches thick so some strength is needed to do the carving. Do not let children do the carving without supervision as the knife can easily slip and cause injury. By slicing across the top you can gain access to the interior. Scoop out the seeds and place a candle in the bottom so the face can glow at night.

There are also mini pumpkins that are fun for children to decorate. One of my favorites is Jack-be-Little because it is deeply ribbed and and attractive as a holiday decoration.

PUMPKIN ROUGE VIF D'ETAMPES – The Cinderella pumpkin.

Actually a squash, Rouge Vif means vivid red in French. A French heirloom from the Etampes region, it stands out because of its flattened globe shape, prominent ribbing and bright scarlet color. Introduced to American gardeners in 1883, the fruits can weigh up to 25 lbs and measure up to 20 inches in diameter. Plants mature in 95 days, eyecatching for Thanksgiving and Halloween decoration. The fruits have sweet, orange, edible flesh suitable for pies and soup.

PUMPKIN NEW ENGLAND SUGAR – Perfect for pie filling and soup.

Numerous pumpkins are good for pie fillings and pumpkin soup (curried pumpkin soup is a personal favorite), including the Jack O'Lantern varieties and various kinds of closely related squash, such as the Crookneck Cushaw that is shaped like a butternut squash, with a thick, crooked neck. The New England Sugar pumpkin is a small pumpkin and suitable for growing vertically up trellis. A vine can produce a dozen fruits that have thick rinds under the hard orange shell.

Radish – All shapes and sizes

These crisp, pungent root crops can be eaten fresh or cooked, varying in size from the size of a cherry to the size of a baseball. Some are round but a whole series of Japanese and Chinese varieties have thick, long icicle-shaped roots called Daikon, requiring a deep sandy soil to grow straight and smooth. An odd-looking turnip shaped radish variously called Red Meat and Watermelon, has a white exterior and watermelon-red interior that is especially attractive when sliced.

Radishes are best when they are crisp and slightly pungent. They can become pithy and hollow if deprived of water during their development, and in hot weather. They must be direct-seeded as they cannot tolerate being transplanted, spaced at least 1 inch apart. Rather than grow in a straight row I like to plant them in a broad band, at least six inches wide. Thinning can be tedious unless you use a pair of pointed scissors to snip unwanted seedlings at the soil line. A sandy soil will avoid mis-shapen roots,

RADISH EASTER EGG - A range of beautiful colors.

Most people are familiar with the fastest maturing radish, Cherry Belle, that's ready to harvest in 20 days of direct seeding. But plant breeders have introduced a whole range of interesting colors so that we now have Sparkler (a red and white cherry-size bicolor), French Breakfast (a torpedo shaped red and white bicolor), Hailstone (a white), Icicle (a white torpedo shaped root), Purple Plum (a cherry size purple) and Gold Nugget (an orange). They taste alike and all have been combined into several radish seed mixtures. Easter Egg features round cherry-size varieties that mature in 30 days.

Rhubarb – Good companions: strawberries and rhubarb.

The British are the masters of growing rhubarb. At Cawdaw Castle, in Scotland (of Macbeth fame), I have seen rhubarb as tall as a giraffe and with edible stalks as thick as my wrist. The British are so fanatical about rhubarb they have a national rhubarb collection at the Royal Horticultural Society's northern display garden at Harrowgate, Yorkshire. There I have seen more than a hundred varieties grown side-by-side for evaluation. Of course, the north of England and Scotland - with their abundant rainfall - is prime for growing rhubarb as one of its chief requirements is lots of moisture. At Cawdor Castle the head gardener revealed that his secret to growing such a handsome planting was cow manure.

Mature plants produce large, flamboyant flower clusters, held well above the foliage. These should be pruned away as soon as they form to direct more energy into the roots.

Rhubarb is grown for its red stalks, although the ruffled part of the leaf is poisonous and must be discarded. The stalks should be peeled and chopped into inch-long segments for cooking. The cubes break down into a delicious moist pudding consistency that requires sweetening to make it taste devine. Perhaps the most famous use for rhubarb is as a pie-filling – either used alone or combined with strawberries for a rhubarb-and-strawberry pie.

Rhubarb is a hardy perennial and one of the first vegetables to be harvested in spring, about the same time as asparagus. Plants can be grown from seed (started indoors 8-10 weeks before outdoor planting) or from year-old roots. The more you pick the stems the more new stems grow to replace them. For storage, rhubarb freezes well. There is considerable variation in stalk thickness and color, some varieties showing a deeper red than others, but generally turning green when cooked. My favorite variety is Canada Red because the red continues up to the tip of the stalk.

Spinach - Fast growing cool season vegetable.

Few leafy vegetables have such a satisfying flavor as spinach, either cooked as a side dish to go with meat and potatoes, or raw in salads. A hardy, cool season vegetable, it germinates at low temperatures (40F and above), but can suffer erratic germination on account of its susceptibility to damping off disease and crusting of the soil.

Spinach likes regular watering to grow quickly, making edible rosettes within 45 days of direct seeding. At the onset of hot weather it quickly goes to seed. In addition to early spring, spinach can be direct seeded in September to be grown as a fall crop, and left in the ground to overwinter. In areas with severe winters, a light covering of straw or horticultural fleece will help it through the cold season.

MALABAR SPINACH - A problem with spinach varieties planted in spring or fall is that they relish cool weather, and when the days get hot and humid they bolt to seed. There are two spinach varieties that relish hot weather. One is the climbing spinach, Malabar. It has red stalks and dark green glossy heart-shaped leaves that are a delicious spinach substitute. It requires strong poles for support and the more you pick the more new leaves grow to replace them. In fall, the plant has gorgeous red flower clusters turning it into a pillar of fire.

NEW ZEALAND SPINACH - The other heat tolerant spinach substitute is New Zealand spinach. It is a low, spreading plant with succulent green leaves, the vines extending to three feet wide. Like Malabar spinach, the more you pick the ivy-shaped leaves, the more it produces, from early summer to fall frost.

Squash – Askutasquash, summer and winter varieties.

The early American colonists discovered squash among the Indians who called these husky fruits *Askutasquash* meaning 'plants eaten raw'. The Indian name became shortened to squash. There are basically two kinds of squash – summer squash that are delicious eaten raw, like a cucumber, or cooked; and also winter squashes that can be eaten raw in their immature stage, but are generally left to mature into larger fruits with hard shells, making them suitable for winter storage. The vegetable marrow, grown extensively in Europe, is a type of zucchini squash that the Europeans allow to grow large.

ZUCCHINI SQUASH RICHGREEN — All female zucchini squash.

I do not know of any vegetable that is easier to grow than a zucchini squash. The seed is large and easy to handle, can be direct-seeding into the garden after frost danger, and within 45 days you can harvest slender, torpedo-shaped green fruits that the French and British call courgettes. The fruits are so tender they can be sliced into salads and eaten raw, or cooked for a tasty side dish. It's vital to pick the fruit when they are young, no more than 6-8 inches long for that is when they are most tender. Left on the vine the fruits will swell to the size of 18 inches or more, and although the interior is still edible and tasty, allowing fruit to reach that size drains the plant of energy and causes it to stop bearing.

Most zucchini squashes bear both male and female flowers. The females have a baby zucchini between the flower and the stem, and when this is cross pollinated from a male flower the fruit will start to form. Unpollinated fruit soon shrivel and die. Although bees generally transfer the pollen you can help nature along by hand pollinating the female flowers. This simply requires picking a male flower, stripping away the yellow petals and rubbing the powdery pollen at the center of the flower onto the shiny center of a female. Generally the male flowers appear first, and it can seem like a long time before female flowers come along, so it makes good sense to choose a zucchini variety that produces more female flowers than males AND encourages the females to appear first. That's the distinct quality of Richgreen.

CLIMBING TROMBONE ZUCCHINI — A Gorilla in the garden.

This is one amazing vegetable. Left to sprawl across the ground the vine will snake out in all directions, suffocating all in its path with large hairy leaves, but given support it has tendrils that allow it to climb naturally. I have harvested fifty fruits in a season, the vines bearing within 60 days and continuing non-stop until fall frost. The fruits start off a pale green color, with a long, narrow curled neck and a bulbous base. The neck is solid flesh with no seeds since they are concentrated in the bulb part. The neck has white interior flesh like a regular zucchini and a tender skin so it can be sliced and eaten raw or cooked like a regular zucchini. I grew one fruit that measured three feet long. When I sliced up the neck it produced over 300 slices.

As the fruits mature they change color to beige and then brown, like a butternut squash. At this stage it even tastes like a butternut. The fruits develop hard shells and are suitable for storage in a cool dark, frost-free place, remaining edible for months.

SUMMER SQUASH EARLY PROLIFIC CROOKNECK – Summer squash galore.

If the Trombone zucchini is the gorilla of the garden then Early Prolific Crookneck is the swan. It is much more behaved in its growth habit and has a curved neck like a swan's, similar in flavor to a zucchini squash. Its tender-skinned golden yellow fruits are produced in great profusion on a bushy plant that needs just three feet of space. Best eaten when small and pale yellow, each fruit can be sliced to eat raw or cooked like a zucchini. Sauteed with onions, the combination is really delicious. Keep the young fruit picked to ensure a continuous supply. If left on the vine they deepen to orange and become warty, at which stage they lose their supreme flavor.

WINTER SQUASH DELICATA – Sweet potato flavor

There are literally hundreds of winter squash suitable for home gardens, in all shapes, sizes and colors, but the flavor is fairly consistent whether you grow an acorn, butternut, or buttercup type – a flavor reminiscent of sweet potatoes. Most winter squash grow long, rambling vines, but some have been bred to produce a short vine or bush habit. Bush Delicata is my favorite because it is mildew resistant, and the two-serving size and oval shape is perfect for small space. Developed by Dr. Molly Zahn and George Moriary at Cornell University, Bush Delicata won an All America Award for its quality. Plants average 8 fruits each, weight up to 2 lbs, white with dark green stripes and an orange interior. Fruits reach maturity in 100 days and store well for several months. The fruits should be baked, sliced in two, and a pool of maple syrup poured into the middle for the most delicious flavor. Space plants at least 2 ft. apart.

VEGETABLE SPAGHETTI SQUASH – Pasta without the calories

When I visited the Japanese seedsman, Takeo Sakata, at his home in Yokohama, in 1974 he was 84 years old. I was served a side dish of steaming vegetable spaghetti in a rich marinara sauce. He found the melon-shaped squash with a spaghetti interior in China, but when he released it to the world in 1934 under the name spaghetti squash, it did not sell. He dropped it from his catalog, and in 1960 re-introduced it as vegetable spaghetti, promoting it as a low calorie substitute for pasta spaghetti. Sales improved dramatically - so much so that every year growers in California around Oxnard plant vast fields for sale in grocery stores throughout America. Because of its hard shell the fruit can be stored for several months in a cool, frost-free place. Moreover, the spreading vines can be grow up trellis to save space, each vine capable of producing a dozen fruit up to 3 lbs

Zucchini Richgreen

Summer squash mix with Early Prolific Crookneck (bottom)

Winter squash, Delicata

Vegetable Spaghetti squash

Chapter 9 - *Variety Selections for Huge Garden Yields*

Mammoth Russian sunflower seeds

Radish, Easter Egg Mix

each. Since a single fruit can cost $5.00 in a grocery store a single vine can produce $60.00 worth of food.

Vegetable spaghetti is such a versatile vegetable that in 1980 I collaborated with a friend, herbalist Phyllis Shaudys, on a Vegetable Spaghetti Cookbook containing 100 recipes, from vegetable spaghetti bread to vegetable spaghetti desserts. Moist and delectable, the bread can be served as a coffeecake or dessert. Here is the book's recipe for Vegetable Spaghetti Bread:

> Delicious with softened cream cheese, the loaves freeze well. The following recipe makes two loaves –
>
> 3 eggs; 1 cup of oil; 2 cups of sugar; 2 cups cooked, chopped and drained vegetable spaghetti; 1 teaspoon of vanilla, 3 cups flour; 1 teaspoon salt; 1 teaspoon baking soda; 1 teaspoon baking powder; 2 teaspoons cinnamon; 1 cup chopped pecans.
>
> Beat the eggs until foamy; add the next four ingredients and mix lightly but well. Add the dry ingredients and the nuts and mix together. Divide into 2 greased loaf pans. Bake at 325F for 60-65 minutes.

Cooking is easy. Simply take a fork and pierce the shell so air can escape and place the whole fruit in a preheated oven at 375F for 45 minutes. Turn the squash over half way through baking for even cooking and to avoid scorch marks on one side. Then remove it and slice the fruit across the middle to make two halves. With a fork remove the dime-size white seeds and begin to unravel the creamy spaghetti-like interior. The 'spaghetti' by itself is rather bland, but when you add a flavorful sauce, such as a clam sauce or a parsley butter sauce, then the strands soak up the juices and the meal becomes delicious.

Direct-sow the seeds 1 inch deep, spacing plants at least three feet apart. Although the vines will extend 6 ft., the stems will knit together to form a dense groundcover that can suffocate competing weeds. Choose a fertile soil with good drainage in full sun.

Sunflower - Nutritious snack food

Sunflowers are native to North America and, as a result of plant breeding, many cultivated kinds have been developed, some for ornamental effect and others as a source of edible seeds (nuts). The variety mostly grown for nuts is Mammoth Russian, a tall-growing plant (up to 10 ft. high) and capable of growing one enormous head, up to 18 inches across, the central seed disk filled with grey and white striped seeds that can be shelled to produce a delicious snack. Mammoth Russian is an annual that likes to be direct-seeded into the garden, 18 inches apart. Within 80 days the flowers open out and become invaded by bees that pollinate the seed disk. When the weight of the seed head bends the disk down it is ready to harvest by cutting off the flower head and shucking the seeds. These can be shelled, eaten raw or roasted.

Sweet Corn – Sugary, Sugar Enhanced and Supersweets.

The North American Indians introduced sweet corn to European Colonists soon after the Pilgrims landed at Plymouth Rock. William Penn, impressed with reports of a beautiful land, arrived soon after, and it was his estate manager, John Logan who discovered the secret of pollination in corn. He refuted a popular garden book of the time which claimed corn was self-pollinating. By excluding pollen from the silks he proved conclusively that pollen from the tassels must make contact with the silks in order for the corn to be pollinated and swell into an edible cob, or ear, full of milky kernels. His findings were read to the Royal Society in London, where his report is still archived.

At the turn of the century there were two kinds of corn – white corn for eating and yellow corn for feeding to cattle. Two heirloom sweet corn varieties were especially popular. They were Country Gentleman and Stowell's Evergreen, both of which are still offered in seed catalogs.

Then along came Golden Bantam, a small yellow sweet corn that was sweeter than any of the whites. Golden Bantam made its debut in 1902 when a Mr. J. G. Pickett in Greenfield, Massachusetts offered his stock seed – a total of two quarts - to a New York seedsman, who in turn sold it to Burpee Seeds for $25.00. It proved to be one of the greatest bargains in commerce for Golden Bantam became famous as "The sweetest and richest corn in all history." It has been variously described as "the tenderest, the sweetest, the most luscious, the most honeyed, the most sugary and the most toothsome" of sweet corns. It is still available from seed catalogs and it lives up to its reputation IF you eat it within a few hours of picking; otherwise its sugars change to starch and the kernels become mealy.

Sweet corn is best direct-seeded 1-inch deep, although many growers will use transplants to get extra early yields. Since most plants produce only one ear, they tend to mature at about the same time, and so succession plantings are advisable at two week intervals until the end of July. For highest germination, delay sowing until after frost danger since sweet corn seed sprouts best at 70F soil temperature. Space rows 8 inches apart in rows at least 3 feet apart. A high nitrogen, high phosphorus fertilizer at time of planting is recommended. Water regularly during dry spells, and especially when the stalks start to show tassels and silks. Poorly filled ears can result from lack of moisture at this stage, also from poor soil, or incomplete pollination. Each strand of sweet corn silk is attached to an embryo – the immature kernels. Only when pollen touches the exposed silk will the kernels swell to fill the ear. Since pollination occurs when the wind blows pollen from the male part of the plant (the tassel) onto the female part (the silk), lack of wind can cause poor pollination, or not having a large enough block of corn stalks. So never plant just a row of corn – rather plant a block of at least three rows.

THE THREE SISTERS. Sweet corn occupies a lot of space and so Amish farmers like to save space by growing three crops in the same row. After the sweet corn has germinated and reached knee-high they will plant pole snap beans beside the corn and alternate the beans with a planting of vining butternut squash. This way, the beans and squash vines will use the corn stalks for support and will not interfere with the corn harvest because the corn ears will mature before the pole beans and the squash vines start to reach maturity. These three vegetables – sweet corn, pole snap beans and butternut squash – are known as the three sisters.

SWEET CORN EARLY XTRA SWEET. I remember Mrs. Lois Burpee, who was a wonderful cook, inviting me to sample a new yellow sweet corn that she had harvested from her garden and I ate three in quick succession. Its name was Illini Xtra Sweet, an All-America Winner and the first of a new race of sweet corns called Sugar Enhanced (SE) for short. It had been bred by Professor John Laughman at the University of Illinois, Urbana, and though he published a report on the advantage of SE corns in 1953, seedsmen were skeptical of its value, until Illini Foundation Seeds introduced the first SE sweet corn, Illini Xtra Sweet in 1970, following an All-America Award. The new corn quickly caught on and a whole series of SE corns followed, including Early Xtra Sweet, that is 15 days earlier than Ilini Xtra Sweet, an 85-day corn.

These SE corns do not convert their extra sweetness to starch as quickly as regular corns. Later, a new type of corn, called a Supersweet (Sh2 for short), established a third category. The Sh2 corns are extra sweet like the SE corns, but they hold their sweetness even longer – especially under storage and for shipping long distances. A disadvantage of the supersweets is that they need isolating from other corns by at least 500 feet, otherwise they can lose their supersweetness. Therefore, an extra sweet corn like Early Xtra Sweet, is a better choice for the home gardener .

In addition to yellow and white sweet corns, there are bicolored and even red varieties.

The biggest spoiler is likely to be the corn ear worm, the larvae of a moth that lays its eggs on the silks for the larvae to hatch and burrow into the kernels. These grey worms can eat their way through the topmost row of kernels by harvest time. Dusting the silks with organic pyrethrum or rotenone dust can control the pest, although most organic gardeners simply slice off the top discolored part of the ear before cooking.

A ghastly looking disease that attacks sweet corn is a fungus called corn smut. It looks like a mass of black blisters coming out of the ears. These burst and release millions of powdery spores resembling soot. In Mexico the blisters are gathered and the powdery contents used as a mushroom-like flavoring for egg dishes. In the International section of your supermarket or gourmet store you may even find corn smut sold in cans.

SWEET CORN SILVER QUEEN is not a sugar enhanced sweet corn and it's not a supersweet sweet corn. It's not even a hybrid sweet corn. Yet it has developed a following among home gardeners as the one to grow for tender kernels and sweet, milky flavor and worth the 90 day wait to harvest. It grows long ears (8 inches) with up to 16 rows of white kernels. The originator, Rodgers Brothers today actually sells more of Jubilee than Silver Queen, but that's because it is favored by food processors. Silver Queen is the biggest selling sweet corn hybrid in America among home gardeners, and even the seed company that introduced it, Rodgers Brothers, cannot explain why this non-hybrid is so sweet. The result of a breeding program in Caldwell, Idaho, Silver Queen was first introduced in 1958 but did not start to receive a following until 1960.

Sweet Potato – Also known as yam.

The sweet potato is a warm season vegetable that is grown from 'slips' – rooted offsets that come up in clusters all around a sweet potato tuber when it is suspended over a glass of water or placed half-submerged in moist potting soil. A supermarket sweet potato can yield dozens of 'slips' for you to propagate your own. Also called yams, they are often confused with an African climbing plant by the same name unsuitable for most US gardens.

The slips must be planted outdoors after frost danger. These should be planted 12 inches apart in a raised bed 2 ft. wide. Earliest yields are assured by growing through black plastic. A member of the morning glory family, the vigorous vines will knit together to create a dense ground cover of heart shaped leaves. Depending on variety, sweet potato tubers can be red, orange, white and purple skinned. The flesh can be yellow, white and orange.

SWEET POTATO BEAUREGARD — Early and disease resistant.

Developed by the late Larry Rolston at Louisiana State University, and named for a Civil War general, Beauregard was released in 1987. The variety quickly established itself as the preferred sweet potato to grow for its extra earliness (90 days), big, elongated rich-red tubers and orange flesh.

Swiss Chard - A heat tolerant spinach substitute.

When I first started gardening there were only two kinds of Swiss chard, a leafy vegetable with crispy white or red stalks, and crinkly, glossy dark green leaves that seemed to ooze nutritional benefits. Fordhook Giant was a favorite, and Ruby (also known as Rhubarb.) Ruby is a crimson variety that many gardeners grow as an ornamental in container plantings. In early 1993 I visited New Zealand for the first time, and not only discovered a population passionate about growing vegetables but an unusual kind of Swiss chard (which New Zealanders call silverbeet). Its name is Rainbow because in addition to red and white, it contained a pink, lemon and yellow-stalked variety. In Australia it became known as Five-color Chard. During my three week tour of New Zealand I learned of an amateur gardener near Wellington, John Eaton who was working on a new kind of Rainbow chard – one with many more colors – and in a telephone conversation he explained that the leaves were much more tender than existing Swiss chard varieties. He sent me a seed sample and I was the first person in America to grow Eaton's new chard mix.

I advised him to contact Rob Johnson at Johnny's Seeds, a seed house in Maine, as a possible distributor. I had visited Johnny's Seeds in Albion the previous year and the company impressed me with its dedication to quality and organic growing methods. Eaton eventually worked with Johnny's to introduce the new variety as Bright Lights, which went on to win an All-America award. Unfortunately, Eaton died shortly after of cancer, but his legacy lives on as one of the top vegetable introductions of the century – on a par with Sugar Snap peas.

SWISS CHARD, BRIGHT LIGHTS. As Rob Johnson explained it to me in a letter, Eaton had separated out 9 distinct stalk colors in addition to the red and white already familiar to American gardeners, and his own breeders perfected a way to isolate the colors and keep them stable. The old Rainbow and Five-color chards never became popular because they were unstable, often producing only two or three colors. Bright Lights includes lemon yellow, canary yellow, gold, pink, apricot, orange, purple and bicolors. The leaves are dark green or bronze depending on the stalk color (the reds tend to show bronze leaves). Moreover, the colors of the leaves and stalks remain with light cooking (preferably steaming). Since its introduction to the world in 1998 seedsmen have separated the gold and orange to sell as separate colors.

Today, Bright Lights chard is often included in mesclun salad green mixes to add flavor and cosmetic appeal. Plants can be direct seeded several weeks before the last frost date, since they are hardy, or the seed can be started indoors 6 weeks before outdoor planting to raise transplants. Even when young, the seedlings show their true colors and so it is possible to select the best colors for your vegetable garden or container plantings. A light picking of young leaves and stalks can be made within 30 days of seeding, and a heavier picking of thicker, longer stalks made within 55 days. The more you harvest the leaves, the more the plant produces new ones for an everbearing harvest. The leaves taste like spinach and the stalks can be used as a substitute for cooked celery, though not with a celery flavor. Bright Lights will remain productive in the garden into fall, and even survive light frosts. A covering of horticultural fleece will extend the harvest to Christmas even in the North.

Tomatillos – Salsa ingredient

This close relative of tomatoes is a warm-season vegetable that produces golf-ball size fruits colored green or purple, and wrapped in a papery husk. Start the seed indoors 6-8 weeks before outdoor planting after frost danger and plant at least 12 inches apart. The plants are spreading and will knit into each other to create a dense ground cover. Maturity depends on variety, but usually the fruit can be harvested in 85 days. The flavor is similar to eggplant when cooked. The green-fruited variety Gigante (4 inches in diameter) requires up to 100 days.

A close relative of the tomatillo is the cape gooseberry or golden berry. The yellow marble-size fruit are smaller than tomatillos, encased in a papery husk and with a much sweeter flavor – so sweet that the berries are eaten raw and even added to fruit salads.

Tomatoes – Love apples

More tomatoes are grown by home gardeners than any other vegetable. Discovered by the Spanish conquistadors growing in the coastal mountains of Peru, the red and yellow fruits were at first treated with suspicion in Europe because of their similarity to deadly nightshade, a poisonous plant. Moreover, early varieties did not taste pleasant except in cooking. That all changed after Alexander Livingstone, a farmer in Reynoldsburg, Ohio discovered in a field of tomatoes a large, red, round, smooth skinned variety he called Paragon. It became the first commercially successful tomato variety, and to celebrate Livingstone's achievement the town of Reynoldsburg calls itself the birthplace of the modern tomato and holds a tomato festival in summer.

Today there are almost 5,000 hybrid and non-hybrid tomato varieties in circulation. Small-fruited varieties are called cherry tomatoes and they include some of the sweetest tasting, such as red Sweet 100 and yellow Sungold. Another large group is plum shaped and called paste tomatoes because they are mostly used for making tomato paste. A popular class with home gardeners is the medium sized tomato such as Early Cascade and Early Girl. These form clusters of up to six fruits and are especially popular in grocery stores. They are

Sweet corn, Early Extra Sweet

Chapter 9 - *Variety Selections for Huge Garden Yields*

Sweet potato, Beauregard

Swiss chard, Bright Lights

ideal for stewing and using fresh, sliced into salads. Then come the large fruited and giant fruited varieties such as Big Boy and Beefsteak. Tastes vary from country to country. In the USA housewives want an all-red round tomato, but in Japan the preference is for a round red tomato with green shoulders. Maroon is a favorite color in Russia.

Tomato plants can be classified as determinate or indeterminate according to their vine length. A determinate variety does not grow tall, but makes a lot of side branches and stays bushy. The short vines often exhaust themselves long before the season is over. An indeterminate variety will make a tall vine that continues to grow indefinitely. Indeterminate tomatoes are best staked, and they are capable of the highest yields. Some varieties like Better Boy will grow to roof high in a single season and yield more than 300 lbs of fruit. The world record for a heavyweight tomato is a Delicious that tipped the scales at 7 lbs 12 ozs.

Tomatoes also possess some really strange colors in addition to red and yellow. There are white, maroon, striped, pink and orange, even a variety that stays green when ripe.

Tomato seed is best started indoors eight weeks before outdoor planting after frost danger. When transferring to the garden, dig a hole up to half the length of transplant so the roots are set deep. This allows extra roots to emerge wherever the stem is in contact with soil. Choose a sunny location with good drainage and set the plants at least three feet apart. The best support for an indeterminate vine is a bamboo stake or a wire cylinder with the plant set in the middle so as the vine grows the side branches push through the wire mesh and become self supporting.

At the end of the season, listen to weather forecasts and when there is danger of frost, you should pick all the unripe tomatoes and place them indoors. At room temperature the green fruits will continue to ripen, and supply you with tomatoes for several weeks after the vines have been killed.

TOMATO TROUBLESHOOTING – Tomatoes in general are relatively carefree, but there are spoilers, mostly to do with blemishes or low yields.

Low yields. Tomatoes – especially the larger fruited varieties – are heavy feeders and poor fruiting is mostly caused by a lack of phosphorus – responsible for fruit formation - and too much nitrogen that promotes foliage growth. To correct for lack of phosphorus rake bone-meal into the upper soil surface at time of transplanting. I also like to give my tomato plants a boost of Spray-N-Grow liquid fertilizer or my compost tea twice weekly during the growing season. Tomato flowers have difficulty setting fruit during cold periods so don't be in such a hurry to plant outdoors in the spring.

Late Ripening. Generally this is the nature of the variety you have chosen to grow. Many heirloom tomatoes, for example, are notorious for late ripening – such as Cherokee Purple. But late ripening can be caused by an infertile soil and poor pollination. Believe it or not, excessive heat can restrict pollination, as well as low temperatures. A tomato is self-pollinating, but sometimes the pollen in each flower needs to be shaken to do its job. In greenhouses where there is no wind, growers will take a battery operated toothbrush and agitate the flower trusses to ensure a good fruit set. Outdoors, simply shake the flower clusters occasionally. Mulching with organic materials such as straw and grass

Tomato, Big Boy Hybrid

clippings can delay ripening since these tend to keep soil cool. To enhance earliness, use black plastic as a mulch. This absorbs heat and holds it in when nights turn cool, promoting early ripening by as much as two weeks.

Sunscald. In the popular movie, the Godfather, the aging crime lord is seen playing with his grandson in his tomato patch and suffers a heart attack. The tomato patch is covered with shade cloth, in spite of the fact that most garden writers advise giving tomatoes full sun. What the shade cloth does is prevent sunscald – a pale blemish on the side of the fruit when it is exposed to too much sun through facing south or lack of foliage cover. The pale blemish spreads to make the fruit inedible. To avoid sunscald you can give your tomato plants a LIGHTLY shaded canopy or avoid heavily pruning foliage so fruits on the sunniest side of the plant are shaded.

Blossom-end Rot. The physiological disease shows itself as a blackening of the fruit at the blossom end. It starts as a black depression and spreads to infect the entire fruit. Lack of calcium in the soil or irregular watering that deprives the plant of calcium are the main causes. Use of a black plastic mulch will help retain soil moisture during dry spells to allow roots to continue taking up calcium during dry spells. Adding eggshells – as some writers suggest – isn't much help because it takes too long to release the calcium in an eggshell (better to add all your eggshells to a compost pile where they have a better opportunity to break down.) Liming an overly acid soil does help.

Cracking. Some tomato varieties are more prone than others to cracking. In particular, cracking commonly occurs on the smaller fruited varieties like Sweet 100 and Sungold.

Cat Faces. This problem is common on large fruited tomatoes like Beefsteaks. A corky pattern develops around the blossom end, or a brown corky streak will develop on one side of the fruit, extending from the blossom end to the stem end. This is caused by poor pollination, either by a cold spell or lack of air circulation to mix up the pollen for self-pollination. Mulching with black plastic will help avoid cat faces, and shaking the flower trusses on large fruited varieties.

TOMATO-POTATO – Tomatoes above ground, potatoes below.

I am the inventor of this remarkable graft between a tomato and a potato. It sounds implausible, but you really can grow full-size red, ripe tomatoes on the vine part of the plant and potatoes among the roots. I first took an interest in grafting tomatoes onto potatoes when I read an advertisement from a now defunct mail order nursery that offered the product. I sent for it and was disappointed to discover that all I received was a potato hollowed out with a pinch of sphagnum moss inside and three tomato seeds located under the sphagnum plug. The instructions said to plant the potato, and the tomato seed would germinate to produce a tomato vine, while the potato would sprout and produce potatoes. But if any of the seeds did actually manage to germinate, the potato grew more quickly and suffocated the tomato vine.

I liked the labor saving idea of growing two crops from one planting, and experimented with grafting techniques. The best success involved growing a Sub-Arctic tomato transplant, boring a hole all the way through a Red Pontiac potato with an apple corer and inserting the transplant into the center of the potato. The moistness inside the potato keeps the tomato from drying out and in effect makes an ideal transplant pot. Transferred to the garden, the two plants grow together at the same rate and reliably produce a fine crop of Red Pontiacs in the soil and a heavy yield of Sub-Arctic tomatoes on the vine.

I took my idea to a national mail order nursery and they set up a production line to manufacture the grafts by the thousand. I also approached the syndicated Sunday newspaper supplement, Parade magazine for some publicity. Bud Pironti, the executive I had to sell on the idea was skeptical but invited me to his office in Manhattan to see a sample. I pulled up two plants from my garden, placed them in two-gallon pots with some soil, and took them in a carrier bag, one in each hand, to the Amtrack train station in Trenton, thence to Penn Station in the heart of New York within walking distance of Parade's offices on the top floor of a skyscraper.

As I walked through the crowded terminal, then out into the bustling streets of New York with the bushy green tops of tomato plants waving out of my carrier bags, policemen looked at me suspiciously, and several street people stopped me to ask: "What you got there – marijuana?" I suddenly realized I could be the first person on earth to be mugged for a pair of tomato plants.

When I reached my destination I took the turbo elevator to the twenty-eighth floor and I was shown to Pironti's office. Not a vestige of greenery was anywhere and he was on his way in from lunch. His secretary allowed me to spread some newspapers on his plush carpet and dump the two sets of plants from their pots. To my amazement both stood bolt upright with tomatoes, potatoes and soil clearly visible, as though they were growing through the floor, with an impressive view of the Empire State Building through the window.

When Pironti walked in he stood there with the most incredulous look on his face. I don't think he had ever seen a potato outside a supermarket, let alone growing around the roots of a tomato plant in his office. Needless to say my proposals were accepted and since then millions of tomato-potato plants have been sold to delight gardeners as a space-saving idea.

TOMATO SUPERSTEAK – Big as grapefruits

This Beefsteak-type tomato was bred by the late Ted Torrey, vegetable breeder. I asked how he bred Supersteak, and he gave all the credit to David Burpee. Torrey said that Burpee just pointed to two tomato varieties one day and suggested he cross them. Torrey did and Supersteak was born. He said Burpee had an uncanny sense of knowing what varieties to mate to achieve a desired result, rather like the uncanny skill that the legendary breeder, Luther Burbank possessed.

Supersteak is superior to all other beefsteak tomatoes by yielding large red fruit (up to 2 lbs in weight) that are smooth and globe-shaped. One slice can cover an entire slice of bread, and if you want to know what a 2 lb tomato looks like put it next to a Ruby Red grapefruit and you'll see they are the same size. I believe that Supersteak has genes of a variety called Delicious running through its cells. Delicious is a Burpee selection from Ponderosa, a giant fruited pink-skinned monster introduced by the old Peter Henderson Seed Co. Delicious has the distinction of holding the world record weight for a tomato – at 7 lbs 12 ozs. It is quite likely that after enough gardeners have grown it, Supersteak will beat that record..

Supersteak's large, round, smooth-skinned red fruits have very few seeds, and the flavor is superb. I have seen it staked with as many as 24 big perfectly formed, blemish free fruits on a single plant at one time. Moreover it is earlier ripening than any of the Beefsteaks.

TOMATO BETTER BOY VFN (also known as BUSHELMAKER) – World record holder for most tomatoes on one plant.

The world record for the heaviest weight of tomatoes from a single vine is 342 lbs, recorded by an Alabama gardener, Charles H. Wilbur. The vine reached a height of 25 ft, using nothing more than his home-made compost to provide nutrients. He grew 110 lbs of tomatoes in a whisky half barrel planter, and 1,368 pounds of tomatoes from just four plants planted side-by-side in a square. Better Boy is a derivative hybrid from Big Boy and Lemon Boy, produced by Petoseed Company, before it merged with Novartis. Big Boy was produced by the late Dr. Oved Shifriss while working as a vegetable breeder for Burpee Seeds. Released in 1949, it was an instant success, combining earliness with large, smooth, round fruit and a meaty interior. Dr. Shifriss left Burpee to teach at Rutgers University and I went to interview him for an article I was writing about tomatoes for Readers Digest magazine. Although the parents of the original Big Boy are known only to Burpee, I asked Dr. Shifress how he bred it, and he said he bred it in the library at Delaware Valley Agricultural College, Doylestown, Pennsylvania reading about the various traits of large-fruited tomato varieties and how those traits are inherited genetically. From his reading he simply picked two parents to cross that he thought would produce the desired result, and PRESTO he was correct. Since Dr. Shifriss's parents were from the Ukraine and emigrated to Israel before moving to the USA, there is speculation that he might have used a Ukranian heirloom variety in the parentage of Big Boy, but I do not believe that is true. The sense I got from my interview was that he used two American varieties, one for large size and the other for smooth, round shape. The VFN after the name, Better Boy means that the variety is resistant to two wilt diseases (verticillium and fusarium wilt) and to nematode infestations.

TOMATO BIG RAINBOW - No two tomatoes exactly alike.

There are a lot of versions concerning the history of this attractive mammoth tomato, and I don't believe anyone really knows its origins. That's because it seems to be identical to several other tomatoes that have different names and claim different pedigrees. To my sensibilities, it seems identical to Flame, Pineapple, Striped German and several other giant-fruited tomatoes with golden yellow skins and red stripes. Also, all have red and yellow marble-ing on the inside. Of all the names, however, Big Rainbow seems most appropriate since no two fruit are ever alike. They can be nearly all red, nearly all golden yellow, or striped half-and-half. Also, the bicolor pattern can take many forms – a red blossom end feathering to yellow, and various gradations in between. It's a beauty and the flavor is superb. I've grown 2 lb fruit with ease, and they have the same smooth, round shape of Supersteak – not corrugated like most other giant fruited tomatoes.

TOMATO POLBIG – Big, early and almost seedless

In the earliness stakes it is usually small-fruited varieties that win – varieties like Sub-Arctic and the cherry size Sweet 100. Everyone wants a big early tomato, but most big early tomatoes have poor flavor. It seems that for a big tomato to taste great, it mustn't be rushed. Polbig is an exception. Discovered in Poland, it has replaced Burpee's Big Early as the one to grow for earliness. It yields more fruit than Burpee's Big Early and has good disease resistance. The name is strange (a contraction of Big and Polish), and is bound to hamper its popularity, but when you want large fruit by July 4th in Northern gardens Polbig is now the favorite among knowledgeable tomato growers.

TOMATO SUNGOLD - Super sweetness

This cherry-size, golden yellow tomato originated in Japan. It was introduced to the Western world by Thompson & Morgan who aren't in the habit of selling yellow tomatoes because traditionally they are not nearly as popular among the public as red varieties. But they featured Sungold on the back cover of their catalog because they had never tasted such a sweet flavored fruit. The fruit is so sweet I have eaten them in a bowl with a scoop of vanilla ice-cream. It's remarkably early and highly productive, more than 1,000 fruit from a single vine.

Sungold does have one slight flaw, however. It is subject to cracking. So don't let the fruit stay on the vine any length of time. Pick them as soon as they ripen before they have a chance to crack. Snack on them like candy. They're a lot healthier for you into the bargain.

TOMATO EARLY CASCADE – 500 tomatoes to a single plant

Not everyone wants a big Beefsteak-type tomato. For salads and making tomato sauce I also want something more substantial than a Sungold. For earliness most people are happy to settle for a tomato as big as a billiard ball as long as it has good flavor. These billiard ball size tomatoes are known as saladettes because they are perfect for slicing into salads. I like to cut mine in half and make four segments from each half, in the shape of an orange segment.

Early Cascade has other advantages. One vine is capable of yielding 500 medium size fruits, mostly in clusters of seven and eight, as perfectly formed and perfectly round as peas in a pod. The clusters hang down the plant like a curtain – a pillar of fruit clusters. Moreover, the vines are exceedingly vigorous and disease resistant. They do not exhaust themselves by the end of summer like many other tomatoes, but have the stamina to continue bearing right up to a killing frost. I grow mine in cylinders of builder's wire so the plants can be self-supporting, poking their side branches through the mesh, and climbing to a height of 6 ft and more.

TURNIPS AND RUTABAGAS

Although these two root crops can look alike in appearance, turnips are much faster to mature (in as little as 40 days), while rutabagas can take 100 days. While I find the flavors similar a lot of people find turnips sweeter than rutabagas. That is certainly true of the new hybrid all-white Japanese varieties which are best harvested the size of a golf ball.

A bonus to growing turnips is the edible green top, known as turnip greens. The most widely planted turnips are Purple Top Globe and Purple Top Milan (with a more flattened

I'll Make You a Gardening Wizard Overnight!

Cape gooseberry

Tomato, Supersteak

Chapter 9 - *Variety Selections for Huge Garden Yields*

Tomato-potato plant

Tomato, Big Rainbow

Tomato, Early Cascade

Tomato, Sungold

globe shape). There are also all-red and all-yellow turnips, also a cylinder-shaped French turnip, Blanc de Crossy. In a loose soil it will produce twice the number of slices as a round turnip. Seed should be direct-sown and the seedlings thinned to stand 3 inches apart. They perform best in cool weather, and should be watered at the slightest hint of a dry spell to keep the root tender. Blemishes on the skin can be caused by worms, but these generally scar the surface and can be removed by peeling.

Remove tops for storage in the crisper section of the refrigerator. Plants are hardy and can be sown several weeks before the last expected frost date. Never allow the soil to dry out as this will affect the flavor.

TURNIP TOKYO CROSS – Sweet and juicy.

Winner of an All-America Award for its rapid growth and sweet flavor, this hybrid variety was bred by the Japanese seed house, Takii. The color of snow, it matures its ping-pong ball size roots in just 40 days. The flavor at that size is incredibly sweet, and the tops are edible as turnip greens. Left in the garden, plants will continue to grow to the size of a tennis ball and still remain sweet.

Watercress - The finest salad ingredient.

Don't be fooled by claims in seed catalogs and books that you can grow watercress in a moist soil or in a bucket of water. For watercress – a hardy perennial - to remain productive it demands a clear running stream, or a shallow pond fed by a clear running stream. At Cedaridge Farm I have several running streams, including a man made stream that uses re-circulated water through a filter so I can specifically grow watercress. The stream opens out to form shallow pools with gravel soil and the watercress loves it, staying productive all year – even in the depths of winter. To grow watercress is easy – just purchase a bunch at the supermarket and you will find that it has wispy white roots already formed at every leaf node. Simply take a sprig, insert the end in a sandy or gritty soil under water, and make sure one of the leaf nodes stays in contact with the soil by weighting the stem down with a stone.

AMERICAN CRESS. There is a type of cress that is very similar to watercress in appearance, which you CAN grow without running water. It is called American cress, and is well worth growing if you crave that piquant flavor that watercress adds to salads. American cress is easily raised from seed either direct-sown into the garden or started indoors 4 weeks before outdoor planting. The plants are hardy and will tolerate mild frosts. They also tolerate crowding so I like to broadcast the seed in a wide row.

Watermelon – Red, Pink, White, Yellow and Orange fleshed.

Given the choice I'd rather have a crisp, honeysweet slice of watermelon than any other kind of melon, but they are not the easiest of vegetable fruits to grow, especially if you want a seedless variety which most people do. In a recent melon book a writer states: "When it comes to melons even plant breeders admit that hybrids have nothing over heirlooms. They're not bigger, better, or more improved. The development of seedless or triploid seems to be the major "advantage". I disagree. I've met a lot of melon breeders in my time and can't think of one that would make such a claim.

WATERMELON YELLOW BABY - I was head of All-America Selections, the national seed trials when the yellow fleshed hybrid, Yellow Baby won an award. I traveled to Taiwan to meet the Chinese breeder, Known-You Seed Company and learned exactly what made Yellow Baby distinctive over any other watermelon. First, it has 50% fewer seeds than similar size 'icebox' watermelons. Second, it was bred at a high elevation, so it tolerates cold better than other watermelons I know. Third, it has extra earliness – usually it's the first variety to ripen. And into the bargain it is extremely sweet. In China yellow fleshed watermelons are even preferred over red because of their extra sweet flavor.

In Taiwan I learning how Chinese farmers test watermelons for ripeness. Standing in the watermelon field with snow-capped mountains in the background, my host picked up a watermelon that had a dried tendril close to the fruit, and thumped the skin with his knuckle. He advised: "If it sounds like thumping your stomach (a soft sound), it's probably over-ripe; if it sounds like tapping your forehead (a dull sound) it's probably under-ripe, and if it sounds like knocking your Adam's apple (a hollow ring) it's just right.

With seedless watermelons, such as Triple Crown, the fact they are seedless increases their sugar content. Since they develop no viable seeds, that energy is concentrated into making them exceedingly sweet. The big question is "How do you make seeds for a seedless watermelon?" It's like crossing a jackass onto a mare to create a mule. The mule is stronger than either parent, but it is a hybrid and therefore sterile. Like many plant hybrids, it cannot reproduce itself. Seed packets of seedless watermelons contain two types of seed – the male parent to provide pollen and the female parent to form the fruit. You can tell the male seed from the female by its color - usually stained blue by the seed supplier with instructions to plant one male vine with every six females. That requires a lot of space and it's the reason why not many home gardeners plant seedless watermelons.

WHEN FLAVOR IS EVERYTHING. Flavor in a vegetable or fruit is affected by many factors: choice of a flavorful variety, sunlight, time of harvest, adequate watering, size of the plant, soil fertility, and other factors. Sunlight makes chlorophyll – the green part of a plant and the greener the leaves generally the more flavorful the vegetable. Sugars move into the edible parts of vegetables, such as sweet corn, in soluble form and therefore adequate moisture is essential. Slug damage can make lettuce bitter, numerous diseases can make fruits inedible – such as sunscald on tomatoes. However, under optimum growing conditions, here's a list of vegetables I have found most flavorful.

Asparagus Purple Passion – tender spears, extra early.
Beet, Burpee Golden – tender roots AND tender greens.
Broccoli, Romanesco – mild, sweet bud clusters in spirals.
Brussels Sprouts, Jade Cross – tight, sweet buttons, hardy to Christmas.
Cabbage, Savoy King – buttery yellow interior, dark green wrap leaves.
Cantaloupe, Ambrosia – so sweet and delicious growers keep its name a secret.

Turnip, Tokyo Cross

Rutabaga

Watercress

Watermelon, Jubilee

Chapter 9 - *Variety Selections for Huge Garden Yields*

Watermelon, Yellow Baby

Carrots, Short 'n Sweet – small core, short crunchy roots.
Cauliflower, Snow Crown – large crisp, white heads.
Celery, Self-blanching – sweet and crunchy buttery yellow stalks.
Chard Bright Lights – tender green and bronze leaves, celery-like mid ribs.
Corn, Silver Queen – milky high sugar content.
Cucumber, Orient Express – bitter free, tender skin.
Eggplant, Dusky Hybrid – tasty fat slices perfect for grilling.
Lettuce Buttercrunch – buttery yellow, crisp interior.
Onion, Giant Walla Walla – sweet and crisp, grow anywhere onion.
Pea, Sugar Snap – sweet edible peas and crunchy pods.
Pepper, Gypsy Hybrid – thick, crunchy, sweet walls to eat like an apple.
Potato, French Fingerling La Ratte – buttery flavor, melt in the mouth texture.
Pumpkin, New England Sugar – best for pie filling and pumpkin soup.
Radish, Cherry Belle – crisp, crunchy mild flavor in record time.
Spinach, Tyee hybrid – succulent, dark green nutritious leaves.
Summer Squash, Early Prolific Crookneck – tender raw or cooked.
Winter Squash, Waltham Butternut – gourmet sweet potato flavor.
Sweet Potato, Beauregard – sweet, nutty flavor. Delicious baked.
Tomato, Supersteak – large fruited smooth round fruits and meaty flavor.
Tomato Sungold – cherry-size fruit as sweet as candy without the calories.
Turnip, Tokyo Cross – sweet and juicy flavor and speedy growth.
Watermelon, Yellow Baby – sweet, yellow fleshed ice-box size.
Watermelon, Triple Crown – large oval fruit, dark red flesh, sweet and seedless.

NUTRITIONAL ADVICE. Fresh vegetables, berries and fruits are a power house of nutrition, including vitamins vital for various bodily functions. One of the most dreaded diseases among seamen on long voyages during the age of sail was to run short of fresh vegetables, and suffer from a delibitating disease called scurvy, where the lips crack and the teeth fall out, followed by delirium and death. Vegetables in particular contain natural substances call antioxidants exclusive to plants. These antioxidants are capable of protecting the body against stress and diseases, such as cancer.

Some of the highest scoring antioxidant vegetables include garlic (very high), lettuce, kale, onions, spinach, broccoli and bell peppers.

In addition, a valuable nutrient called beta carotene is found in carrots, green leafy vegetables, squash, peppers and sweet potatoes. Lycopen – found mostly in tomatoes – helps humans ward off cancer, especially prostate cancer in men. Lutein reduces risk of breast cancer risk. It is contained in kale, collard greens, spinach and yellow squash.

To preserve these nutrients in vegetables, eat them fresh wherever possible, like in a salad. Never overcook as overcooking can destroy them. Avoid juicing vegetables as this destroys their fiber content and can cause an undesirable surge in blood sugar. Stir fries using olive oil, soups that are allowed to gently simmer and not boiled for hours, and stews where the greens are added at the last moment so as not to destroy their nutritional value, are all good ways to enjoy vegetables. Enjoy head lettuce, sweet bell peppers, baby

Chapter 9 - *Variety Selections for Huge Garden Yields*

Silver Queen sweet corn

summer squash, carrots, celery, cherry tomatoes and melons as snacks rather than processed foods.

To store leftover vegetables for a short period, cover in plastic wrap and place in the crisper section of your refrigerator.

TIPS ON STORING POPULAR VEGETABLES

The United States Department of Agriculture, through the government printing office, makes available free, or at low cost, helpful information about the storage and preserving of home garden fruits and vegetables. Listed below are the most useful of these informative books. To obtain copies simply send a postcard request to: Superintendent of Documents, Government Printing Office, Washington DC 20402. Or visit the Catalog of Government Publications on the internet.

The Complete Guide to Home Canning
The Beginners Guide to Home Canning
Home Freezing of Fruits & Vegetables
Making Pickles and Relishes
Storing Vegetables & Fruits in Basements, Cellars, Outbuildings & Pits

CANNING (the use of glass jars to preserve vegetables) is a popular way to preserve many vegetables. However, it is essential to follow canning instructions for each class of vegetable in the above bulletins. Vegetables for home canning must be at the peak of freshness and blemish-free – no bruises, cracks or signs of disease. Wash all vegetables before canning.

Except for high-acid red tomatoes, vegetables should be processed before canning in a steam pressure canner, not merely boiling water, since higher temperatures than boiling point are needed to kill potentially harmful bacteria, and pressures must be adjusted depending on your elevation above sea level (the higher the altitude the longer the steam pressure processing time needed).

Before using jars, check for chips and cracks, and test lids for a tight seal after cooling by pressing the center of the metal lid. The lid will feel rigid and will not depress if a successful seal has been made. Label and date sealed jars, remove screw bands from two-piece lids, and store canned foods in a cool, dry place. Examine all jars of canned goods before use. Discard any showing signs of spoilage – bulging lids, leaks, spurting liquid, foul odors or mold. Boil home-canned vegetables, except pickles, at least 10 minutes in a covered saucepan before serving.

FREEZING is easier than canning. All vegetables intended for freezing should be freshly picked, washed thoroughly, and be free of blemishes.

Containers for freezing are usually made from rigid plastic or moisture-proof, pliable polyethylene bags that can be sealed and made air-tight. Before freezing, vegetables need to be 'blanched' or scalded with boiling water to inactivate enzymes responsible for further ripeness and aging. Heating times vary according to the vegetable so check consumer bulletins for this information. After blanching, vegetables need cooling quickly under cold, running water, then packed immediately for freezing.

Following are the most common vegetables used for storage.

Asparagus - Excellent for freezing in bunches. The tender tips are also suitable for canning.

Beans, Snap - Pods of green, yellow and purple varieties are good for canning and freezing, although freezing is easiest. The dried pods can be shelled and the beans stored in glass jars.

Beans, Lima - Pods should be shelled and the dried beans stored in glass jars in a dry cupboard. The large, buttery beans are also suitable for feezing.

Beets - Roots with tops chopped off will store well in a box of moist sand or peat moss in a cool basement. The round roots are good for canning and freezing, peeled and then boiled, in whole or sections. Baby beets make delicious pickles. Larger roots should be sliced into rounds.

Broccoli - Good for freezing. Cut the large rounded heads into small sections. Wash thoroughly to dislodge any small worms hiding among the bud clusters.

Brussels sprouts - These hardy vegetables will remain useable in the garden until the ground freezes. The buds are good for freezing. Discard any loosely folded leaves.

Cabbage - Firm heads will keep in good condition for a month in the crisper section of the refrigerator. Otherwise, preserve by shredding the head to make sauerkraut, steeped in brine. Red cabbage makes an excellent pickle.

Carrots - Carrots are hardy and will stay in the ground during winter months until the soil freezes. Otherwise baby carrots can be peeled and frozen; larger carrots can be cut into thick slices for freezing.

Cantaloupe - Slice firm, ripe melons in half, discard seeds and scoop out balls with a melon ball scoop for freezing.

Cauliflower - The firm, rounded heads are good for freezing. Wash thoroughly to dislodge small worms that might be hiding among the bud clusters, and cut into small sections. Also makes a tasty pickle.

Celeriac - The globular root will remain edible in the garden until the ground freezes. It also keeps well in a cool basement and in the crisper section of the refrigerator.

Chard - Remains a long time in the garden during winter, until the ground freezes. The glossy green leaves will freeze like spinach.

Cucumber - Small 'dill' cucumbers preserve well as pickles. Larger fruits can be sliced into rounds or cut into sticks for pickles.

Eggplant - Freezes well if cut into 'sticks', but to prevent the white flesh from turning brown on exposure to air, immerse in saltwater before processing.

Lettuce - Can be grown in a cold frame to hold during winter months. Rows of lettuce in the garden will also stay firm well into winter months if protected with a covering of clear plastic or in a cold frame.

Kale - Stands in the garden all through winter, providing fresh greens without need to can or freeze.

Kohl-rabi - The swollen stem sections should be peeled and diced for freezing.

Leek - The stalks will stand in the garden a long time during winter, until the ground freezes.

Mustard - Smaller, tender leaves are suitable for freezing, like most leafy green vegetables.

Okra - Freezes well providing the pods are picked when young and tender. Also makes delicious pickles.

Onion - Kept cool over winter in the crisper section of a refrigerator or in a cool basement, onions will remain firm and edible for several months, providing they are 'keeper' varieties. Shallot onions make excellent pickles.

Parsley - This hardy plant will tolerate heavy freezes and remain growing in the garden until the ground freezes. Freeze the chopped leaves for longer storage. Cut into 2 inch segments and freeze.

I'll Make You a Gardening Wizard Overnight!

Peanuts, Jumbo Virginia

Parsnips - The plants can be left in the ground until the ground freezes. The roots will store in the crisper section of a refrigerator for several months, and longer stored in moist sand or peat moss in a dry basement.

Peanuts - Dried peanuts will keep in their hulls indefinitely. Locate a recipe for peanut soup on the internet and freeze.

Peas, Black-eyed - Shell the peas (actually beans) when the pods dry and store in glass jars in a dry cupboard.

Peas, English - Edible pod varieties like Sugar Snap and snow peas freeze easily. Shelled peas can be frozen, dried peas will store indefinitely in glass jars in a dry cupboard.

Peppers - Slice the big, blocky bell peppers into strips and freeze. Dry hot peppers and store as ropes or wreaths.

Potato - Both the Irish potato and sweet potato store well over winter in a cool, dry basement.

Pumpkin - Make pumpkin pies and freeze as cubes.

Radish - The large Japanese 'Daikon' radish stores well in a box of moist sand or peat in a basement.

Rhubarb - Excellent for freezing. Slice the stems into 1-2 inch segments.

Spinach - The leaves freeze well stripped of stalks. Spinach will stand in the garden until the ground freezes. To afford longer protection, grow in a cold frame or under a clear plastic tunnel.

Squash - Winter squash will store well in a cool basement. Be sure the stem section is not soft before storage, otherwise rot may enter the fruit through the rotten stem. Cut zucchini and crookneck squash into rounds for freezing.

Strawberries - Suitable for freezing whole.

Sweet Corn - Freezes well, either on the cob or as whole kernels cut from the cob with a sharp knife.

Tomatoes - Green tomatoes picked before frost will ripen over several weeks at room temperature. Whole tomatoes can be peeled and canned, or frozen without peeling. With a large surplus of tomatoes, bring to boil in a large pot and allow to simmer until they make a thick sauce for freezing.

Turnips and Rutabaga - These root crops will survive even heavy frosts left out in the garden. They store well in the crisper section of a refrigerator, and also in moist sand or peat moss in a cool basement. Large specimens can be peeled and cut into sections for freezing.

Carolyn's Comments:

"Of all the vegetable varieties we have grown, Derek's tomato/potato has astonished more visitors than all his giant vegetable successes. In summer when we have visitors, he likes to show them his tomato/potato plants, grip the main stem with one hand and pull it up to reveal potatoes among the roots. It's like a magic trick. It really works. One day on television we watched a news reporter open up a box of four tomato/potato plants, highly skeptical of the advertised claims. But when she removed from its wrapping four healthy green tomato/potato transplants already collecting chlorophyll, she exclaimed excitedly: 'Oh, my goodness. This might work!' She could hardly wait to plant them and follow their progress through the growing season. Derek lectures a lot and though it is time consuming, he values meeting with gardeners of all kinds, from beginners to experienced because it gives him contact with others who are passionate about gardening, and he is always receptive to new ideas and variety recommendations. This contact with gardeners across the country also helps him foresee trends before they occur. For example, the current trend in vertical gardening is one he recognized several years ago because of the interest in saving space, and even before that he foresaw the interest in container gardening."

Vegetable garden harvest at Cedaridge Farm

CHAPTER 10
Sell Your Surplus at a Profit

> *"When people pay to sample your home-grown produce you will feel an incredible sense of pride."*
> - from my article in **Nouveau** magazine about Farmers' Markets

Most of us have no intention of selling our vegetables and fruits, but it's good to know that if we wanted to there is a ready market out there for home-grown produce. I have a neighbor who cultivates a large melon patch each year and sells only melons from a table beside her driveway. The money she earns (as much as $5,000.00 in a good season) pays for her local property taxes.

ORGANIC FARMING -When I first started growing vegetables there was a lot of discussion in the press about Organic Farming and whether it was possible for organic farmers to compete economically with chemical farming and its ability to produce picture-perfect produce (even at the expense of health concerns, nutrition and flavor).

J. I. Rodale, founder of Organic Gardening magazine, based in Emmaus, Pennsylvania, was often ridiculed for his belief that farmers could grow good-looking produce without chemical fertilizers (using compost) and without chemical pesticides (using natural insect controls). J. I. Rodale died of a heart attack while conducting a television interview with Dick Cavett in which Rodale predicted a wider acceptance of organic gardening for health reasons. J. I. Rodale's son, Robert continued to take the magazine and publishing business to greater success.

Robert and I became friends after I became executive director of All America Selections (his research farm was an All-America test garden and Robert was a judge). I remember his giving me a personal tour of his own garden at his home near Emmaus, and a new research facility in Trumbaursville, where I observed experiments into fish farming and growing potatoes in different beds to determine whether various mulching methods produce greater yields. He was impressed with my report of a trip I had taken to Taiwan where one of the agricultural institutions had collected together every known tomato variety (3,000 varieties at that time) for breeding purposes, and we planned a trip together to see other initiatives by Chinese plant and soil scientists. Before we could make the trip, however, Robert was killed in a car accident in Moscow.

An indication of how strong the organic gardening movement has become was brought home forcefully when I attended the Sanibel Island Farmer's Market, Florida, held Sunday mornings between City Hall and the Sanibel Public Library. I saw that one of the vendors had customers three abreast lined up across the parking lot to purchase vegetables labeled organic, with a USDA seal of approval prominently displayed above the name of their enterprise, Worden Farm. There were four other vendors selling fresh vegetables but they were not nearly as busy. Actually, I didn't need to be told the produce was organic; I could SEE it in the color and vitality of the produce. I questioned one of the clerks manning the table, and he explained that the farm was located near Punta Gorda, owned by a husband-and-wife team – a pair of Ph.D.'s, Chris and Eva Worden, who had taken over a cow pasture of 60 acres and turned it into a viable organic growing operation. After only six years in operation they have 30 acres in production and a thriving business growing organic vegetables.

Several days later I visited Worden Farm and interviewed the youthful owners, both still in their late 30's. Eva graduated in Ecosystem Management from Yale University, and Chris in Soil Science and Crop Nutrition from the University of Connecticut. Eva is a bright, cheerful, vivacious brunette who likes nothing better than teaching organic gardening principles, and ways to use vegetables creatively. Chris is tall, tanned, athletic-looking, modest and fully focused on the farming operation. At the core of their financial success is a farm membership program whereby they agree to grow under contract for private individuals sufficient vegetables to supply a small family for an entire season (basically October through May.) They have 300 subscribers who pay $600.00 for the season, with the choice of picking up produce at the farm one day a week, or at various drop-off points in the area. They also attend five local farmers' markets.

After I turned onto a country road that ran straight as a gun-barrel through citrus orchards, cow pastures and horse farms, I drove onto a sandy driveway and parked on the grass verge in front of a barn where fresh vegetables were displayed in wooden bins for customers to pick up their weekly supply. Eva conducted me around and I was amazed to see how healthy everything looked – rows upon rows of cabbage, kale, lettuce, broccoli, cauliflower and arugula in neat rows that disappeared into infinity. Every plant exuded health and vitality, and hardly a bug bite could be seen.

Most of the crops were grown in raised rows, 3 ft. wide and 6 inches high, covered with a white plastic mulch to keep the fields weed free. The white also reflects heat. On certain crops (such as melons) they use black plastic to warm the soil. A tractor cultivator hoes between the rows. Drip irrigation hose runs the length of each bed under the plastic, providing moisture on an as-needed basis. Eva explained it is a system perfected in Israel.

For fertilizing they use mostly compost made from poultry and horse bedding (they buy 150 tons a year from local horse farms), which they mix with landscape debris such as wood chips. To supplement the nutrient content in the compost they also add an organic fertilizer, Microstart 60, which mostly provides additional nitrogen. To help control diseases, they practice crop rotation, ensuring that a particular plant family like cabbage and root crops are not grown in the same place for four years. In between plantings they also grow a cover crop (such as Sudan grass and cowpeas) and plow it under to help raise the nitrogen level and to provide what Eva calls 'spatial diversity.'

Chris believes the key to their success in keeping down insect pests and disease is the health of the soil, also the application of a fish emulsion fertilizer that deters insects by its odor. Occasionally, if aphids or a beetle pest looks like it might become a problem, Chris will use an insecticide approved by the Organic Materials Review Institute, a non-profit organization that approves organic products. This may be a biological control like BT to reduce caterpillar populations, or pyrethrum or insecticidal soap, both of which work well on aphids and other soft-bodied insects.

Another key to the Worden's success is variety selection. Their favorite seed source is Johnny's Seeds, located in Maine, a breeder and prime producer of vegetable seeds raised organically. The Wordens test for performance and stick with the earlier or higher yielding varieties, some of which may be hybrids. They raise their own seedlings under plastic hoop houses.

Chris grew up in Maryland on a farm, and Eva grew up in Coral Gables, Florida. Eva's parents also have a fruit grove in the area of Homestead, Florida, a big farming community. She taught horticulture at the University of Florida, got to know the Punta Gorda area well enough to realize it was the perfect location to fulfill their love of the land by farming responsibly. Today, the flavor of their produce and the crowds that converge on their stalls at the local farmers' markets are testimony to their success. To learn more about the Worden Farm membership growing system visit www.wordenfarm.com.

SELLING TIPS - Whether you are a home gardener with surplus produce to sell, or a farmer growing vegetables for a livelihood, local farmers' markets are good places to sell fresh produce. The fees to set up a table are usually low (as little as $5.00). Here are some tips for selling vegetables and fruits:

1. Make your table display as colorful and attractive as possible. Bunch red radish next to green lettuce, red beets next to orange carrots, white kohlrabi next to yellow squash; green zucchini next to golden beets, purple asparagus next to green sugar snap peas, and so on.
2. If everything you sell is organically grown and you choose not to be certified organic by the government (it costs money to be certified), then call your produce NATURAL – no chemicals used!
3. Make your display LOOK organic by displaying root crops in peach baskets rather than plastic crates. Use brown paper bags instead of plastic bags. Keep the tops on beets and carrots and use a spray bottle of water to make their skins shine. A dry root vegetable soon loses its luster, and the green tops will wilt unless you keep them moistened.
4. Offer as wide a selection of produce as possible. The bigger your display the more customers you will attract because people like to choose. Learn local preferences. In areas with a strong Asian population sell Chinese vegetables like bok choy and snow peas. In areas with a Latino population sell tomatillos, hot peppers and cilantro.
5. Grow for earliness. By using horticultural fleece and black plastic as a mulch, for example, it is possible to ripen strawberries two weeks ahead of normal. By transplanting corn seedlings rather than direct seeding you can beat other vendors by two weeks.

6. Offer small samples, especially of your sweetest melon varieties or tastiest strawberries. Slice open some root varieties to show the interior color since the interior often has more eye appeal than the outside. Display some beet chips for people to sample and explain how they are simply deep fried in olive oil. To sell vegetable spaghetti, show the cooked vegetable sliced open and the interior spaghetti-like strands fluffed up with a fork. Place a sign next to it saying LOW CALORIE SUBSTITUTE FOR PASTA and you will sell out quickly.
7. Some heirloom vegetables can look ugly, especially tomatoes. Consider selling them as a collection of four varieties in a quart container, rather than individually.
8. Sell VARIETIES not vegetable classes. For example, instead of a sign saying fresh lettuce, say fresh Buttercrunch lettuce; instead of sweet onions, say Giant Walla Walla sweet onions since people will consider these special and buy from you rather than a competitive vendor who just sells the vegetable as a class.
9. Build up anticipation. For example, Ambrosia cantaloupe is not an early variety, and may be two weeks later than an extra early variety like Fastbreak. So put up a sign saying – NEXT WEEK: Ambrosia Melons! Come early.
10. Don't sell each vegetable variety at the same price. Sell melons and squash by the pound. Charge more for golden beets than red beets. Bunch different colors of vegetables together and sell at a higher price – a radish mixture, a carrot mixture, a beet mixture, a chard mixture.
11. Know what sells. Strawberries sell quickly, also early asparagus, raspberries, blueberries and blackberries in season. Tomatoes, peppers, eggplant and sweet corn command good prices. Offer vegetables other vendors might not have – for example, edible soybeans, a colorful mesclun mix, long oriental cucumbers, yard long beans, blue potatoes. If you sell lima beans or fava beans, don't shell the pods. You can earn more by selling the beans in the pods, but do open up some pods for customers to see the size of the beans inside. Besides, shelling takes valuable time.
12. If you have sales staff, educate them on the difference between varieties, and encourage them to suggest ways to use a particular vegetable – like spaghetti squash which picks up the flavor of any sauce it is served with, such as marinara sauce or a parsley butter sauce.

Some local communities have a farm stand ordinance that allows you to sell fresh produce from a roadside table or farm stand. Check the local ordinance to see how they want you to comply with safety rules, such as an easy-on-easy-off access.

Carolyn's Comments:

"Our visit to the Worden Farm around the New Year and meeting the owners was one of the most pleasant memories of our time spent in Florida. It was a warm, sunny day and the health and vitality of the organically-grown vegetables was plain to see. Chris Worden had his parents visiting from up north and they were very proud of his success. Eva was extremely knowledgeable about the growing and cooking of vegetables, and we left with armloads of produce to test for flavor. It warmed my heart to see such a worthy enterprise and proof that organic farming — as well as organic gardening — can be a viable enterprise. The Wordens attend five local farmer's markets, and we are delighted to see so many farmer's markets close to Cedaridge Farm. Derek was responsible for the very popular Doylestown Farmers Market, after writing about the success of one he visited in Monterey, California. The president of the local Doylestown Merchant's Association, after reading Derek's article called him in to ask for advice about establishing one in the center of Doylestown as a means to attract more traffic to the retail area, and it has been running now from Easter through Thanksgiving for more than 20 years, offering not only fresh vegetables, but also baked goods, goat cheese, bison meat products, cut flowers, herbal soaps, skin creams, jams, honey, relishes and a host of other home-made products."

I'll Make You a Gardening Wizard Overnight!

CHAPTER 11
How to Turn Your Hobby into a Tax Deduction

"The monetary value of vegetables from a home garden is not taxable."
– *official* **IRS** *ruling*

There are few investments in life that the IRS does not attempt to tax if you make a profit. It's comforting to know that growing fresh vegetables is such a healthy, worthwhile activity that the government does not consider it a taxable event. Where else can a modest $100.00 investment (for seeds and tools) produce a $3,000.00 return in value from a few hours of healthy activity each week in a small backyard space?

This may sound hard to believe but the IRS encourages Americans to turn their gardening hobby into a business and take legitimate business deductions for seeds, equipment, fertilizer, mulch, fencing etc. To verify this enter Summertime Tax Tip 2009-18 as a web search.

It's also possible to apply for government grants for gardening. Yes, there are government grants for gardening. In particular the government has money for numerous small farming and gardening projects such as community gardening and charitable work such as growing produce for underprivileged families. Whenever you seek to sell produce or benefit the community by starting an educational or community service program, you may be able to qualify for government subsidies.

HOW TO TURN YOUR HOBBY INTO A TAX DEDUCTION. Here's what the IRS has to say about gardening as a hobby (which is not deductable) and a business (which is deductable on your tax forms): "Summer is a time when many Americans take their... gardening tools out of storage. Hobbies... are often done for pleasure, but can result in a profit. If your favorite activity does make a profit every year or so, there may be tax implications. You must report income to the IRS from almost all sources, including hobbies. Here are eight questions that will determine if your activity is a hobby or a business:

1. Is the purpose of your activity to make a profit? Generally your activity is considered a business if it is carried on with the reasonable expectation of making a profit.

2. Do you participate in your activity just for fun? Hobbies – also called not-for-profit activities – are those activities that are not pursued for profit.

3. Do you depend on income from the activity? If so, your activity is likely considered a business.

4. Have you changed methods of business to improve profitability? If so, your hobby may actually be a business.
5. Do you have the knowledge needed to carry on the activity as a successful business? People who carry on hobbies as an activity often do not have the business acumen to turn their not-for-profit activity into a profitable business venture.
6. Have you made a profit from similar activities in the past? This may indicate that your activity is a business rather than a not-for-profit activity. An activity is presumed a business if it makes a profit in at least three of the last five tax years, including the current year...
7. Does the activity make a profit in some years? Even if your activity does not make a profit every year, it may still be considered a business.
8. Do you expect to make a profit in the future from the appreciation of assets used in the activity? This indicates your activity may be a business rather than a hobby.

If the activity does not make a profit, allowable deductions cannot exceed the gross receipts for the activity. If you are conducting a trade or business you may deduct your ordinary and necessary expenses.

Although I am not a tax professional (and you should check with your tax preparer since IRS rules are constantly changing) it is easy to see that if you can make your gardening activity a business rather than a hobby, you can receive favorable treatment from the IRS. For example, say that in a given year you have decided to make your gardening hobby a business by the following activities:

1. You contact restaurants and agree to supply them with fresh produce.
2. Once a week from Easter or Thanksgiving (or even less), you pay for a table at a local Farmers Market and sell your produce.
3. You have a table at the end of your driveway with an honor system for people to pay for fresh vegetables.
4. The purpose of this activity can be for any number of reasons - to help pay your local taxes, to send your children to college, to pay for health care, to augment loss of income from being out of work (and a multitude of other reasons).

Say that as a result of this activity the first year, you earn $5,000.00 that helps to pay your local school (or other) taxes or helps augment the family income, and the cost of growing and selling that produce totals $6,000.00 (for cost of seeds, plants, fertilizer, soaker hose, lumber to make a compost bin, Farmers Market fees, purchase of a table and a canopy for rainy days, cost of gasoline and wear and tear on your car driving to and from the Farmers Markets and the restaurants, and other expenses), then you have suffered a loss and can claim these as legitimate business deductions.

Because start-up costs are generally heavy the first year, the next year you might make a profit. Even if it's a modest profit – say $1,000.00 after expenses – it has still proven worthwhile to turn your gardening hobby into a business. In order to claim deductions, do the following:

KEEP A DIARY showing the dates when you attended the Farmer's Markets, the days you made deliveries to restaurants, and the daily income from your table at the end of the driveway. Show the date the selling season started and when it ended.

KEEP ALL RECEIPTS. Place business receipts (even gasoline expenses) in a manila envelope marked BUSINESS EXPENSES and place domestic receipts in a separate manila envelope marked DOMESTIC EXPENSES. Obtain receipts for deliveries to restaurant customers.

That way, if you are ever audited, the IRS can see that you operated your gardening enterprise in a business-like manner.

You can also contribute surplus vegetables to a local soup kitchen and your tax preparer may be able to write off certain expenses on your tax return. Consult with your local IRS office for details if you prepare your own taxes, as the rules can vary from one year to the next.

GOVERNMENT SUBSIDIES. First, go to the government's website by entering Government Subsidies as a search or CSREES.usda.gov, which stands for Government State Research, Education and Extension Service and click on Grants. The grant program is operated by the USDA, and their website explains how to qualify for a grant to fund a gardening or small farming project. Enter several search possibilities. For example, you might enter 'Grants for individuals', 'Grants for small businesses', 'Grants for an educational program' and others. The Government hands out 10 billion dollars in subsidies A MONTH, and has millions of unclaimed subsidies for which you may qualify by filling in a simple application. Show that your proposal will benefit the community or prove educational and there's a possibility you can receive non-returnable grant money.

The website offers detailed information about applying for grants and even supplies free a disk with step-by-step instructions and advice.

For example, you might live in an urban area with a high incidence of teenage crime caused by lack of cultural or creative amenities. The establishment of a community garden could be seen as a means of channeling that teenage energy into gardening and away from crime. By presenting case histories of other initiatives that have resulted in lowering teenage crime, and enlisting the endorsement of community leaders like clergymen, teachers and the police, and also presenting a plan that includes a budget and realistic expectations, it's possible that a government grant might be made.

HOW TO START A COMMUNITY GARDEN. Community gardening is popular in Europe, especially in Britain, Germany, Denmark and Holland. These community gardens (called allotments in Britain) have been established mostly in and around cities where backyard gardens are small or non-existent. They are located along railroad embankments, on vacant lots, in public parks, around public schools and on church land. Some are quite beautiful with greenhouses, potting sheds and even gazebos.

As a first step to creating a community garden in your area, contact the American Community Gardening Association (info@communitygarden.org) where you can obtain useful instruction and download a list of community gardens in your area. The Association can advise you how to generate interest, deal with local government and other landowners, and establish rules for management of the site, including annual fees, a water source, establishing a fence to keep out intruders, and individual responsibilities.

Carolyn's Comments:

"Derek has a higher travel expense than any garden writer I know, and twice he has satisfied the IRS that it is justified. For example, Derek often visits New Zealand to study their progressive gardening methods (the Government has a strong organic farming policy), and it was there he first discovered Bright Lights chard, which later won an All-America award and has become the highest-selling chard of all time. Also, New Zealand's spring and summer growing seasons occur when it is fall and winter in the US so he can continue shooting plant specimens and gardens for his stock photo library. He attends most annual meetings of the Garden Writers Association and in order to maintain one of America's most diverse photo libraries he must visit trial gardens throughout the country. He lectures widely and has a special relationship with the Monet Museum, at Giverny, France. For twenty years he has produced a calendar about Monet's garden for sale in their gift shop and throughout the world. This requires frequent trips to France for fresh photographic images. Also, he has written about the restored gardens of other Impressionist painters, including Cezanne's Garden, in Provence and Renoir's Garden, near Nice. Monet and Renoir both had extensive vegetable gardens and Derek was the first to write about them. We even own a beautiful oil painting by the American Impressionist painter, Willard Metcalf, of Monet's vegetable garden. It is an extraordinary picture, showing Monet's plots of lettuce and cabbage all surrounded by hedges of peonies in full bloom.

During Derek's last tax audit the auditor concluded the sessions by saying he was satisfied with Derek's return but could not understand why Derek had not entered any business expenses for city water. 'That's because we are on a well system,' Derek explained. The auditor, who had lived in the city all his life, replied: 'You mean your water COMES OUT OF THE GROUND?' Derek said 'Yes, and it's free so that's why I don't show it as a business expense.'"

For years Derek produced garden articles for Architectural Digest magazine, and he has been sent on assignments all over the world. Twice he went to Bermuda, once to Hawaii; also he found beautiful gardens in Morocco, Scotland and even the Sub-antarctic where he photographed mega-herbs on Campbell Island. On a trip to South Africa, photographing the garden of a vet at in the Kruger National Park, Derek asked the owner what was his biggest problem and he replied: 'Our teenage boys are constantly leaving the gate open and you cannot imagine the destruction that a hippopotamus can do.' Derek wanted to photograph Kruger's biggest baobab tree, and he was driven three hours to see it along dirt tracks. He asked permission to leave the jeep and climb up into the tree and the ranger clapped his hands to see if any lion's heads popped up out of the grass. Derek hadn't been in the tree more than a few minutes when he heard the driver honking, and screaming: "Get back in the jeep. The lions are coming!"

CHAPTER 12
Herbal Magic

"If you fail with vegetables and fruits, try herbs."
– from my book, **Herb Gardening for Beginners** (Friedman/Fairfax)

Most herbs come from inhospitable places – regions of the world with poor soil, long periods of drought and insect pests. Many of the scents and flavors in them were developed to ward off chewing insects or browsing animals. They are survivors and you should have little difficulty growing most of them in your garden. The cardinal rule is to provide full sun, good drainage and spare the water. Basil, for example, is susceptible to frost and root rot from overwatering. Lavender should not be watered until it looks dead.

In Colonial times herbs were important not only to flavor bland food, but also as medicines (some of these claims have since been proven false), and to mask household odors, like a modern day air freshener. Moreover, it doesn't take a lot of a particular herb to provide flavorings since most are quite potent and only a leaf in some cases is needed to produce a desirable flavor. Many herbs are suitable for container gardening both indoors and outdoors.

The great difficulty in growing herbs is that the majority are not very ornamental. Except for lavender, nasturtiums, garlic chives, and a few others, they mostly have inconspicuous flowers, and so we must rely on creating a tapestry effect with leaf colors, leaf shapes and leaf texture for a pleasing design. There are some ingenious designs for herb gardens. One is the cartwheel, whereas brick paths radiate from a central space to create pie shaped beds like the spokes of a wheel. This design (shown here) was made famous by the Findhorn Community, a group of organic gardeners that live in the north of Scotland.

My personal favorite design, and the one used at Cedaridge Farm, is the Colonial Quadrant Garden, a layout that actually extends way back in time when Medieval monks established physic gardens behind monastery walls to grow healing herbs. This design consists of a simple square dissected by paths that cross in the middle to create four smaller squares as planting beds. Each square can represent a theme, if you wish – one for medicinal herbs (such as mint, for the relief of congestion), a second for culinary herbs (such as basil and chives), a third for dye plants and a fourth for fragrance (for example, lavender, lemon grass, and cloves).

An herb garden does not need to be all herbs. In mine I like to add salad crops like frilly Lollo Rosso lettuce, Red Acre red cabbage and hot Cayenne peppers for a little extra color and interest.

HERB KNOT GARDEN

Suitable perennial hedging plants for the design:

Boxwood
Germander
Lavender cotton

Fill the spaces between the hedges with all-one herb, using different leaf colors and textures for best effect, for example, purple basil, silver sage, golden oregano, dark green parsley, variegated mint, blue rue, silver lavender, lemon balm and others.

HERB GARDEN DESIGN. Although herbs can be grown in rows or blocks like a traditional vegetable garden, many herbs have interesting leaf textures, leaf colors (even gold, silver and bronze) and leaf forms that are conducive to creating interesting patterns and themes. Some useful herbs – like chives and nasturtiums – even have colorful flowers. Some common herbs that display plain green leaves (like thyme and mint) have varieties that are variegated with silver and gold to add extra appeal.

The most alluring herb garden theme is an Herbal Knot Garden, with low boxwood hedges creating a labyrinth design of squares or curves. The low hedges create decorative shapes that form beds into which you can plant all one variety of herbs, or a mosaic of different varieties.

Herb knot garden

COOKING WITH HERBS - Even the most common meals can taste gourmet quality by the addition of an appropriate herb. For example, what a difference chopped chives can make to a breakfast of scrambled eggs, or coarsely chopped basil leaves to a dish of stewed tomatoes, or finely chopped parsley to mashed potatoes. Consider the improvement that a sprig of crushed mint leaves can make to a glass of iced tea, and a sprinkling of oregano to a plain tomato and cheese pizza.

PRESERVING HERBS - Usually the topmost leaves on a stem impart the best flavor. This is especially true of mint, lemon balm and basil. Drying is the easiest way to preserve most herbs, and drying intensifies the flavor. Simply rinse the stems under cold water and hang them upside down to air dry for 7-10 days. Or spread the leaves on a cookie sheet and place in an oven at 200F for an hour or less. Drying is complete when the leaves feel crisp and crumbly.

Some herbs can be frozen. These include parsley, chives, chervil, coriander, oregano, mint and rosemary. Wash in cold water, then blanch by steeping in boiling water for 50 seconds. Cool quickly in ice water, drain and pack into freezer bags. Basil, chives and dill don't need blanching.

USEFUL HERBS. The following is what I consider to be a list of beneficial herbs to grow in a herb garden, mostly culinary.

Design for a Quadrant Herb Garden

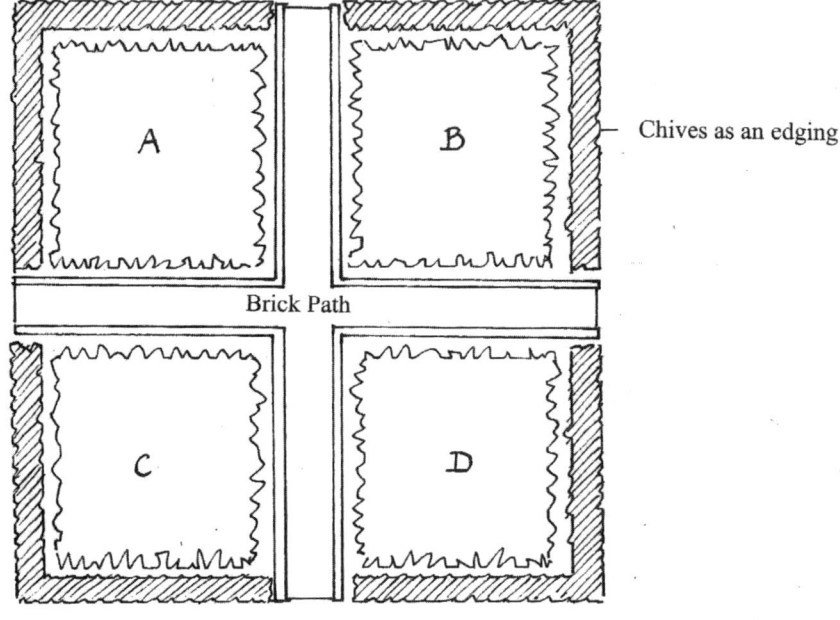

Bed A- Mint, Thyme, Rosemary, Tarragon, Chamomile, Lavender, Garlic
Bed B- All Basils (purple-leaf, green leaf, curly leaf, green mound etc)
Bed C- Parsley, Cilantro, Chervil, Garlic chives, Dill, Chili peppers
Bed D- Sage, Fennel, Marjoram, Oregano, Lemon Balm, Lemon grass

Chapter 12 - **Herbal Magic**

Quadrant herb garden, Cedaridge Farm

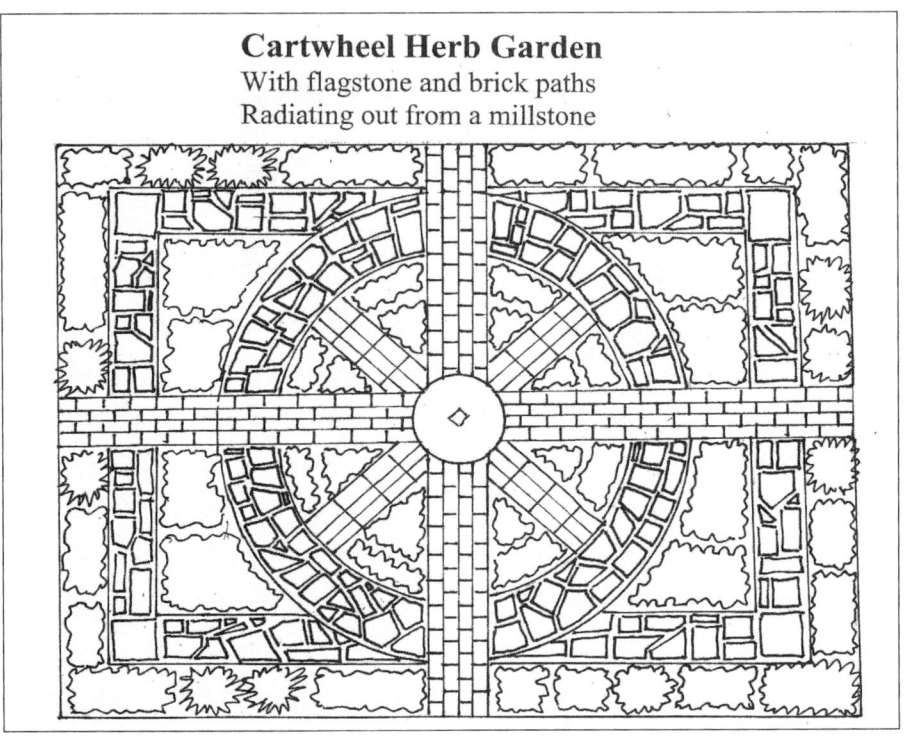

Cartwheel Herb Garden
With flagstone and brick paths
Radiating out from a millstone

Aloe vera – a tender perennial from the deserts of Africa, with succulent, spiky leaves filled with a clear gel. Helps to heal burns and itchy insect bites. Keep a pot on a sunny kitchen window during winter and place outdoors during frost-free months. Mature plants produce an attractive poker-like yellow flower spike. The easiest way to propagate an Aloe vera plant is to take a piece of leaf and root it in a moist mix of vermiculite and perlite, or break off an offset with as much root as possible and transfer to its own pot.

Anise - There are two kinds of anise – true anise and anise hyssop. True anise resembles the wayside weed, Queen Anne's lace or wild carrot. A hardy annual, it is grown mostly for its licorice-flavored seeds that are used in baking, to add flavor to sweet rolls and home-made bread. The seeds can be chewed as a breath freshener and to aid digestion at the end of a spicy meal, such as chili and curry. Propagate from seed sown directly into the garden.

Anise hyssop is a hardy perennial related to mints. It produces beautiful blue and white flower spikes that are so ornamental they are grown in perennial flower gardens for decorative effect. The entire plant, including stems, leaves and flowers has a strong anise fragrance, reminiscent of root beer. The leaves make a refreshing anise-flavored tea, and the dried seeds are a substitute for true anise.

Propagate by division and by starting seeds indoors 6 weeks before outdoor planting.

Chapter 12 - **Herbal Magic**

Herb garden with bee skip accent

Basil - a tender annual grown mostly to add a sweet, clove-like flavor to raw tomato and to create pesto sauce for flavoring pasta dishes and pizza. Use the leaves soon after harvesting as prolonged storage – even in a refrigerator – will turn the leaves black. There are many forms of basil, including the common lettuce leaf basil with broad, pointed glossy green leaves, bronze-leafed basil that can be used ornamentally in flower beds, and a low bushy variety, Green Bouquet that makes a decorative edging for flower beds. Depending on variety the flowers can be white, pink and purple. Thai Queen, an All-America Award winner, displays a beautiful bouquet of deep purple flowers and lustrous dark leaves.

Basil seed is best started 6 weeks before outdoor planting after frost danger. Transplant the seedlings to stand at least 6 inches apart. Pinch out the lead shoot to encourage side branching and a bushy habit. Basil is sensitive to overwatering, so be sure to give the plants good drainage. Basil also looks good in a pot.

Here's my favorite recipe for pesto sauce:

2 cups loosely packed basil leaves.

1/3 cup of pine nuts or crumbled walnuts.

2 cloves of garlic.

1 cup of Parmesan cheese.

1 cup of olive oil.

Salt, pepper, and lemon juice to taste.

Process to a rough paste in a food processor or blender:
basil leaves, pine nuts, garlic and cheese.

With the machine running, slowly pour in the olive oil through the feed tube. If paste seems too dry add a little more oil.

Add salt, pepper and lemon juice.
Use or freeze topped with a thin layer of olive oil.

Bay Laurel – a tender evergreen shrub that produces shiny, leathery camellia-like leaves that are pungent. It is valued as a flavoring for soups and stews, especially fish soups such as bouillabaisse. The leaves are so strongly aromatic that one leaf can flavor a gallon of soup. Remove after simmering as the leaf is unpalatable. Bay laurel is best planted in a decorative pot that can be taken indoors during winter months. During frost-free months it makes a good focal accent for an herb garden.

Plants can be trained into topiary shapes, especially topknots. Propagate from tip cuttings rooted in a peat-based potting soil (see page 259).

Chamomile – a hardy perennial with aromatic apple-scented leaves and small, white daisy-like flowers. The dried bud clusters make a refreshing tea when steeped in boiling water. Also a popular fragrance for face creams and massage oils. To use as an insect repellent, simply rub the cooled tea on exposed parts of your body. Direct-sow seeds in early spring

Chapter 12 - *Herbal Magic*

Dried herbs in storage jars

Basil varieties

or start indoors 6-8 weeks before outdoor planting. Root divisions are also a way to obtain new plants. Space 6 inches apart.

Chervil – is similar in appearance and flavor to cilantro. It is a hardy annual that produces finely divided leaves similar to parsley, and a pungent flavor that enhances soups, stews, egg and meat dishes. Seed is best direct sown and thinned to at least 3 inches apart since the plants tolerate crowding.

Cilantro – also known as corianda, is a hardy annual best direct-sown and thinned to at least 3 inches apart since the plants tolerate crowding. The young fan-shaped leaves are broad and serrated when young, but become more divided and slender when old, with no loss of flavor. The fresh leaves are mostly used to flavor meat dishes, soups, egg dishes, pizza and Mexican food.

Echinacea – also known as purple coneflower, this prairie wildflower is a hardy perennial that produces purple daisy-like flowers on 4-ft tall stems. Many health benefits are attributed to its ground dried root. Ingested as a tea, Echinacea is an antibiotic and stimulates the immune system. Plants are hardy, may be direct sown in early spring, or started indoors 6-8 weeks ahead of outdoor planting. Three to four year old roots contain the strongest healing powers. The roots also divide easily to make new plants, spaced at least 12 inches apart.

Garlic - So many health benefits are attributed to garlic, it is called "The Miracle Herb." These include relief of toothache, blood purification, and as a cold remedy. Slivers of garlic are also used as a flavor enhancer, especially for spicy foods like curries, pasta sauce and meat dishes. The strong onion-smelling active ingredient is contained in the white pear-shaped bulbs which divide into segments called cloves. To ward off infections simply shave slivers of three cloves into a quart of chicken, beef or mushroom broth and simmer for ten minutes after bringing to the boil.

Garlic is a hardy perennial best grown from cloves that can be planted in fall or early spring to mature later in the summer. Cover with 2 inches of soil, spaced 4 inches apart. When the leaves bend over, dig the bulbs and clean them of soil. Air dry in the sun for two days to cure them, and store in net bags until ready to use. The dried leaves can be removed or braided to make garlic ropes for hanging in the kitchen.

There are many different varieties of garlic, including some with a purple or pink skin color, and different degrees of pungency. Elephant garlic, with white bulbs as big as an apple, is one of the milder strains.

For an insecticide, combine a cup of garlic cloves and a cup of cayenne (or equally hot) peppers with a quart of water and liquefy. Transfer the liquid to a quart capacity spray bottle and spray over plants susceptible to soft bodied insects, such as fava beans, Brussels sprouts, snap beans, cabbage and anything that deer are likely to eat.

Garlic Chives are similar in appearance to chives, but with flat leaves and white flowers instead of pink. It is a hardy perennial that produces a strong flush of new leaves early in the season, and remains productive until well after fall frost. It is used mostly chopped like chives to flavor anything that might benefit from a mild garlic flavor.

Geraniums, Scented Leaf - The family of scented leaf geraniums contains dozens of varieties. Tender perennials best grown in pots, the list includes mint scented, coconut scented, lemon scented, orange scented and rose scented. In addition to the interesting aromas and flavors possible from growing these easy-care plants, many of them have beautiful flowers and even more fascinating leaf shapes. Most of the leaves are deeply indented, and many have a velvet-like texture. To add a particular flavor to muffins, for example, place a small leaf or two (such as the coconut-scented geranium) in the bottom of a cookie tray before baking in the oven, and the intricate outline of the leaf will decorate the underneath. To propagate, take tip cuttings and root in a potting soil (see page 259).

Ginger - is a tender perennial best grown in a pot and overwintered indoors. Ginger has almost as many health claims as garlic, including a defense against catching colds when imbibed as a refreshing tea. The edible portion is a lumpy brown root called a rhizome. Peeled, the root can be shaved to add a snappy flavoring to fish, meat and Chinese dishes. There are many forms of tropical ginger, but the species *Zingiber officinale*, is the most widely grown. Plants are best propagated from root division, spaced 6 inches apart.

I'll Make You a Gardening Wizard Overnight!

Chamomile

Chervil

Garlic

Chapter 12 - **Herbal Magic**

Garlic chives

Ginger roots

Ginseng roots

I'll Make You a Gardening Wizard Overnight!

Coriander (cilantro)

Ginseng – is a hardy perennial that is a challenge to grow because it is slow growing from seed and prefers a shady, fertile, humus-rich, constantly-moist soil . The forked root takes five to seven years to reach mature size. It is then chopped into tiny cubes to make a refreshing tea with many reported benefits, notably an energy boost and as a ward against colds. Start seeds 8-10 weeks ahead of outdoor planting. Germination can be erratic and some seeds may take two years to sprout. Space plants at least 6 inches apart in shaded raised beds.

Horseradish - is valued for its thick root which is spicy hot and good to flavor meat dishes like beef and ham. The outer brown skin is peeled and the white interior grated to make piquant sauces. Add to mayonnaise for a horseradish dip, and make a delicious cocktail sauce by adding the grated root to a mix of tomato ketchup and lemon juice.

Horseradish has broad, upright, wavy leaves that can grow to three feet high. Like watercress, it will grow with its roots permanently submerged in shallow water. Propagate by root division.

Lavender – one of my most memorable moments was hiking a trail beside the Gorge du Verdun, in Provence, cresting a hill and discovering an entire mountainside of wild lavender growing in stony shale. One of the most pleasant fragrances in all of nature, lavender is used to scent soaps, perfumes, air fresheners, face creams and shampoos, though flowers and leaves also make a refreshing tea and an insect repellent.

Although plants are regarded as hardy perennials, the variety Lavender Lady will bloom the first year from seed started indoors 6-8 weeks before outdoor planting after frost danger in spring. Thereafter it may perform as a perennial. Different varieties have different degrees of hardiness. In my experience the pale blue lavender, Munstead (zone 6), is a zone hardier than the deep blue variety Hidcote, and the tall-growing mid-blue lavender, Grosso. Lavender demands sharp drainage and is best planted in a bed of pure gravel.

Lemon Balm – resembles mint in appearance and spreads like a weed if you allow it to set seed. Plants grow to 2 ft. high, form a bushy clump of aromatic leaves. There are several forms, including green, golden yellow and variegated. The leaves, when crushed impart a pleasant lemony fragrance and flavor. Use as a garnish with fish, salads and fruit dishes and as a flavor enhancer for iced tea. Although the plants die down in winter they are hardy perennials and tolerate poor soil.

Lemon Grass – a tender perennial that is best grown in a large pot and moved indoors during winter months. The arching yellow-green leaf blades are highly decorative and make a beautiful accent for the center of an herb garden. Use the base of the leaves as a replacement for lemon, especially in fish dishes, curries and Thai cooking. To propagate simply divide up the roots. In addition to culinary use, lemon grass is an effective mosquito repellent rubbed onto skin.

Marjoram - Except for frost-free locations, marjoram is best grown as an annual from seed started 6 weeks before outdoor planting. In appearance and flavor it is similar to oregano. The two mostly differ in their flowering characteristics. Oregano has small, white, insignificant flowers, while marjoram can have beautiful pink flower clusters. Both produce serrated green leaves used fresh or dried to flavor Italian meals such as marinara sauce and pizza. Personally, I think oregano adds the best flavor.

Mints - Spearmint and peppermint are both hardy perennials mostly used to make a refreshing tea and to relieve congestion from colds and sinus allergies. Mints also make a delicious flavoring for numerous drinks like lemonade, and as a sauce to enhance the flavor of lamb, mashed potatoes, carrots and peas. Simply chop up a cupful, pour in malt vinegar to the brim and add a teaspoonful of sugar. Then spoon onto your lamb chops.

I detect no difference in flavor or fragrance between spearmint and peppermint. I can tell them apart, however, by the shape of the leaf – a narrow, serrated, glossy leaf in the case of peppermint, and a broad, velvety leaf for spearmint. The roots can be invasive, so confine plants to a sunken container or a part of the garden where they won't bother other plantings. Any section of root with a node can be used to start a new planting. Simply layer a stem horizontally and cover with 3 inches of soil, spaced 6 inches apart. The best flavor is concentrated in the top whorl of four to six leaves. Also, the mint flavor will intensify when dried.

Mints and several other herbs – such as chamomile, lavender and lemon balm - make a refreshing tea. Simply gather the fragrant parts (about half a cup) and place in the bottom of a tea pot. Then pour boiling water over them and allow to steep for two or three minutes. Add sugar, honey or maple syrup if you need a sweetener.

CHOCOLATE MINT — In almost all herb families there are varieties that impart a special aroma or flavor that's distinct. Among mints Chocolate Mint is one of my favorites. Discovered in Mitcham, Surray (England), Chocolate Mint resembles spearmint but smells like chocolate when the leaves are crushed, especially when the leaves are dried. It is easy to grow — even in a pot on a windowsill - and it is extremely hardy. The plant is more compact than spearmint and the leaves have a chocolate sheen. It prefers full sun and tolerates heat, poor soil, even crowding, making it useful as a groundcover. Unlike spearmint and peppermint it is not a rampant spreader and is easily contained by mowing it at the edges. Dainty purple flower spikes appear in mid-summer, held well above the foliage. Chop a leaf finely and add it to cakes, cookies, desserts and drinks for a chocolate minty flavor. I especially like it sprinkled over ice cream and over a fruit salad. Drying Chocolate Mint intensifies the aroma, making it suitable for potpourri.

Parsley — is a hardy biennial that produces a mound of aromatic leaves the first year, then stretching into a long flowering stalk the second season. Related to carrots, the seed is fine and germination can be erratic when direct-sown. Higher germination is assured if you start the seed indoors at 70F room temperature, 6-8 weeks before outdoor planting. Parsley will tolerate mild frost, and also winter freezes. Space plants at least 6 inches apart, and pinch out the lead shoot to encourage side branches. There are curly-leaf and plain-leaf forms. I prefer the curly form as it is easier to chop into fine pieces than the flat leaf type. But I know many good cooks who prefer the flat leaf for its stronger flavor. The more you pick the leaves, the more leaves will grow to replace them. The low-growing plants make an excellent edging for flower beds and a decorative container accent. Parsley is best used as a garnish, sprinkled over egg dishes, mashed potatoes and salads. One form, called Hamburg, not only produces aromatic leaves but also white roots that taste like a parsnip.

Rosemary — is a fairly hardy woody plant best grown from rooted cuttings. The slender needle-like leaves have a pine fragrance used to flavor pork, duck, chicken and other meat dishes. There are weeping forms for planting to cascade over a terrace. In a sheltered, well drained soil, rosemary may survive a mild winter, but in gardens north of zone 8 grow in a pot and move it indoors during winter months. Plants are drought tolerant, should be planted at least 2 ft. apart. To move indoors, mature plants can be pruned back to within 4 inches of the soil line, dug up, potted and moved indoors where they will sprout new bushy growth. Rosemary makes a flavorful vinegar. Simply take a bottle of store-bought clear vinegar. Heat, pour into attractive bottles and insert sprigs of rosemary. Within several days the rosemary leaves and stems will impart their spicy flavor to the vinegar for use on salads, potatoes and meat dishes.

Savory - There are two kinds of savory: summer savory and winter savory, and it is summer savory that good cooks prefer as a seasoning. The leaves and crushed dried stems are used mostly as a flavoring for bean dishes; also soups, stews and potato dishes. Plants grow upright to three feet high and display small insignificant tubular white flowers. Winter savory has a spreading, cushion shape, just 6 inches high, covering itself in masses of small white flowers in late summer. Propagate either by direct seeding or starting indoors six weeks before outdoor planting.

Sweet Cicely – is a hardy perennial herb that has an uplifting licorice aroma, and every part of its leaves, stems, roots and flowers are edible. It is a majestic plant, growing to five ft. tall with globular chartreuse flower heads. These bear spherical clusters of green seeds that turn brown when dry. They can be eaten raw in salads and as a breath freshener. The dried seeds are good to add to soups and stews for flavor. The roots can be peeled, grated and eaten raw like candy. Propagate from seed direct sown or started indoors 6-8 weeks before outdoor planting.

Sweet Leaf - Also known as Stevia, this compact, bushy, tender perennial grows leaves that can be used as a substitute for cane sugar or artificial sweeteners. For centuries the Japanese have used it to sweeten drinks and foods. Grow the plant in a pot near a sunny window during winter. Pick the leaves and chew them for a quick sugary taste treat. Or dry and store to use in drinks as a sweetener, including coffee and tea, cakes and cookies. Two or three leaves are sufficient to sweeten a strong cup of coffee. The author of a book about Sweet Leaf says: "The largest user of sweet leaf is Japan. When the Japanese government banned certain artificial sweetners due to health concerns the use of sweet leaf as a natural alternative increased dramatically. Sweet leaf's useage has also increased due to health concerns towards dental problems, obesity and diabetes." Plants are propagated from tip cuttings.

Tarragon - There are two kinds of tarragon: French tarragon, the kind that is preferred by good cooks, and Russian tarragon, an inferior product because of its weaker flavoring potential. French tarragon has an anise-like aroma and its slender green leaves are used mostly to flavor salads, soups and sauces; also fish and poultry. Both are hardy perennials. The plants form clumps of spire-like, leafy stems up to 4 ft. high. French tarragon does not set seeds and is propagated by division.

Thyme – is a hardy perennial that improves the flavor of many foods, particularly meat dishes. There are various forms of thyme, some more pungent than others. Most have a low, spreading habit and in early summer produce white, red, pink or purple flowers. Plants have small, oval leaves and wiry stems and it is these that are used to make a refreshing tea for the relief of headaches and sore throats. Sow seed indoors 6-8 weeks before outdoor planting or divide up the roots of established plants, spacing them at least 6 inches apart. Plants are easy to grow in a pot and tolerate drought. The dried stems, crushed and steeped in water make an effective insect repellent.

EDIBLE FLOWERS. Both broccoli and cauliflower are members of the cabbage family with edible bud clusters, so it's not surprising that in the world of plants there are many more edible flowers, especially among plants that are often classified as herbs. The following are mostly used to dress up salads by adding color, and also interesting flavors.

Borage – blue, star-shaped flowers add a cucumber flavor to salads.
Calendula – orange and yellow petals add a pleasant piquant flavor to salads.
Carnations – pink and red petals add a mild, lettuce flavor to salads.
Chives – pink flowers add an onion flavor to salads.
Hibiscus – pink and red flowers add a lettuce-like flavor to salads.
Lavender – blue flowers make a pleasant, fragrant, bitter tea.
Marigold – yellow and orange petals add a spicy flavor to salads and egg dishes.
Nasturtium – yellow, red and orange petals add a piquant flavor to salads.
Pansies and Violets – mostly blue flowers add a mild, lettuce like flavor to salads, and may be candied.
Roses – most colors add a pleasant, lettuce flavor and fragrance to salads.
Squash blossoms – yellow petals add a pleasant mild flavor to salads and may be sautéed.
Yucca – white flowers add a lettuce-like flavor to salads.

Carolyn's Comments:

"At Cedaridge Farm we use a lot of herbs in cooking. One of Derek's favorite breakfast meals is an herbal omelet using orange-yoked free-range eggs from our own chickens. For this savory treat Derek picks chives, parsley, coriander and basil, chopped fine and added to the omelet or scrambled eggs at the last moment. When the children were young we established a tradition of every Sunday serving a pizza made from a home-made tomato sauce, fresh sliced tomatoes, chopped peppers and onions, grated Cheddar cheese, Portobello mushrooms and chopped basil. I remember one time Derek lamented we had no Portobello mushrooms to include in the topping, and the two youngest children Vicki and Derek Jr, asked what they looked like. Derek explained they were brown on top and black underneath and the size of a saucer. They yelled excitedly that they knew where to find Portobello mushrooms and returned with two beauties – one the size of a dinner plate. Derek had been growing Portobellos in the basement and when the production declined he threw the contents of the growing box onto a compost heap in the woods. The children had been playing in the woods earlier that day and seen the Portobellos but thought they were poisonous. What a delicious pizza topping they made, and the children have never forgotten that experience."

Chapter 12 - **Herbal Magic**

Lavender bouquet

Lemon balm

Chapter 12 - **Herbal Magic**

Oregano

Spearmint

Chapter 12 - **Herbal Magic**

Chocolate mint indoors

211

Parsley, Curly Leaf

Chapter 12 - **Herbal Magic**

Weeping rosemary

Thyme used as a ground cover

Chives in a container

CHAPTER 13
Healing Ointments & Skin Creams

"Alas, that the mind can be overthrown by bodily frailness. When serving in court he was seized by severe paralysis and all his powers failed and left him, and he lost mind, mobility, all enjoyment from life itself for a time, and eyesight for a year. He struggled however to surmount these many obstacles. He emerged from darkness and when he realized that every moment was precious to him, he returned to gardening."
– Epitaph on a gravestone, Bury St. Edmunds

Skin creams and soothing oils offer relief from dry skin and tension. You can control what goes on your skin by making your own skin creams and massage oils from herbs. Here's one of my favorites using the gel inside the leaves of an *Aloe vera* plant:

SKIN CLEANSING LOTION. Fill a cup with gel from inside the leaves. Add a tablespoon of mineral oil to the gel which has a cucumber-like aroma. If you want to change the fragrance, add two drops of lavender oil from an eye dropper (or some other favorite fragrance, like gardenia or orange blossom). Mix the oil and gel thoroughly. The mix should turn nearly white (or show the color of the scented oil). Cleanse your face and pat dry. Dab a dime-size spot of cream on your face and massage into your skin, using a circular motion. Store extra cream in a glass jar and refrigerate.

SIMPLE CALENDULA SALVE. This recipe is from the Blueberry Hill Inn, Goshen, Vermont: Ingredients needed are 4 oz of calendula petals infused in almond or olive oil and .75 oz of beeswax. Combine these ingredients in a double boiler or crock pot and heat until the beeswax melts. Immediately transfer to salve jars or shallow tins, allow to cool, and label. Calendula salve can be used to relieve cuts, scrapes and skin irritations such as insect bites. The calendula fragrance is itself pleasant and spicy. If you wish to change the fragrance apply a few drops of an essential oil such as lavender or chamomile (see next recipe).

HERB INFUSED OILS. Place dried herbs of your choice – such as lavender – in a glass container and cover with the oil of your choice, such as olive oil. Start with 1 part herb to 4 parts of oil. Add as much oil as necessary to completely cover the herb in order to avoid mold. It is essential to use dried herbs to avoid spoilage from excess moisture in the herb parts. Cover and allow the jar to sit in sunshine for 3-4 weeks. The sunshine allows infusion of the herbal essence into the oil. After the infusion period strain the herbs from the oil using wire mesh strainer lined with cheesecloth. Allow the oil to drip through and squeeze residue from the cheesecloth. If little bits of herb squeeze through the strainer, strain again until you have a pure, potent liquid. Store herbal infused oils in the refrigerator when not in use. Oils can turn rancid and if this happens, discard.

AROMATHERAPY is the use of fragrant oils to alleviate stress. Numerous herbs possess spicy or sharp aromas that open up the nasal passages and produce a feeling of relaxation and well being. In particular are various kinds of mints (spearmint, peppermint, lemon mint for example; also lavender and chamomile). An easy way to use the fragrant oils in aromatic plants is to simply pluck a handful of leaves, bruise them to release the oil, and steep in hot water. As the water boils place a towel over your head to form a canopy over the rising steam. This then concentrates the essence around the face and nose.

HERBAL VINEGARS are easy to make by starting with a clear vinegar or a red vinegar of your choice. Use herbal vinegars not only to improve the flavor of salads but also as a refreshing facial rinse, after shave lotion and mouthwash. As a general rule use 1 cup of fresh herbs to two cups of vinegar. First, wash and dry the herbs of your choice and place in a jar with a tight fitting lid. Pour the vinegar (5% acidity preferred) over the herbs and seal the jar. Set in a cool, dark place and shake the jar every two days. After 2 or 3 weeks, strain the vinegar into a stainless steel pan and bring to a boil. Put a sprig or two of the chosen herb into a sterilized bottle or jar and pour the hot vinegar into the bottom, leaving 1/4 inch of room at the top. Seal, cool and leave in a cool, dark place. Stored this way herbal vinegars will keep for up to 3 months. Food coloring can be added to create an appealing color, for example green added to a basil vinegar, red for a chili-pepper vinegar, yellow for a dill or garlic flavored vinegar. Also, the use of certain herbs will naturally color a clear vinegar: purple leaf basil for example will produce a pink hue.

HERBAL SOAPS. To make lavender soap you will need the following ingredients: 4 ozs unperfumed white soap, grated; 5 tbsp water; a cup of dried lavender flowers finely ground; 1-2 drops of essential lavender oil; 1 drop of blue food coloring (optional).

Take empty cardboard toilet roll tubes to use as a mold and block one end with masking tape so the soap mixture does not run out.

Place soap and water in a large bowl and put in the microwave on high for 2-3 minutes (or melt over a pan of simmering water). Stir the mixture and add the lavender oil and color; mix well. Using a funnel, pour the mixture into the toilet roll tubes, and stand upright until the soap sets (2-3 hours). Remove the soap and cut into 1 inch 'rounds'.

POTPOURRIS. Before the invention of aerosol air fresheners, herbs were valued for masking household odors. Some herbs, like lavender and mint, are strong enough to deodorize a room by themselves, but the value of a potpourri (a mixture of fragrant dried herbs) is not only the rich aroma possible from many mingling scents, but also a beautiful visual experience from colorful petals, especially rose and lavender petals.

Begin by collecting together an assortment of herbs – choosing a balance of colorful

Chapter 13 - *Healing Ointments & Skin Creams*

Herbal vinegars

flower petals, leaf textures and seeds – and dry in batches. The drying process is best accomplished by drying them in a warm, dark, dry place since the sun will weaken their aromatic properties. Good ventilation is essential to avoid rot. An easy way to dry is to bunch the herbs by their stems and hold them together with an elastic band, and hang from a beam. Otherwise hang from a clothes rack. Some herbs – like anise and dill – have aromatic seeds that need to be shucked from the seed head to dry on a tray. The drying time can take two to three weeks. After which separate the leaves and flowers from the stems and store in separate jars with airtight, screw-top lids.

When ready to make your potpourris, select a decorative bowl and combine as many dried herb parts as desired, choosing some with sharp, spicy fragrances like mint and some with a fruity fragrance like scented rose petals. To prevent the aroma fading too quickly consider adding a fixative such as ground orris root or sweet flag root.

Place the bowl of potpourri near an entrance hall or on a vanity table and scoop up a handful to provide an uplifting fragrance whenever you feel like it. You can also pack a potpourri into a cloth bag, heat it in the microwave for 30 seconds to intensify the aroma, and place it near a pillow for a pleasant perfumed night's sleep.

Carolyn's Comments:

"Derek occasionally writes for Vermont Life magazine even though we live in Pennsylvania. One beautiful summer we stayed at the Blueberry Hill Inn, Goshen. The main attraction for us was the fact the property had a large blueberry orchard and a large organic vegetable garden with hiking trails leading off into a pristine wilderness. The inn also featured an herb garden in a cartwheel design, located directly below our bedroom. The owner's wife gives classes in making facial creams (see above calendula salve recipe), and I recall taking one of the classes, involving calendula petals as the main herbal ingredient. Derek subsequently wrote an article about the inn and its beautiful gardens. Whenever we travel we like to seek out bed & breakfast inns that feature a vegetable garden and/or herb garden because that generally is an indication the accommodations will be comfortable, the food will be good, and the owners will be interesting people to talk to with a shared passion for gardening. New Zealand is full of places like that, but here in the US we enjoyed staying at the Stanford Inn, overlooking the Pacific Ocean at Mendocino, California. The beautiful sloping site on the edge of a redwood forest features a spacious organic vegetable garden in raised beds. Also in an idyllic coastal setting is the Goose Cove Lodge, Deer Isle, Maine where herbs grown on the property are used to flavor the best fresh seafood dishes I have ever tasted.

A short drive away, at Harborside we visited another remarkable organic garden - the home of the late Scott and Helen Nearing who wrote the best-selling book about self-sufficient living, titled Living the Good Life. Forest Farm, their home and garden is perfectly preserved and open to visitors. It overlooks a powder-soft beach and the slate-blue waters of the Atlantic Ocean. A special feature of the property is a large walled enclosure for the vegetable garden that Scott laid stone by stone to keep out critters, and a home-made greenhouse to raise seedlings and grow food crops out of season. Scott lived to be 100 and Helen was killed in a car accident, aged 91. Their book struck a cord with many who yearned for a life of self-sufficient living, especially young people disenchanted with the pressures of city life, international strife and the proliferation of government into every facet of our lives.

Just prior to Helen's death she had signed papers deeding the property to a foundation that continues to maintain the garden as Helen left it, and opens it to the public for spiritual enlightenment. The property had been much bigger but as the Nearings got older they sold off sections to friends. Garden book authors Eliot Coleman and his wife, Barbara Damrosch bought one piece and today they maintain a self-sufficient lifestyle in the Nearing tradition. Another part of the property – the original Nearing homestead - was sold to Stanley Joseph who helped the Nearings in their garden. Shortly after buying it he married freelance photographer Lynn Karlin, and they developed a thriving business selling organic vegetables, cut flowers, dried wreaths, wicker baskets and Lynn's photographs to local outlets. Lynn documented almost every day of their life together with her camera, learned to fly, and recorded some beautiful aerial views of the property and surrounding cape. Stanley wrote Main Farm (Random House) using Lynn's photography, showing the property through four seasons. The book ends on a jubilant note, and yet there is an unhappy postscript because Stanley ended his life at age 50.

A tribute to Stanley, written by the owners of Goose Cove Lodge, reads: 'A trip to Harborside on Cape Rosier was something hundreds of our guests did to meet him so they might grasp a piece of local wonderment...we will think of him every time we look at one of his dried flower wreaths or see a copy of his book...every time we see a delphinium or a dahlia we will be reminded of him. Happy memory!'"

CHAPTER 14
Grow Delicious Fruits, Berries & Nuts for an All Season Harvest

"If you have room for only one berry bush make it a blueberry and if you still have room for a fruit tree, make it an early peach. The two in combination in a fruit pie is a flavor experience that is hard to forget."
– from my article on home orchard fruits in **Nouveau** magazine

Fruits such as apples, pears and peaches are not the easiest of trees to grow, mainly because they can fall victim to host of pests and disease. Most fruit trees need more than one tree to act as a pollinator, they need good drainage and air circulation, and judicious pruning is generally required at the end of the fruiting season in order to ensure worthwhile yields the following season. On the other hand, berries – such as strawberries, raspberries and blackberries - are relatively carefree and do not require so much space. For both fruit trees and berries choose a sunny site and fertile soil. In a lightly shaded location you might try a blueberry bush or a pear tree. Following is my experience of growing a fruit orchard and a berry patch.

Apples – An entire orchard of fruit on one tree!
Paul Barnett, of Chidham, West Sussex, in England, developed a hobby grafting different varieties of apples onto a single Bramley's Seedling apple tree that had stood in his backyard for many years. At last count the tree bore fruit of 250 different varieties. If Barnett had tried to grow those 250 apple varieties on individual trees, he would have needed more than an acre of ground.

Actually, there are other ways to grow apples in a small space – by selecting columnar trees that grow short upward facing branches. These require nothing more than a whisky half barrel to grow in. You can also choose special dwarf apple varieties to grow in a container. These are grafted onto a dwarf root stock that keeps the tree low and compact. Dwarf varieties generally stay below 8 ft. high and allow you to cover them with horticultural fleece so you don't have to spray once the blossoms have set fruit. The lightweight fleece acts as a barrier against most insects pests, birds and disease organisms. The lightweight see-through fabric is put in place after flowering occurs, and removed after harvest. The only precautionary treatment before fruit set might be an organic dormant oil spray to kill early insect visitors

Although most apples require another different variety for pollination, be aware that an ornamental crabapple can act as an excellent pollinator. Most apples need a minimum

Honeycrisp apples

Chapter 14 - *Grow Delicious Fruits, Berries & Nuts for an All Season Harvest*

Jumbo apple and Red Delicious

Dwarf apple, Golden Delicious

I'll Make You a Gardening Wizard Overnight!

Thornfree blackberries

number of 'chill hours' - or 'cold nights' (temperatures close to freezing) in order to set fruit. However, some varieties, like Granny Smith, do better in southern states than others. So, in mild winter areas, check with local nurseries about varieties requiring fewer cold nights.

I recall when I first started gardening that Red Delicious was the favorite apple variety for flavor, to be usurped by Fuji from Washington state, Gala from New Zealand and Braeburn, also from New Zealand. Today the crown has passed to Honeycrisp, developed by the University of Minnesota. A large yellow apple with a red blush, it has a clean, sweet flavor and remarkable hardiness – best suited for zones 3 to 6 (most other varieties are suited for zones 6-8). An apple that's capable of making an entire pie filling from one fruit is the variety, Jumbo. Grown on a dwarfing rootstock, it can grow yellow apples with a flush of red up to three times the size of a regular apple.

Apples, like most other fruit trees, can be sold bare root, balled in burlap, or in containers. Bare root stock normally consists of year-old grafts with the soil washed off the roots and delivered by mail order. The tree should be planted as soon after receiving it as possible into a sandy loam soil. Be sure to keep the graft union (a swollen stem section above the root) above soil level and prune away any sucker growth that appears below it. Plants that are balled in burlap are usually a minimum of two years old, and the same is true of plants in containers. Remove the root ball with as little soil disturbance as possible and tease any matted roots so they have freedom to grow in their new home. Roots enclosed in burlap need the burlap to be cut away in strips without damaging the roots; otherwise the burlap can restrict the roots. Any broken branches or broken roots should be trimmed away and soil kept moist (but never saturated) until the tree is well established.

IMPORTANT TIP: Never plant a fruit tree without wrapping the trunk with a product called Tree Wrap, a plastic spiral that encircles the lower trunk; or encircle the lower trunk with burlap to create a barrier against damage by borers – insect larvae that hatch from eggs laid on the bark and which burrow into the tree, causing it to die – especially on peaches, cherries and plums.

Blackberries – Although I planted a small pea patch at the back of the row house where I lived with my parents, at age five and became hooked on gardening the moment I tasted those sweet green peas, another defining moment was at the age of nine when we moved to a semi-detached development house with a sizeable back yard, composed mostly of builder's rubble. As other homeowners graded and planted lawns, I helped my father transform the site into a beautiful rock garden. The garden backed onto an older property with a well-established garden, owned by a gray-haired Scottish widow, Mrs. Mackintosh, who I rarely saw. One day in summer I walked to the bottom of the garden and spied the biggest bush of blackberries I'd ever seen, arching their canes from her property onto ours, and loaded with luscious ripe fruit the size of small plums. As I stood there tempted to pick some blackberries, Mrs. Mackintosh came outside and told me kindly: "You may pick any of the berries that grow on your side of the fence."

I picked a bag full and my mother made the most delicious blackberry pie from the berries. I decided there and then that when I grew up and had a place of my own I would grow a bush of blackberries just like Mrs. Mackintosh.

Even though blackberries grow wild in many parts of North America, they rarely can grow as big as a cultivated variety. What's more you can grow them on thorn-free canes. The berries turn from green to red to black when fully ripe, but a black blackberry doesn't necessarily mean perfect ripeness. If the berry shows any sign of resistance when you try to pick it, chances are it will be sour. Only when the berry literally falls into your hand the moment you touch it, is it likely to be sweet. To save space, blackberries can be splayed out flat against a south facing wall or up trellis.

Blueberries – These bushy woody plants are native to the north-eastern states of North America. They like an acid soil, and full sun or light shade. They generally need protection against birds, so either grow them in a wire cage, or cover the bushes at harvest time with horticultural fleece. My preference is the variety called Blueray since it can produce berries as big as a nickel in generous clusters that hang down the plant like bunches of grapes. Plants are relatively slow-growing but a modest harvest can be expected the second season after planting year old rooted cuttings. Like blackberries, they are extremely high in anti-oxidants. Eat them fresh off the vine or use for a delicious pie filling. Blueray is self-pollinating so one bush can produce fruit, but will yield more heavily if cross pollinated by another variety.

Cherries - A cherry tree can grow exceedingly large, but there is one variety, Stella – a dark red sweet , semi-dwarf variety introduced from Canada in 1968 – that can bear dark red fruit the second season after planting. Moreover, it can be pruned to stay compact. It is the only variety I know that is self-fruitful and will grow and fruit reliably in a whisky half-barrel. Another way to save space is to espalier the pliable branches against a south facing wall or fence. The cherries produced by Stella can be exceedingly large, so much so that I have seen farmer's markets sell the fruits by size – regular size and large.

Cherries are classified as sweet and sour – the sweet cherries eaten fresh off the tree. Moreover, they can be a dark red, bright red, yellow and yellow with a red blush. Sour cherries have a tart-sweet flavor that also allows them to be eaten fresh off the tree, but they are valued more as a pie filling.

Give cherries full sun and a fertile soil with good drainage. It's possible to buy trees that contain three grafts – a dark red, bright red and yellow cherry all on the same tree. The biggest problem with cherries is keeping the birds off them. This I do by covering the trees with horticultural fleece once the fruit has set.

Currants & Gooseberries - Currants and gooseberries are closely related and many states discourage their planting because they harbor a disease called pine blister rust that kills pine trees. Currants can be red, black and white with the red most popular for making jams and pie filling. Gooseberries are larger than currants and also make excellent jam and pie filling. They are mostly green and purple depending on variety and prefer a climate where summer temperatures are cool and moist. The bushy plants are thorny and can make a decorative low hedge.

Kiwi - The New Zealand kiwi we see in stores, with an oblong shape and brown fuzzy skin surrounding a sweet green interior actually comes from China. It is not reliably hardy north of zone 8. The plants grow long, rambling vines that require strong support, and a male for every seven female vines to set fruit. There is a smaller-fruited kiwi, commonly called an Arctic kiwi (that actually comes from Siberia), which produces bushels of green fruits the size of a large grape (and with a similar flavor). Although there is a self-pollinating variety called Issa, I prefer the variety Ken's Red for ultimate sweetness, even though it requires the planting of a male vine to pollinate the females. Both kinds of kiwi ripen their fruits in late summer and autumn. Kiwi vines can be grown over arbors like grape vines, and they are easily espaliered against a fence or south facing wall.

Paw Paw is a native hardy American deciduous tree that is attractive in the landscape. It grows into a pyramid shape with upward facing branches and broad leaves that turn buttercup yellow in fall. The maroon cup-shaped flowers occur in early spring before the leaves appear and attract flies for pollination by imitating the smell of dead meat. The fruits are generally oval, sometimes resembling a mango, with a blue-green skin that turns yellow when ripe. The interior has a soft, yellow filling with the texture of custard and flavored like a banana. Large black seeds can be discarded or used to grow more trees. The entire filling can be eaten as a dessert. Plants grow to 40 ft high, are highly variably in the quality and size of the fruit, and two trees are needed for pollination.

Pears - Generally speaking, pears are easier to grow than apples. My biggest problem growing pears has been a tendency for crows to descend on the trees before the fruit is ripe and strip the tree clean. Therefore, a covering of horticultural fleece is recommended once the blossoms have set fruit. Pears can take a little shade, producing fruit in conditions where an apple tree will fail.

Like apples, pears require a fertile soil and good drainage. Frequently, a tree will set far more fruit than it can adequately support, and so rigorous thinning of the fruit is required. When you see a tree burdened with fruit, thin it down to leave a third of the fruit on the tree, otherwise the fruits will remain small, or the tree may shed all its fruit prematurely.

To save space you may wish to consider a three-in-one pear whereby three varieties are grafted onto one trunk. Usually, this would involve a Bartlett type (a large yellow pear with a pink blush), a Bosc type (a long brown skinned French pear with a slender neck) and a red (such as Red Bartlett). When you grow three varieties on one tree each variety will pollinate the other.

Dwarf pears are suitable for growing in a whisky half barrel. Also they can be espaliered against a sunny wall or fence to save space. When I started gardening Bartlett was the favorite variety (it is still extremely popular) but it is susceptible to a serious pear disease, fireblight. This virulent disfiguring disease causes fruits to blacken as though they have been scorched by fire. Moonglow – a Bartlett look-alike - has better fireblight resistance.

Asian pears are not difficult to grow, and yet they command the highest prices in stores, often wrapped individually in a foam sleeve to keep them blemish-free. The major difficulty is getting Asian pears to grow big. They generally set huge quantities of fruit that remain small unless rigorously thinned. Also, be aware that an Asian pear will pollinate a European pear and vice versa. Like apples, pears require at least a hundred cold nights to set fruit in spring, and so in mild winter areas, check with local nurseries on what varieties are recommend for your area.

For best flavor allow Asian pears to ripen on the tree, but pick European pears like Bartlett and Bosc so they have a few days to ripen off the tree. Planting instructions are the same for apples.

Peaches - What's a garden without a peach tree? I have planted daffodils under my peach trees so that in spring the daffodils bloom with the peach blossoms. Like apples and pears, there are dwarf peach trees that can be grown in a whisky half barrel. They demand full sun and a fertile well drained soil, and thinning of the fruit if too many blossoms set fruit, otherwise the size will be small and the tree may drop its fruit before they have a chance to ripen. There are several special peach varieties I have grown for delicious flavor. The standard for excellent is Redhaven, a dark red-skinned sweetly flavored, medium size peach that ripens in August. Then there is the ugly-duckling of peaches, Stone Mountain. A lime green color at maturity, it is incredibly sweet, and the last of peach varieties to ripen (usually late September).

Peaches are suitable for growing flat against sunny walls, the branches splayed out like a fan, and espaliered against a fence. Several varieties can be grafted to share the same trunk. One of these is usually a nectarine, which is a fuzzless peach. For planting instructions, see apples.

FLAMIN' FURY PEACHES. Paul Friday, a private Michigan peach grower and breeder, has developed a series of large-fruited peaches that has resulted in 32 new peach and nectarine varieties from a twenty year breeding program that started when he and his cousin, Jim (each with a BS degree from Michigan State University) decided to start breeding peaches. Paul set as his goal the breeding of extra large fruit, using mostly large fruited selections of Redhaven to cross with other varieties. The most recent release is named Big George that is remarkably sweet, weighing up to 1 lb. and ripening late in the season when most other peach trees are finished bearing .

Plums - Personally I do not think there is a better tasting plum than an old fashioned English Damson, with its blue skin and sweet green flesh. Basically, plum types can be classified as European and Japanese. The plant breeding wizard Luther Burbank did a lot of breeding with Japanese plums. They are large and usually red with a red or orange interior or black with an orange or yellow interior. For my money I prefer a particularly precocious bearer, Shiro - a yellow skinned plum about the size of a golf ball.

To save space plums can be heavily pruned and grown in whisky half-barrels, the trees covered with fleece after fruit set in spring.

For planting instructions, see apples.

Blueray blueberry

Stella cherries

Kiwi vine

Chapter 14 - *Grow Delicious Fruits, Berries & Nuts for an All Season Harvest*

New Zealand kiwi

Hardy Arctic kiwi

Paw-paw fruit

Raspberries - These cone-shaped fruit grow on canes, like blackberries. Although the most common color is red, there are black, yellow, orange and purple varieties. Most raspberries crop in late summer and early fall, but the variety Heritage crops in early summer on old canes and fall on new canes, yielding medium-size red fruit. I grow Heritage for its long harvest season, but prefer the giant-fruited varieties, Titan or Royalty. They bear berries the size of a thimble and dusky, purple fruit in mid-summer. Raspberries can be planted in spring or fall and spread by underground runners so that after only three years an initial patch of only three or four plants can expand into a thicket. Cut out old brown canes that bore fruit in summer, leaving new green canes to bear next season's crop.

Strawberries – All Four Seasons

Of all the berry fruits, strawberries are the universal favorite. They are hardy perennials, flower and fruit early in the season and are easy to grow either in the garden or in containers. They are highly rated for flavor and even the fragrance of ripe strawberries is uplifting. Traditional strawberry plants crop once a year, in June over most of the USA but now there are THREE kinds of strawberries to extend the season. 'Everbearers' are a misnomer for they are not truly everbearing, but produce a crop twice a year, in late spring and again at the onset of cool weather in fall. A built in time clock that measures the amount of daylight hours stops June bearers from bearing at the onset of long days during summer months and restricts everbearers to cropping only during the shorter days of spring and fall. However, a new race of strawberries, called 'Day Neutrals' are true everbearers, producing several flushes of fruit in spring, summer and fall irrespective of long day length and high heat. However, this repeat cropping is possible only if the plants are kept watered and nourished with booster applications of a foliar fertilizer during summer months. It seems quite strange to be picking tomatoes and strawberries at the same time, but it's possible with a variety such as Tri-Star or Brighton.

Tri-Star is one of several day neutrals developed by Dr. Gene Galetta, a strawberry breeder with the USDA's fruit research station in Beltsville, Maryland. The fruits of Tri Star are sweet and delicious, mostly cone-shaped. Genes for the true everbearing qualities of Tri Star and Brighton were provided by day neutral wild strawberries discovered in Alaska and Brighton Canyon, Utah.

Irrespective of variety, the trick to growing good strawberries is to first buy virus free plants from a reputable supplier. They can be planted in spring or fall, preferably into a well-drained, sunny, sandy soil. To keep the bed weed-free, plant through black plastic, or spread straw around them. If one year old roots are planted in spring, flowers and fruit will start to form immediately, the fruit ripening within 60 days. However, in order to grow the largest fruit and highest yields it is best if the first flowers are removed in addition to any runners that form, until midsummer. This ensures that the roots are given time to develop fully and support a heavy crop. You can stop removing the flowers by mid-August. When planting in the fall it is not necessary to remove the flowers as the roots will continue to grow after the top growth has gone dormant.

A covering of horticultural fleece applied in the fall and left over winter until mid May will encourage early ripening of the fruit by up to two weeks especially if plants are grown through black plastic.

Strawberries are suitable for growing in containers, particularly whisky half barrels and special terracotta vase-shaped strawberry jars with pockets around the sides. As strawberry plants mature they set runners – long slender stems that radiate out from the mother plant in all directions. When the tips of the runners come in contact with soil they root and produce more strawberry plants. If the runners do not touch soil, but are left dangling in mid-air – such as from a hanging basket – the tips of the runners are still capable of forming leaves, flowers and small fruit, providing the mother plant is watered and fed. The effect can be extremely decorative.

Another type of strawberry to consider is the alpine strawberry, bearing small, sweet cone-shaped fruits in June. The compact, bushy plants are suitable for edging flower beds and will tolerate light shade.

NUTS. There are nut trees to suit every garden size. Filberts (or hazelnuts), for example grow on a small, multiple-trunk tree that will thrive in a whisky half barrel, while English walnuts can grow to more than 40 ft. wide and equally high. Pecans also make tall trees, although they start fruiting when young and can be kept compact by pruning. The following most popular hardy nut trees require full sun and a fertile soil with good drainage. Most require two trees for pollination, although there are exceptions, as noted.

Almonds are closely related to peaches and do well wherever peaches grow. In fact, the shell of an almond nestles inside a green peach-like fruit that is not edible. Plants grow to 20 ft high, can bear within three years. The variety All-In-One is self-fruitful.

Black Walnut is a hardy tree whose wood is valued for making furniture, and though it can be highly productive of nuts, it has several disadvantages in a small garden. First, the roots of a black walnut contain a plant poison call juglan that inhibits the growth of plants growing under or near it. Second, the leaves in spring appear later than most trees, and they drop earlier than other trees in fall. The nuts are located inside a green case that smells pleasantly of lemon soap, but when the nuts fall they split open to reveal a black, oily interior that will stain clothing and make a mess of lawns or driveways. The nuts themselves are delicious, but the shell is extremely hard and difficult to crack unless you choose a thin-shelled variety like the Thomas Black Walnut. Plants grow to 40 ft high and equally wide, will bear nuts in 2-4 years. The flowers are green and called catkins, hanging down from the branches in spring. They need pollinating by another walnut to set fruit.

English Walnut is a hardy tree that has similar disadvantages to the black walnut. Its roots produce a plant poison, the green nut cases produce an oil that stains clothing and the nut cases can make a mess of driveways and lawns. However, the shells are easier to crack than a black walnut. The flowers are similar to black walnut and can be pollinated by a black walnut and vice-versa. The variety I recommend is Champion, a heavy-bearing tree that will grow to 40 ft. high. Plants can bear in six years.

Butternut is one of the most delicious of all nuts. Closely related to the black walnut, it is similar in all respects, except the green nut case is oval and the nut is oval. It is just as difficult to crack as a black walnut. Like all walnuts, be sure to plant these large, messy trees away from the main garden – preferably at the edge of the property and never as an avenue to line a driveway.

Chinese Chestnut - When the majestic American chestnut fell victim to a devastating blight that killed millions of trees, the disease-resistant Chinese chestnut was imported as a source of nuts. It is not as big as an American chestnut, and the nuts are not quite so large, but it is a beautiful tree in the landscape, creating a spreading canopy and covering itself in white flower clusters in mid-summer. The nut cases are spiny and the brown, shiny nuts must be peeled to reveal the edible interior. Eaten raw, the nuts have a bitter flavor, but roasted or boiled they turn sweet and delicious, especially if a felt-like membrane around the meat is scraped off. The variety to grow is Colossal, a special selection that grows the largest dark skinned nuts – 14-18 to a lb. Plants grow to 30 ft high, can bear nuts in three years.

Filberts - Also called hazelnuts, vast orchards in the Pacific Northwest produce tons of nuts that are round when shelled. The nuts form inside a hard brown shell that itself is enclosed by a sheath. The yellow, dangling flower clusters are called catkins and appear in early spring. Plants form a small tree, 10 ft high by 8 ft wide. They can be pruned to grow in a whisky half barrel and to create a dense hedge. Filberts need cross pollination. Make one of them Casina, a thin shelled variety capable of 50% higher yields than others. For a pollinator consider Barcelona, the most widely planted filbert before Casina.

Pecans are associated with southern states where large plantations are devoted to growing the tall trees. However, there are hardy varieties that can be grown in northern states, such as Missouri Pecan. Hardy to zone 4, it requires another tree for pollination. The nut itself is a reddish brown inside a hard oval shell that is surrounded by a green outer casing. The trees bear young (in their third year) and can be kept compact by heavy pruning.

BEES FOR POLLINATION - Finally, a special tip concerning pollination: most pollination of fruit trees is conducted by bees, but the honey bee has experienced a serious decline in numbers in recent years. There is another bee, similar in appearance to a honey bee, called a mason bee because the female lays her eggs in holes that she seals in with a plug of mud. The mason bee is capable of pollinating ten times more flowers than honey bees, and the best way to attract the mason bee to your garden is through installing a mason bee nest. The nest consists of small tubes packed horizontally inside a waterproof cylinder that is best placed 6-7 ft. off the ground, on its side facing the sun, and under some shelter like the eaves of a shed or house. The females crawl along the tubes to lay their eggs at intervals, with a ball of food for the larvae. Each mason bee lives only a year, and so its survival is entirely dependent on the next generation. The difference a single mason bee nest can make to fruit yields is enormous.

I'll Make You a Gardening Wizard Overnight!

Stanley prune plum

Carolyn's Comments:

"Our first attempt at a fruit tree orchard was a disaster. We chose a spot that we thought had good drainage, but it puddled with water in winter, and as a consequence the fruit trees were always stressed. That led to our experimenting with growing fruit trees in containers filled with good garden topsoil and compost and the results have been astonishing. In particular has been our success in growing figs. We have several varieties including the yellow-skinned tender Kadota, the yellow-skinned St. Michael that produces the largest fruit of all, and Brown Turkey which has survived outdoors in a sheltered position. The biggest yields from Brown Turkey are possible by growing in a container that can be moved inside during winter. The plant merely requires frost exclusion as it does like to have a cold snap as a resting period. The potted figs are moved into our conservatory where they lose their leaves. They are watered sparingly, just to keep them alive, and then in February they start to sprout new leaves. There are two flushes of fruit — one in spring from fruit that forms as soon as the plants break dormancy, and again around Labor Day when the bigger harvest occurs.

Harvesting black figs always reminds me of a wonderful trip Derek and I took to the South of France when he was researching Renoir's garden for a book of the same name. We stayed at the Chateau Eze, a beautiful hotel on a cliff overlooking the Mediterranean, in the village of Eze on the border with Monaco, and in the morning Derek picked up the telephone to order breakfast in our suite. I heard him ask the concierge what was on the breakfast menu and the concierge answered 'Just tell me what you want.' Derek let his imagination run wild. He asked for scrambled eggs with smoked salmon, two slices of Charentais melon, red grapes, goat cheese, chocolate filled croissants, fresh squeezed orange juice, two Ruby Red grapefruit halves, Kona coffee, whole wheat toast with redcurrant jam and BLACK FIGS. In my half-awake state, my head buried into the pillow I chuckled as it was obviously Derek's idea of a joke; but the concierge made no reply and when he arrived with the breakfast tray EVERYTHING DEREK HAD ASKED FOR WAS THERE. We ate it on a balcony outside our bedroom overlooking the sparkling waters of the Mediterranean with a bunch of red carnations in a vase, freshly picked the previous day from Renoir's garden."

Chapter 14 - *Grow Delicious Fruits, Berries & Nuts for an All Season Harvest*

Moonglow pears

Redhaven peaches

Chapter 14 - *Grow Delicious Fruits, Berries & Nuts for an All Season Harvest*

Jumbo Royalty raspberry (left)

Earliglow strawberry compared to a peach

Pecan nuts

CHAPTER 15
Container Gardens for Big Yields Fast

> *"A whisky half barrel is a versatile container, roomy enough to grow an apple tree or 100 lbs of tomatoes on a single plant."*
> - from my article on container gardening in **Nouveau** magazine

More Americans are staying home, entertaining at home, and willing to dress up their patios and decks with container grown flowers and vegetables. There's no weeding, no digging, and watering and fertilizing are easy. Moreover, critters like deer are unlikely to bother plantings so close to the house, and insect pests like slugs are less of a problem. Container gardening allows you to enjoy growing vegetables almost anywhere there is adequate sunlight.

I don't think anything proves the potential of container gardening for high yields more than results from growing tomatoes. Our own have been impressive enough - 500 Early Cascades from a single plant, but the world record for tomatoes grown in a whisky half barrel is 110 lbs, accomplished by Charles H. Wilbur of Crane Hill, Alabama and described in his book *How to Grow Record Tomatoes* (Acres USA). Key to his success is choice of variety (Better Boy) and his home made potting soil. This consists of one part home-made compost and three parts garden top soil.

When choosing a container - ALWAYS ensure you have drainage holes otherwise water will collect in the bottom and rot plant roots. If the container doesn't have a drainage hole (for example a metal cauldron would not), then drill several holes in the base and use some broken clay crocks over them to avoid soil clogging them.

Many types of containers can be obtained inexpensively from goodwill stores and garage sales like junked metal wash tubs, enamel bath tubs, metal, wood or plastic buckets and used wooden shipping crates; even old boots. I've even seen beautiful planters made from damaged row boats. Just remember that the larger the container the better, since small containers will dry out more quickly than large ones.

A company that has done more to promote the popularity of container gardening in America is the Kinsman Company, headquartered in Pipersville, Pennsylvania. The owners, Graham and Michelle Kinsman are near neighbors and publish a comprehensive catalog featuring 100 pages of garden tools and accessories of which 30 pages are planters - the largest selection in North America. They have often photographed their products at Cedaridge Farm. In particular the Kinsmans have popularized the hay rack planter which can be a free-standing unit or attached to the side of a house. These units are more attractive than regular window box planters. They are roomy, have steel ribs fitted with a

I'll Make You a Gardening Wizard Overnight!

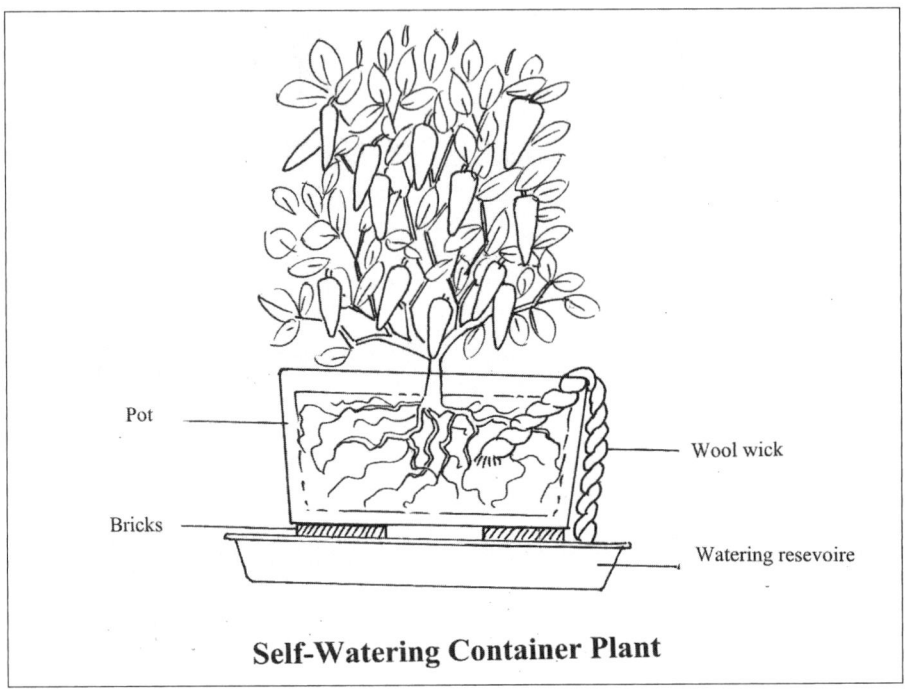

Self-Watering Container Plant

coco fiber liner so that plant roots can breathe, and they are ideal for creating striking plant combinations. A Kinsman customer, Pamela Crawford improved on these hay rack planters by punching planting holes in the liner so plants can be grown out of the sides as well as the top, creating a lush cascading effect and in some cases a complete sphere. Pam went on to write a series of popular books about her methods, with an emphasis on side planting. The Kinsmans now use Pam as a consultant. I visited Pam at her home north of Atlanta and saw for myself the incredibly beautiful display she has made by mounting metal cradle planters on pedestals. See the appendix under sources for more information.

Ever since I began gardening I have experimented with a vast array of containers and plant permutations. Gone are the days when I would be content with a few lettuce, geraniums or strawberry plants in a whisky half barrel. Now I prefer the sophistication of combining vegetables and flowers in Versailles planter boxes and English lead planters. Not only is the choice of planter important for a dramatic display, but also the placement. Rather than have one container commanding a place on a deck, I like to see them in clusters, so there is a variation in heights. Texture is important, too. Common textures like plastic can look monotonous, but a mixture of rusty metal, wood with peeling paint, and terracotta with a patina of moss or algae can add tremendous visual appeal.

Within the containers, try to create several layers of color, leaf shape and leaf texture. First, there is the rim of the container which might call for a compact spreading plant like strawberries that can extend their runners over the rim, or the shiny chocolate and chartreuse forms of sweet potato vine, capable of draping their long stems and heart-

Peppermint in whisky half barrel   *Herbs in decorative containers*

shaped leaves down the sides of the container like a curtain and producing edible tubers into the bargain.

Within this outer rim I like to use something strictly decorative that's upright or mounded - but still relatively compact, like Saber coleus or New Guinea impatiens. For a third level of interest I use a tall plant like an erect Bright Lights Swiss chard or stalks of sweet corn. Banana plants, with their explosion of paddle-shaped leaves and purple-leaf mustard also make beautiful central accents.

The potting mix used in containers is extremely important. Avoid garden topsoil alone as it has a tendency to pack down and restrict plant roots. I also avoid pure potting soil as I find it is too lightweight and offers poor anchorage for some plants. Rather, I prefer to use a mix of garden topsoil and commercial potting mix, or garden topsoil and Starbucks coffee grounds since the combination costs nothing. To keep soil mixtures from drying out too quickly consider using a hydro gel. This acts like a sponge to retain moisture and resist rapid evaporation.

Regular feeding is essential to keep container plants looking healthy. At time of planting I add to the potting mix a granular all-purpose fertilizer, like 10-10-10, and follow this up with a liquid foliar feed or a liquid soil drench. A long handled watering wand is useful for watering containers - especially hanging baskets - as it allows you to poke the nozzle through lush foliage and water directly at the root zone.

RECOMMENDED CONTAINERS. When considering which containers to use for growing vegetables, you must decide whether you plan a mixture of vegetables or a single plant, such as a tomato or a dwarf fruit tree. Although hanging baskets are attractive they are the most difficult for growing vegetables since they tend to dry out too quickly. Here is a review of containers I have found most suitable for growing vegetables:

WHISKY HALF BARREL. As well as looking attractive, it has sufficient room to grow a fruit tree such as a dwarf peach or a dwarf apple. Also consider a cluster of vegetables, such as several pepper plants, tomatoes and eggplants, or a cluster of salad greens like mixed lettuces, or a cluster of herbs like parsley, chives and basil. Since whisky half barrels are made of wood, do not allow the base to rest on soil as it will rot. Instead, raise the bottom off the ground using bricks or special clay feet that slip under the bottom.

VERSAILLES PLANTER BOXES. These are a French design originally used at Versailles Palace in France, to grow palms and fruit trees. They come in a range of sizes, small ones with legs and large ones with casters so the boxes can be moved about. These boxes are usually colored grey, green or white and mostly used for plants like citrus that need to be moved indoors during winter.

BATH TUB. Enamel bath tubs are excellent planters for a wide range of plants, especially for growing herbs on a hard surface. They can be used with the legs set on concrete or flagstone or they can be buried up to their rims in soil. They make a good centerpiece for a patio grouping, the bath tub in the middle and an arrangement of various containers around the sides to hide the expanse of enamel.

DINGHY. Small row boats such as dingies can be used as planters after they become unseaworthy. Gardeners living along the coast may often find a wrecked dinghy washed ashore after a storm, or find them for sale in boatyards and at garage sales. Whether made of plastic, glass fiber or wood, a small dinghy can grow a large number of vegetables and culinary herbs.

TERRACOTTA POTS are the most attractive of all containers in my opinion. Their warm, natural earth color is ideal for decorating a patio or deck. Although they are available in a variety of sizes and shapes, my favorite is the wide rimmed rounded pot because it will accommodate a lot of plants. These pot-bellied urns are especially good for collections of herbs, with vining scented leaf geraniums cascading down the sides.

METAL HAY RACK PLANTERS can be mounted against a wall. They have metal ribs and must be lined with a nesting material such as sphagnum moss or coco fiber. The moss and fiber holds in the soil and helps keep the roots cool.

TOPSY TURVY PLANTER. We have grown several tomato varieties in this upside-down planter, including a yellow cherry tomato, a red plum tomato and a medium-size Early Cascade. They all produced worthwhile yields. The container itself consists of a flexible plastic column with a hole in the bottom into which you plant a tomato seedling. In the early stages the tendency of the tomato plant is to bend up and grow skyward, but eventually

Chapter 15 - *Container Gardens for Big Yields Fast*

Tomato-Potato in a Pot
Tomatoes on the vine; potatoes in the pot.

the weight of stems, leaves and fruit force it to grow down. The growing instructions must be followed carefully. For example they tell you not to use garden topsoil, but to use lighter weight potting soil. When it becomes wet, the garden soil can become too heavy and rip the unit off its hanger. I generally watered the unit every day and fertilized every two weeks.

Actually, you can create your own upside-down planter by simply taking a deep hanging basket with wire ribbing and make a nest of sphagnum moss, through which you can push a tomato seedling. Fill the basket with a potting soil and mulch the top to prevent rapid evaporation. Placed side-by-side I found the wire basket as productive as the Topsy Turvy.

Carolyn's Comments:

"I think we have had more fun experimenting with growing plants in containers than any other aspect of gardening. Twice our container gardens have been featured in magazines, in Flower Gardening and Container Gardening, sold through bookstores. We have several good places to display plants in containers - a flight of stone steps leading from the kitchen to the garden, a flagstone patio off our guest cottage and a deck off our sunroom. Container gardening allows us to be creative in several ways - with the choice of plants and the way we partner them, the choice of container to compliment the plants and their surroundings, and of course the location. Each display area features a different theme. For example, for the guest cottage patio we like to group tropical plants that spend indoors during winter, while the sunroom deck features cradle planters with cascading plants that drape over a balcony to create a curtain of color. I think the most successful container plantings are those that combine flowers with a vegetable as an accent. I especially like to use either golden chard or crimson chard as a vertical accent in the middle of a container because the stalks are so bold and the crinkly green leaves so shiny and flamboyant. Also, we like to use curly blue or black kale as a wonderful textural contrast to flowers. Parsley makes a good edging and contrast to flowers, as do the curly kinds of lettuce like bronze leaf Lolla Rossa and curly leaf varieties of basil. One year we used a yellow pear tomato as a component and the bright yellow fruits looked like Christmas lights.

Derek has mentioned the Kinsman catalog as an excellent source for planters. Of particular value to container gardeners are their Trug tubs, with handles. These are a dual purpose product, useful as a carrier for large loads, like leaves and grass clippings and as a 14.5 gallon planter for growing anything up to the size of a small fruit tree, such as a peach. The Trugs are watertight, but by poking a red-hot poker through the bottom you can make drainage holes to use as a planter. We grow two figs in a pair of black Trugs and it's easy in fall to pick them up by the handles and carry indoors for surviving the winter."

CHAPTER 16
Indoor Harvests Made Easy

"I feel I have joined a higher order of mortal having fruited a banana tree indoors."
– From an article in **Nouveau** magazine on Indoor Gardening

For several years I was president of the Hobby Greenhouse Association. At the time I had a small glass-framed greenhouse that I used mostly to start seedlings in spring and over-winter some tender perennials. Today I continue gardening indoors with the aid of a Victorian style conservatory imported from England and a sun room. The sun room is an American redwood and glass structure that serves as a breakfast room off the kitchen, with heat and air conditioning that allows me to grow tender exotic plants year round, such as Australian tree ferns and several potted plants of Dwarf Cavendish banana. Around the sides it has shelves where I can start seedlings, and a beautiful view along a lawn vista down to a wildlife pond. It's a comfortable place for up to four people to have breakfast, surrounded by greenery.

My conservatory is bigger and is mostly a reading room. It's big enough for six people to sit around a table and have a conversation with a view of my flower garden and a Victorian gazebo. It is home to a pair of fruiting figs, several potted tomato plants, a pepper plant, a Bismarck palm with silvery-blue leaves, an everblooming hibiscus, and a yellow flowered Charles Grimaldi honey-scented angel's trumpet. It also has shelves for me to start seedlings.

There are times I have lived in homes without a conservatory or a greenhouse, and grown plants on sunny windowsills. In those days I also owned an indoor grow light unit for raising seedlings in early spring, also African violets during summer and culinary herbs in winter.

Over the years I have read a lot of claims about growing edibles indoors, such as growing tomatoes on a windowsill during winter in northern climates. It can be done but there are only a few tomato varieties that will tolerate the low light and increased cloud cover of northern homes.

INDOOR TOMATOES. After experimenting with growing numerous tomato varieties indoors over winter on windowsills, worthwhile yields were possible using only a few varieties. These included both red and yellow cherry tomatoes and the remarkable Pixie Hybrid. A dwarf, bush variety, Pixie can grow tomatoes slightly smaller than a billiard ball in a 12 inch pot. Because of its low light tolerance it became popular to grow in England where cool summers and dense cloud cover make outdoor conditions difficult for tomatoes. To harvest tomatoes during reduced daylight hours, such as February and March, seed of Pixie should be started indoors before the end of October in an enriched potting soil and the plant sprayed with a liquid, high phosphorus foliar feed every two weeks.

INDOOR CUCUMBERS. A very good variety to grow indoors is Spacemaster, one of several compact, bush varieties that have short vines. It can be grown in a 12 inch pot with a short trellis, and also in a hanging basket, with fruit hanging down the sides of the plant. I've actually seen tall vining cucumbers grow in roomy window box planters, the vines trained up a tall trellis to produce an amazing number of fruit. Orient Express, a tender, bitter-free Burpless variety is especially good for climbing.

PEPPERS. Bell peppers are highly intolerant of poor light and cool temperatures. The bell pepper Gypsy hybrid is the only one I know that is suitable for growing indoors during winter. It's extremely decorative since the fruit have three stages of maturity – lemon yellow, flame orange and bright red. There are also a number of hot peppers that can look beautiful in pots, such as Thai Hot, with 1-inch cone-shaped fruits held upright like Christmas lights. McMahon's Bird Pepper is another good one to try. McMahon was a Philadelphia nurseryman who wrote America's first garden book, *The American Gardener's Calendar*, in 1806. I have a copy of the first leather bound edition. Containing 666 pages, it is an amazing volume that covers every aspect of home gardening. MacMahon was entrusted with the care and propagation of seeds from the Lewis & Clark expedition to the West Coast of America, and he received the Bird Pepper from Thomas Jefferson, then president. The bright red fruits are only 1/2 inch long, oval, and stand up above the foliage like miniature lollipops. The smaller the fruit of a hot pepper, the more likely you are to harvest a decent crop indoors.

CULINARY HERBS. I doubt there is anything easier to grow indoors than culinary herbs. Most of them come from places with harsh soils and a lack of moisture, and so a sunny windowsill or a Grow Light unit is suitable for a small collection. Here are plants I have grown in 12 inch pots: all kinds of basil, parsley, chives, thyme, stevia (also called sweet leaf since it can be used as a low-calorie substitute for sugar), and cilantro. I have also grown several together in a window box planter, like basil, parsley and cilantro. The flavors may not be as strong as plants grown outside in full sun, but they make a cheerful decorative accent with their beautiful leaf shapes and textures.

MUSHROOM KITS. At one time the only mushrooms that could be grown indoors, in special mushroom soil, were the white button mushrooms. But today it's possible to grow big brown-skinned portobellos (my favorite), shitakii and others, either on specially treated logs impregnated with spawn or in waterproof boxes with a specially prepared growing medium. The directions are fairly easy to follow. The kits for portobellos and button mushrooms come with a dry compost containing spawn that needs moistening to activate, and covering with a moist potting mix (supplied with the kit). Placed in subdued light or darkness, and a temperature below 70F, but above 50F, fine white threads and a

Cayuga grape

Button mushroom harvest

Banana outdoors in Florida

white fuzz will cover the soil. Shortly thereafter tiny pinheads will appear and swell into mature mushrooms. Time to harvest will vary according to variety, moisture and temperature, but a crop of button mushrooms (the easiest to grow) can be expected within just 40 days.

SPROUTS. Many kinds of seeds are good to grow as sprouts indoors, for adding to salads or using as sandwich filler. There are special sprout containers to grow them in, but most sprouts are so easy to grow all you need is a shallow bowl and some moist soft paper tissue to grow them on. The most popular type of sprout is cress and it's fascinating to see how the seed coat splits almost the instant you add water. It has a pleasant mild, peppery flavor. Other good seeds for sprouting include broccoli and wheat grass – both of which have a clean, pleasant flavor, and fenugreek, a bean with a mild curry flavor.

GRAPES. I have grown some good quality dessert grapes indoors in a two gallon bucket around a large sunny picture window and also in my conservatory. The vine needs planting in fertile potting soil, and trained along a vertical or horizontal string so it receives good direct sunlight. My favorites for growing indoors are black Fredonia (larger than Concord) and white Cayuga. Both have seeds inside the berries, but in the case of Fredonia the flavor is sweet and fruity, and in the case of Cayuga the bunches are very long. A high phosphorus fertilizer needs to be worked into the soil at planting time, followed by a foliar feed every two weeks to get a good fruit set.

DWARF BANANA. I was very pleased with myself when I fruited my first dwarf Cavendish banana tree indoors in my conservatory in Pennsylvania. I remember when I suggested to Thompson & Morgan they sell banana trees in their catalog, and a British consumer protection group later complained that their catalog copy was deceptive because the British could not expect to fruit them in the reduced daylight of the British climate. But by the time they received the complaint Thompson & Morgan already had dozens of letters from overjoyed customers reporting success at ripening the fruit. To fruit reliably indoors a banana plant should be three years old, in a 10 gallon capacity tub. Mine produced a long, purple arching flower stalk in March. Where the flower meets the stem, there are dozens of green immature bananas that look like tiny fingers. After frost danger I move the plant outside so it can bask in summer heat. The bananas will grow to ripen before the first fall frost in October. The dozen bananas I picked were delicious and more flavorful than those I buy at the grocery store. I'm told I could have hastened ripening and produced more bananas by tying a clear plastic bag over the flower stem. After fruiting, the main stem dies, but offsets around the base can be removed and potted up to obtain more bananas. To encourage flowering, I sprayed the large, paddle-shaped leaves with Spray-N-Grow liquid plant food, and continued to spray the undersides every two weeks until harvesting.

SUGAR CANE. This tropical grass is killed by frost, but it makes a handsome foliage accent in a pot. There is the green leafed kind with canes that turn yellow when ripe, and one with purple canes, called Pele's Smoke. To mature the cane, grow in a large tub and move outdoors during frost-free months. Plants will grow to 10 feet tall. The bamboo-like canes are full of sweet juice when the leaves turn brown. You can either chew on a cane to extract the juice or squeeze it into a cup. Mix with rum and a dash of lime and you will experience one of the fabulous drink specialties of Tahiti.

PINEAPPLE. There are two kinds of pineapple that are easy to grow indoors in a sunny location – the regular green pineapple that turns yellow when ripe and a variegated pineapple that produces a red fruit. See the next chapter about growing a pineapple indoors and encouraging it to fruit.

I often see in advertisements and on television shopping channels, claims that you can grow other tropical fruits indoors, such as pomegranate, avocado, guava, lychee and papaya, but I have never been successful with these, except to grow leaves and no fruit. There is a dwarf pomegranate that produces orange flowers and small red fruit, but not large enough to be edible.

Indoor gardening under grow lights is a fascinating hobby. There are dozens of units to choose from, including carts with several levels of lights strong enough to grow a wide variety of plants, even in a heated basement area.

Carolyn's Comments:

> "When we moved to Cedaridge Farm and lived in the farmhouse we found the rooms to be cozy and dark as you would expect of a 200-year old farmhouse. There are deep window ledges where we were able to start seedlings and have collections of herbs to grow through the winter, but we craved a bright, sunny room to be surrounded by more greenery, especially during winter months. Our first improvement was to add a sunny breakfast room off the kitchen and this allowed us to grow a lot of house plants during winter and a hanging basket or two of Pixie or Tumblin' Tom tomatoes. Later, with the success of Derek's books and calendars on the Impressionist painters and their gardens, we added a conservatory which has become our favorite room as it allows us to experience the garden in all weather. I especially like to sit in the conservatory with a good book to read while a thunderstorm lights up the dark sky and rain slashes at the window panes. But most of all, the conservatory allows us to experiment with growing plants indoors. The farmhouse also has an unheated, but screened-in sun porch that got very little use until Derek returned from a trip to New Zealand where he had seen similar porches used as an outdoor bedroom. So that's what our sun porch has become – a place to sleep in summer with the sights and sounds of the garden close by, and the rafters filled with the fragrance of dried herbs and dried fruit."

CHAPTER 17
Children's Gardens

*"Children who receive lessons in gardening at school
achieve higher grades than children who do not.
The same is true of children who attend cookery classes."*
– findings of a study among schoolchildren reported in the Pittsburgh Press

When children garden they not only learn the benefits of self-help, they often learn to enjoy eating healthy foods they might otherwise resist – salad greens, tomatoes, green beans and especially Sugar Snap peas. My three children – Tina, Derek Jr and Vicki - all enjoy gardening now that they are adults. I recall when I was a youngster, my father called me into the garden one day and invited me to pick peas. As I picked he encouraged me to sample some and they were delicious. Ever since that time there has hardly been a year of my life when I didn't find time to plant a patch of peas.

With my own children, I would take them to a local u-pick strawberry operation and offer them a reward for finding the biggest strawberry. We would

Dwarf apple, Granny Smith

pick quarts, and of course sample a few handfuls along the way. Then, in the fall I'd obtain some strawberry plants and give each six plants to grow. We would clear a site, mound the soil, plant the year-old roots, mulch around them and water, and then in the spring they would check out the strawberry patch regularly for the thrill of finding the first ripe berry. Of course, there are certain vegetables that most children seem to dislike, such as onions. But it depends on how they are prepared. When they see a giant onion their curiosity is aroused and they may discover a liking for fried onions with sausage and potatoes, or sprinkled sparingly over a pizza. Out in the garden one day my son watched me photographing a group of onions and wondered what was so special about them as they looked no different from the round, brown-skinned kind he had seen in the grocery store. I explained they were a special variety that could be stored a long time without spoiling, and for that reason they were called 'sleeping onions.' Whenever I prepared a meal with onions after that he would ask specially if they were 'sleeping onions' and venture a bite.

When children learn early in life that fresh fruits and vegetables are easy to grow from seeds the desire to garden can remain with them all their lives. By making the care of a garden a family affair, and allowing children to feel responsible for the growth of a mammoth cabbage or a giant tomato you can instill in them a strong sense of self-worth and respect for nature.

Here are some ideas to help engage a child's interest in gardening:

A SIMPLE SOIL EXPERIMENT. Take a handful of topsoil, place it in a glass jar and fill the jar with water. Then shake the contents and allow them to settle. After the water turns from cloudy to clear, have your children examine the contents. They will see that the largest soil particles – sand and gravel – have settled in the bottom, while fine particles – clay – create a layer above them with the coarsest grains at the bottom and the finest on top. Then, floating at the surface will be a layer of organic matter – pieces of compost, stems, decaying leaves, grass blades and pieces of root. Teach your children that the right balance of sand and clay particles helps make an ideal soil, but that the most important ingredient is the floating organic matter because this contains nutrients and moisture-absorbing ability that plants need to grow healthy.

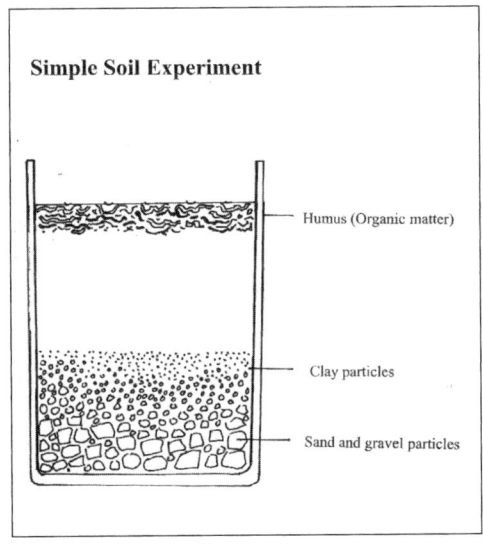

Simple Soil Experiment

A GERMINATION TEST. Fill two glass jars with crumpled paper tissues, moisten and place several bean seeds around the edge between the glass and the paper. In one jar place the beans in a vertical position and in the other jar place the curved edge facing down. Then place the jars in bright light. In a few days the children will observe the seed coat split and a root emerge, growing down. Then a sprout will unfurl and grow up towards the light. They will see that this occurs whether the bean is planted the right side up or upside down – roots always grow towards the source of gravity and the sprout will always grow up towards the sunlight.

PLAY THE BEE. Teach children the process of pollination by having them play the part of a bee. Show them a zucchini squash plant and how the flowers differ depending on whether they are male or female. On the female flower show them the immature embryo fruit underneath the flower and the fact that the female has a shiny center. Then show them a male flower with no embryo underneath and a powdery center. Have them pick the male flower and rub the powdery pollen on the shiny centers of several females. Then several days later show them how the fertilized female has produced a mature fruit good to eat. This participation in the growth of a zucchini fruit can turn them on to eating zucchini.

FREE TOMATO-POTATO GRAFTS. Show your children how to make a tomato-potato by taking a potato tuber about the size of a tangerine and coring it through the center with a sharp pointed blade. The hole must be large enough to accommodate the roots of a tomato transplant. Push the roots of the tomato transplant into the hole and make sure the roots poke out through the bottom. Then plant the two together into fertile soil in a sunny location, making sure the potato part of the graft is completely covered and the tomato is above ground. Water immediately and keep moist until the tomato plant grows strong and leafy. Sometimes the potato part of the graft will prove more vigorous than the tomato, threatening to suffocate the tomato. If that happens simply thin out the potato shoots by cutting off the longest stems so the tomato can get enough air and light. Eventually, the tomato will start to flower and fruit. When the tomatoes have ripened dig up the entire plant and harvest the potatoes.

BLUE POTATOES. Make the endeavor of gardening more interesting by growing some vegetables with unusual colors. Here are some of my favorites – golden beets, purple asparagus, purple podded peas, purple podded beans, orange-headed cauliflower, white cucumbers, red-leaf lettuce, black bell peppers, blue potatoes, black radishes, crimson chard, white tomatoes and yellow watermelons.

Jumbo cabbage, O S Cross

GIANT VEGETABLES. Teach children how to grow giant vegetables. Here are some that never fail to thrill children: Earliglow strawberries will grow as big as a peach; Supersteak tomatoes will grow the size of a grapefruit; OS Cross cabbages can grow to 100 lbs and more; Big Max pumpkin will grow to 100 lbs and more; Royal Jubilee and Royal Windsor watermelons will grow to 100 lbs and more; Big Bertha bell pepper will grow blocky fruits up to 10 inches long; Mammoth onion will grow to 22 inches in circumference; Titan and Royalty raspberries will grow fruit as big as strawberries; Flaming Fury peach will grow peaches as big as grapefruits; Jumbo apple

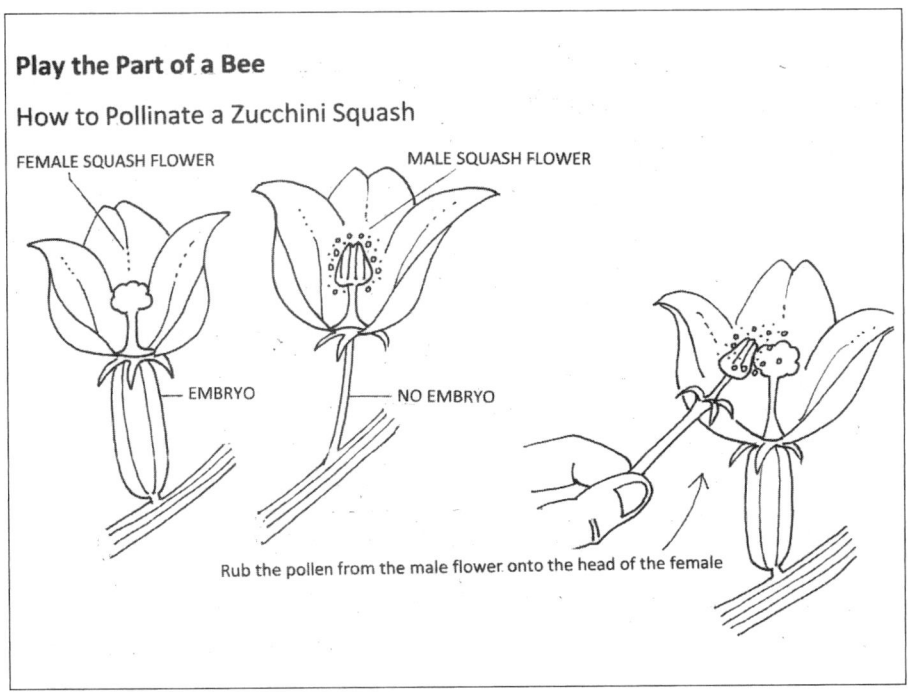

Play the Part of a Bee

How to Pollinate a Zucchini Squash

FEMALE SQUASH FLOWER — EMBRYO
MALE SQUASH FLOWER — NO EMBRYO

Rub the pollen from the male flower onto the head of the female

will grow to three times bigger than a Red Delicious; Mammoth Russian sunflower will grow to 10 ft high and produce a seed head as big as a dinner plate.

GROW A PINEAPPLE. The next time you purchase a pineapple – or an avocado pear – show your children how to propagate these tropical fruits. Normally, to eat a pineapple you would slice off the crown of spiky leaves with a 1 inch layer of fruit and throw it away. Instead, transfer the crown to a pot filled with potting soil. Under the crown is a fibrous core capable of sprouting roots and growing a new pineapple. Place in a sunny window, allow the soil to dry out between watering and feed with a weak house plant fertilizer every two weeks. After two years you can encourage your pineapple to fruit by covering it with a clear plastic bag with a ripe apple inside. The apple gives off a natural gas that can spur the pineapple plant to produce a fruit stalk. The fruit will start off green and turn yellow when completely ripe. Indoor fruited pineapples are generally small, but sweet and delicious just like the parent.

GROW AN AVOCADO. To grow an avocado pear tree indoors simply fill a drinking glass half-full with water. Then take the large brown pointed seed inside the fruit and stick toothpicks around the side like a cartwheel. Place over the mouth of the jar so the toothpicks suspend the seed just above the water level. Within a few weeks the fruit will split, sending out a root into the water and green leaves that grow up towards the light. When the shoot has grown to about six inches, transplant it into a pot with potting soil.

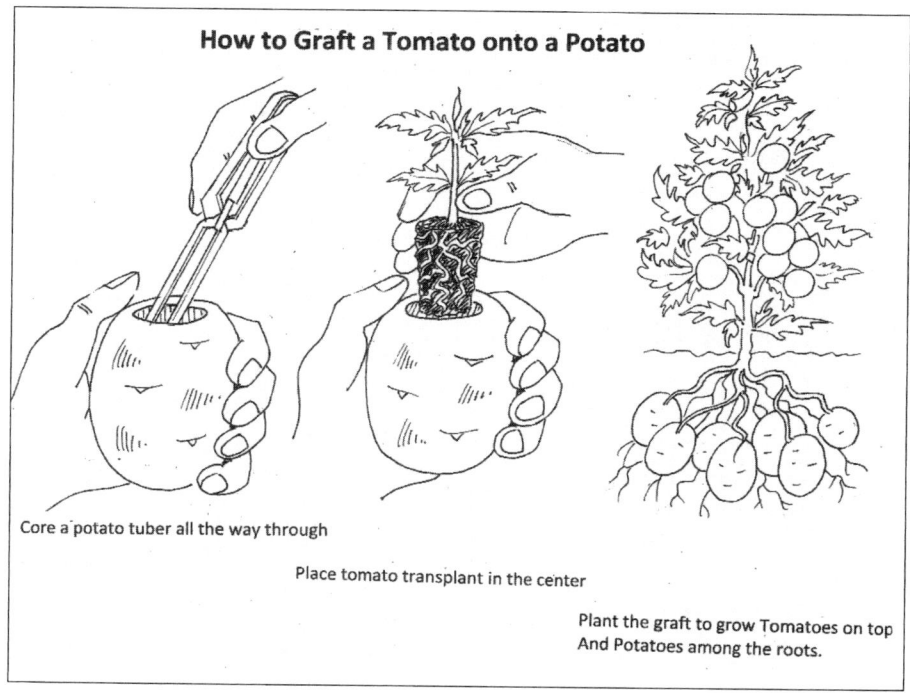

How to Graft a Tomato onto a Potato

Core a potato tuber all the way through

Place tomato transplant in the center

Plant the graft to grow Tomatoes on top And Potatoes among the roots.

Pinch out the lead shoot to encourage side branches and you will be rewarded with an attractive evergreen foliage plant. In nature avocadoes can grow into big trees, so keep pruning to maintain a compact habit. Seeds from lemons and oranges are also easy to sprout in moist potting soil. With sufficient light these can flower and fruit.

FREE PLANTS FROM CUTTINGS. In Greek mythology the strongest man in the world, Hercules had to fight a savage swamp monster called a Hydra. The monster had nine heads and every time Hercules cut off a head, two more would grow in its place. Hercules finally killed the monster with a firebrand, burning the neck each time he cut off a head until it had no more heads. Many fruits and vegetables are like the Hydra. You can cut off a section of stem (called a tip cutting) and root it in moist potting soil. I have done this with tomatoes and figs. It's also possible to take a raspberry or blackberry cane, bend it to the ground, scrape some bark off a two-inch section about six inches from the tip and pin the scraped section so it remains buried in soil but the leaves at the tip remain above the soil. Where the stem meets the ground, roots will sprout and within a month or two you can cut the rooted portion away from the mother cane to transplant in another part of the garden.

FOOLPROOF AIR LAYERING. Another fascinating form of propagation for children is called air layering. This is especially easy to accomplish with figs, but you can try it with any woody plant – like a peach, apple or pear tree. Simply take a slender section of branch, scrape the bark off a two-inch section and wrap it with a moist kitchen sponge. Secure with a rubber

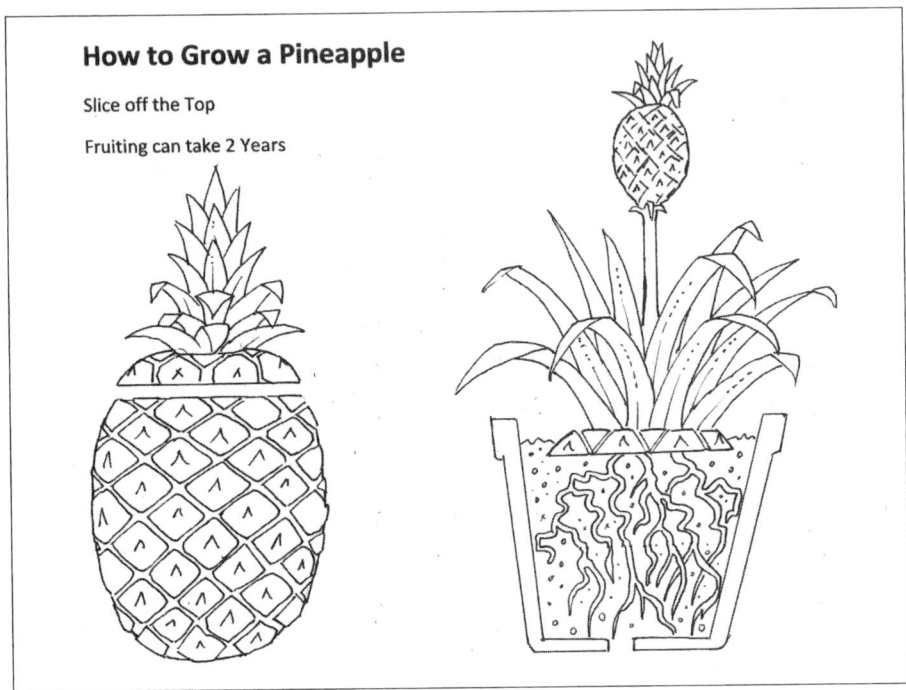

How to Grow a Pineapple

Slice off the Top

Fruiting can take 2 Years

band and enclose the sponge in clear plastic to trap the moisture. Depending on the fruit tree (figs take about four-six weeks) you will see the sponge become a mass of roots, at which time you can prune away the cutting and root it in another part of the garden or in a pot.

FREE CHIA PETS. Cut the top off an eggshell and fill it with potting soil. Then paint a face on the shell and plant lettuce, cress or chives seed on the surface. Keep the soil moist and the eggshell container will sprout green hair just like a Chia pet. When the sprouts grow tall give the face a haircut with a pair of scissors and use the edible greens as a garnish on foods.

MAGIC PEANUTS. Peanuts are not really nuts – they are legumes, related to peas and beans and they have a magical way of producing the 'nuts'. Plant some seeds in a large pot (about 12 inches wide) and look for the first yellow flowers to form. Then examine them closely each day and you will see the center of each flower send out a long, slender probe that digs into the soil and forms the peanuts underground. After four or five weeks you can pull up the entire plant and see dozens of nuts among the roots.

BEAN WIG-WAM. Arrange four or more poles in a square and secure them at the top with string to form a pointed frame. Then plant pole beans at the base of each pole and watch the beans quickly cover the frame all the way to the top. You can then cut a space between two of the poles for children to climb inside and use as a shelter or secret hideaway.

Chapter 17 - *Children's Gardens*

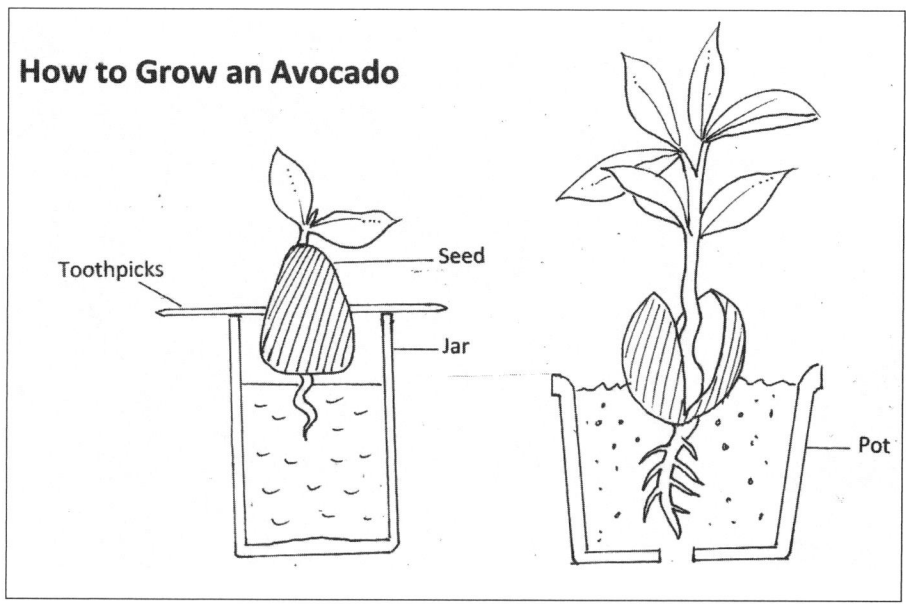

THE EASTER EGG PLANT is an eggplant, closely related to peppers. It produces fruit that so much resemble hen's eggs you can hardly tell the two apart. The fruits generally start off white and turn yellow when fully ripe. You can pick them and paint them to serve as Easter eggs, or you can peel them and fry the inside to eat like fritters. Some seed catalogs call it the Golden Egg Tree.

GROW MUSHROOMS INDOORS. The activity of growing mushrooms, described in the previous chapter, is extremely appealing to children. Help them start a mushroom growing kit indoors, especially button mushrooms to chop fine and use as a topping for pizza.

Carolyn's Comments:

> Derek has a grandson named Owen. His parents live nearby and during summer his daughter Tina often brings Owen to the farm for amusement. He likes to feed Derek's collection of koi and play in a 'Hobbit house' that Derek built for him in the woods. Before they leave for home, Derek always invites Tina to help herself to anything in the garden, and she takes Owen with her to pick whatever is in season. Lettuce in spring and sweet corn in summer are some of her favorites. One day, in winter when his grandson was only three years old Derek asked Owen what he planned to do in the spring, and to Derek's surprise Owen announced 'I want to plant a vegetable garden.' Derek asked him what he wanted to grow and Owen replied: 'Everything you grow.' Later, we learned that when Tina arrived home with the vegetables from her father's garden, she and Owen's father would rhapsodize over the flavor of the vegetables, and so Owen learned from observation that fresh vegetables from Pop-pop's garden always pleased his mother. I'm sure that the happiness he saw as a result of his parents savoring Derek's vegetables is why Owen — at age three - wanted to plant a vegetable garden 'Just like Pop-pops.'"

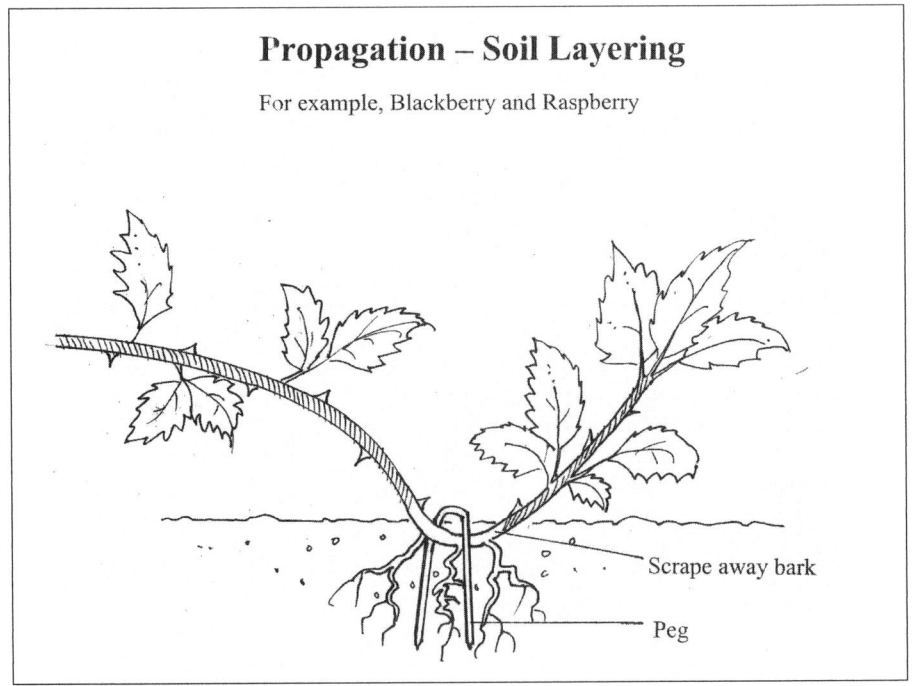

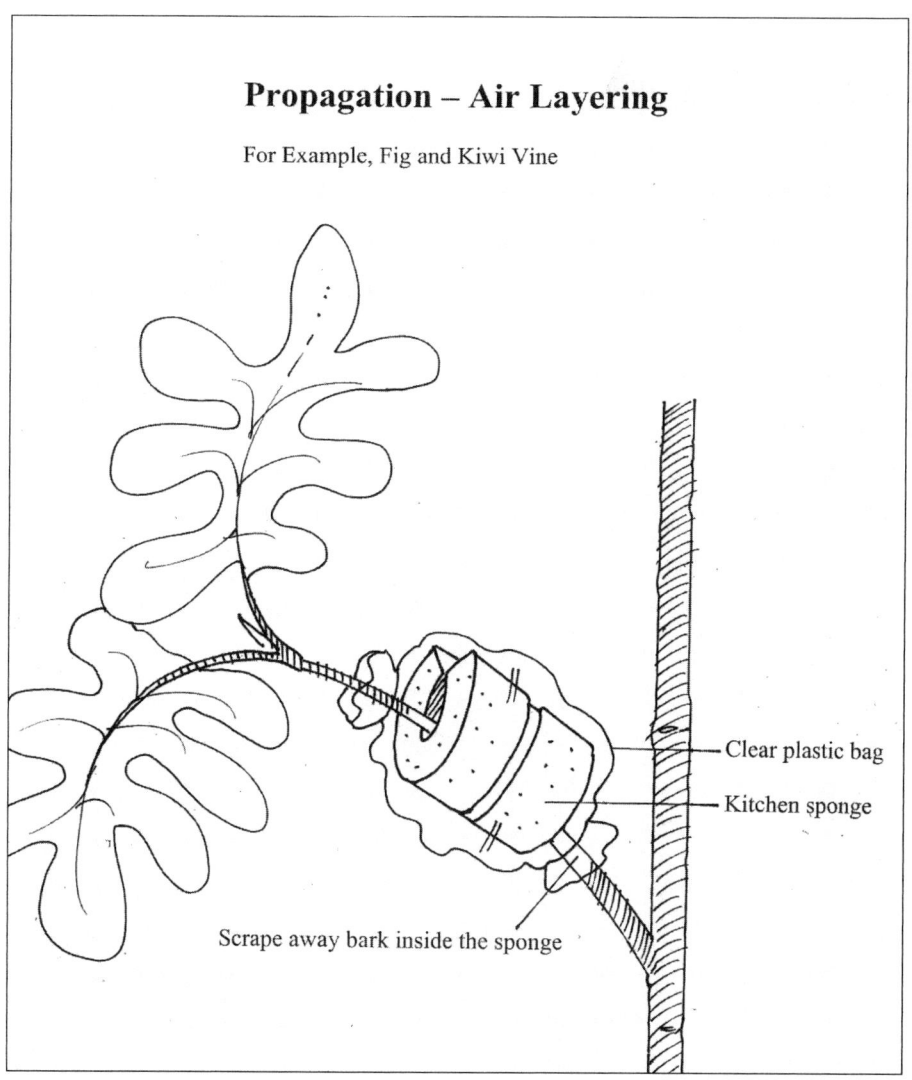

I'll Make You a Gardening Wizard Overnight!

CHAPTER 18
Garden Myths You Need to Know

"I think a garden should delight the eye, warm the heart and feed the soul."
– Prince Charles

Over the years I've seen a lot of misinformation published about gardening. Here's a typical example I found in two garden books: "To improve fruit set on tomato plants, take a camel's hair brush and transfer pollen from one flower to another." That's poor advice because tomato flowers are SELF POLLINATING so tediously going from flower to flower with a brush is a waste of time. Simply shaking the flower trusses will release enough pollen to achieve improved pollination. Invariably, when one writer makes a mistake another writer will copy it. The following advice is even more ridiculous: "Rub a nylon petticoat to build up static electricity, and lay it on the blossoms of one plant. Then take it off and shake the pollen onto another plant. You'll get 100% pollination every time – I guarantee it." Actually, you will simply perform an unnecessary, time consuming chore and if the temperature is too cold no pollination will take place.

What's the point of telling someone to mix 1 cup of sour milk, 2 tablespoons of flour and 1 quart of warm water to control aphids if you don't say WHY these ingredients are supposed to work? I've tried most of these 'miracle' brews and they don't work. Many of them have been tested at scientific institutions and their conclusions are the same as mine. "Don't let the facts get in the way of a good story" seems to be the credo of many authors of home remedy books.

Some of the home remedy controls recommended by self-described gardening gurus, to combat pests and diseases, are ridiculous and can actually harm plants since their application is not as easy to control as a properly formulated organic product (and a lot more expensive than a commercial organic control).

Jeff Gillman PhD, associate professor in the Department of Horticulture, at the Univeristy of Minnesota, has conducted numerous tests on household products and many of his conclusions are the same as mine. He published these in a book, *The Truth about Garden Remedies – What Works, What Doesn't and Why* (Timber Press). He analyses more than 100 common home remedies and finds that most of them are myths, and sometimes even harm plants.

Take household ammonia, for example. It is often recommended as a fertilizer for leafy crops. Ammonia contains nitrogen, which is a plant food. But the nitrogen in ammonia can be toxic to plants, especially seedlings. Buttermilk and other milk products also contain nitrogen, but rather than apply directly to plants these products are best applied to a compost pile where the nitrogen will feed microorganisms that produce a form of nitrogen plants can better assimilate. Epsom salts are also recommended as a fertilizer because they contain two trace elements, magnesium and sulphur. However, in soil where these elements are deficient the soil is generally acidic, in which case dolomitic lime would be more helpful.

How about citrus peels to repel insect pests? The theory is that since citrus peel contains limonene, a natural insect toxin, they will repel all kinds of troublesome insect pests. But the amount of repellent in a few citrus peels is too small to be of any use, and besides, the peel has to be *squeezed* to have any repellent effect. Instead, delegate your citrus peels to a compost pile for rotting down into an all purpose plant food.

Baby shampoos are recommended as a soil amendment, sodas containing high sugar as a pick-me-up for plants, but again these are of questionable value according to Gillman.

Can you imagine being told to rid your garden of pesky squirrels by spraying your property with a mixture of various kitchen products mixed with human urine, and that the most effective urine comes from having consumed too much alcohol? How about using birth control tablets to fertilize your house plants? Or using Tabasco sauce as an insect repellent? Doesn't the author of that nugget of misinformation realize how tiny a bottle of Tabasco sauce is, and how ridiculously expensive it would be to use it as an insect spray, compared to properly formulated organic insect controls available at a fraction of the cost from a garden supply store?

The same book recommends using birth control tablets to feed ailing house plants! Even if a birth control tablet could feed an ailing house plant, does it make economic sense when you compare its cost to the cost of an inexpensive, properly formulated fertilizer tablet? Yet millions of these books have been sold to a gullible public.

HYDROPONICS. Although soil in nature is necessary to anchor plants, provide nutrients and store water, it's possible to grow plants in a mostly liquid medium using soluble nutrients. However, it's not normally a good system for home gardeners because of the expense. The amount of plumbing you need, and the constant attention a hydroponic system demands, is time consuming and expensive for a home garden with one exception: a system of stackable styrofoam pots that nest together to create a tower 4 ft. high with 16 planting stations made by Hydro Harvest Farms, Ruskin, Florida.

COMPANION PLANTING- There is a lot said about 'companion planting' among vegetables with claims that certain varieties do well together and others do not, but there is no substantiation for these claims. I believe it was Ruth Stout who said she did not believe in companion planting, because "All my vegetable plants get along fine." Do not waste time studying lists showing what vegetables are good neighbors and which are bad. There are more important considerations to growing good vegetables like improving your soil. A widely read book on vegetable gardening has a section devoted to companion planting, but their advice is useless because they couch their statements in weasel words, for example: tomatoes *may* (my italics) benefit from parsley; and garlic planted near carrots *may* confuse the carrot fly. I don't want mays and maybes in gardening advice – I want facts by an author who has the experience and substantiation to back up his claims.

PLANTING BY THE PHASES OF THE MOON. My comments on companion planting can be said for planting by phases of the moon. There is simply no evidence that the moon has any effect on germination or seedling growth. Seeds simply need the correct amount of water, a suitable temperature and oxygen to germinate. Too much water will cause them to rot, too little will keep them dormant; too low or too high a temperature will also keep them dormant. Also, a compacted soil that deprives the embryo of oxygen is a primary cause of seeds failing to germinate. Give seeds the proper planting depth, a cool or warm soil temperature according to whether they are warm or cool season type, water (without drowning the seed) and you CAN'T STOP THEM FROM GERMINATING.

The cardinal rule in purchasing garden products – especially SEEDS – is to purchase only from reputable companies. Seeds, for example, all look the same whether they are freshly harvested or they are old and no longer viable. The best seed companies have test gardens where they not only evaluate varieties but invite the public to visit on open days. I also like to deal with seed companies that do some of their own seed production.

Carolyn's Comments:

"Derek looks at the world through the lens of his camera. Constantly he is seeking photogenic compositions whether we are in a park, out for a walk in the woods, visiting friends or travelling. I always enjoy helping him as a stylist. He used to travel with a bulky camera bag over his shoulder and loads of film, but in the new age of digital photography he needs no film and his favorite camera fits into a coat pocket. Photography is an important part of his livelihood, and it is his photography of plants and gardens that has made his garden books so successful in an age where visual impact is often valued more than the written word. But for all his recognition as a photographer, Derek still values the written word more. He gets more pleasure out of good writing than good photography and likes to explain that the 10 books that changed the word, such as Charles Darwin's Origin of Species and Thomas Pane's Common Sense, did not contain a photograph. One time I remember that the Garden Writers Association considered changing its name to the Garden Communicators Association, since some of its members were not writers, but managed websites or took photographs. The issue was controversial and two members were invited to give opposing arguments for a vote by the membership. They were Jeff Lowenthals, President of the Association and an attorney who favored the change, and Derek, who favored no change because he felt that good writing was still key to all kinds of communication. Derek's argument that the term Garden Writer earns more respect than Garden Communicator, and that every picture needs a caption, and every spoken claim often requires written substantiation, garnered 70% of the vote in his favor."

I'll Make You a Gardening Wizard Overnight!

CHAPTER 19
Recommended Reading

"I wrote my book, The Magic of Monet's Garden *because I thought
I could produce a better, more informative book than several that were
already in print, and when both the wife of the curator,
Mme Florence Van der Kemp and the head gardener, Mns. Gilbert Vahaye,
wrote complimenting me on my work, I believe I succeeded."*
– From my lecture, Monet's Garden

I confess to an addiction to good gardening books. I have never written a book because I thought the subject would make a lot of money. Rather, I write books because I believe the book is needed and I can do a better job than anything else on the market. Very few garden books enter the best selling lists. Few sell more than 25,000 copies. The majority sell 5,000 copies and less. Several of mine have sold more than 100,000 copies, and collectively I have sold more than two million books.

Gardening information is full of contradictions. One person will claim a particular deer repellent works; another will say it's useless. Very often there is a valid reason for the contradiction. As I point out in my chapter on pest control, deer are neophobic – (they have a fear of anything new) – and so naturally a plant new to a garden may be ignored for several years until suddenly the deer develop enough courage to try it, and then – bingo – the whole planting will disappear overnight. The same may be true of hanging strips of aluminum to fruit trees. The deer will avoid the strips because of their neophobia, but after a few seasons they overcome that fear, and the strips suddenly become ineffective.

GARDEN BOOKS FOR THE COMPOST PILE. There are a lot of books that should never be in print. I won't name them as there are hundreds, but I can tell you in general what books to avoid.

First, you should realize that many garden books sold in North America were written for another market altogether – usually British or Australian gardeners. Some American publishers are in the habit of making superficial changes to the text and calling them American gardening books for distribution through bookstores. It's not enough to take a book written for another country and climate and simply alter the text. For example, a recent book that purported to be a book of American vegetables was packaged in England and contained glaring omissions – no lima beans whatsoever (extremely important for American vegetable gardens), no peanuts, no soybeans, no cowpeas (a favorite Southern vegetable), no sweet potatoes, no okra for example - and an emphasis on varieties unavailable in the US, like King Edward potatoes and Excalibur runner beans. British born books on vegetable gardening also give poor or incomplete advice on growing warm season vegetables such as tomatoes, peppers and sweet corn, recommending brands of fertilizers and starter mixes not available to US gardeners, and using terminology alien to American gardeners, like calling Swiss chard silverbeets, eggplant aubergines, and arugula roquette.

The other kind of garden book to avoid is the 'sensational' tome, often illustrated with cartoons and icons so numerous the icons become confusing. The authors of these books generally make outrageous claims about home remedies, for example – using mouthwash to cure a pest problem, or birth control pills to fertilize house plants, or household ammonia as a fertilizer. Invariable, these claims have not been tested, and if they have been tested they have proven to be false. Moreover, the authors rarely explain why a particular household product works miracles on plants, or the dosage. "Whatever helps sell the book is justified," seems to be the creed of these 'sensationalists.'

I also avoid 'sponsored' books, like books with a familiar company name in the title, like a well-known chemical company or a seed company. These books receive tremendous distribution – especially through department stores and garden centers – but I want a book with information that is IMPARTIAL – not slanted towards a particular brand of garden chemicals or even a particular brand of seeds because no one company has the best selection for home gardeners.

BOOKS WORTH READING. Here are my top ten choices of favorite books. For the sake of brevity I have chosen books that are a pleasure to read and teach sound gardening practices, rather than overly illustrated coffee table-type books or books intended to be light hearted and humorous. Add these books to your library and you will accumulate knowledge beyond comparison. For a separate lists of the books I have authored see page 268.

Lasagna Gardening (Pat Lanza). The author tells me her soft cover black and white book has sold more than a million copies. It explains her no-dig system of gardening, by composting in layers (like making lasagna) in situ. To begin she instructs her readers to choose a site and lay down a thick carpet of newspapers to kill off turf and weeds down to bare soil, and then to build up a planting bed from garden and kitchen waste. This book won an award from the Garden Writers Association.

Square Foot Gardening (Mel Bartholomew). The original book is in black and white, 348 pages, soft cover and it is a classic. A revised version is in color, but I still prefer the original version. Mel promoted his small-space block planting system through a popular television show of the same name, and invited me three times to be a guest. He also explains how to grow flowers and vegetables without digging, and also NO FERTILIZING through the use of enriched commercial potting soil or making your own from his special formula. I don't quite buy the notion of using no topsoil and no fertilizing, but Mel's system has won a lot of admirers, and the book offers good practical advice that's easy to follow. It won an award from the Garden Writers Association.

Home Grown Vegetables, Fruits & Herbs (Jim Wilson and Walter Chandoha). Wilson succeeded me as executive director of All America Selections and left to host The Victory

Garden television show for many years. Chandoha is one of the most experienced vegetable gardeners I know and his color photography for the book is superb. The cultural information for variety selections is thorough, and a special chapter on Community Gardens makes this an instructional book for beginners. Wilson admits to not being completely convinced that organic gardening works, but Walter is 100% in favor of organic gardening, like me. Soft cover, 192 pages.

Four Seasons Harvest (Eliot Coleman) This soft cover 236-page book with black and white pages is 100% organic in its advice. Coleman has gardened for more than 40 years with his garden writer wife, Barbara Damrosch (see next listing). He describes how to extend the vegetable harvest year round even in the short growing season of coastal Maine. He shows how to make a moveable greenhouse that can be extended to cover hardy outdoor crops during severe weather, and high poly tunnels for growing not only salad crops but root crops of cool season vegetables. I visited the Colemans one autumn and admired their near self-sufficient lifestyle on a property that was once part of the Nearing estate, where the late Scott and Helen Nearing wrote their popular book on self-sufficient living, titled *Living the Good Life*. This is another book I urge you to read for its sound advice.

The Garden Primer (Barbara Damrosch) - On the cover of her soft cover, 820-page book carrying a basketful of fresh vegetables, the author looks far too young to be an expert vegetable gardener, but she has had almost as many years of hands-on experience as I have. The scope of The Garden Primer can be realized by the length of the index – 37 pages – showing where to find all kinds of reliable gardening information, from growing vegetables and lawns to flowers and tools. Like her husband's book (see previous listing) she is 100% organic, and resigned from the Garden Writers Association when they began endorsing garden products that were not organic.

Maine Farm (Stanley Joseph and Lynn Karlin) – Although this handsome full color volume, with 250 inspirational photographs by Karlin, has been long out of print it is still available from second hand sources on the internet. The authors were influenced by their neighbors, the Scott Nearings, to establish a largely self-sufficient lifestyle on a farm on the Maine coast. Eventually the marriage dissolved and Joseph killed himself, but the book is one of a kind, in hardcover, beautifully written to explain the couple's gardening methods and skills at making traditional arts and crafts for a livelihood.

Edible Landscaping (Roslyn Creasy)- The author, whose incredibly beautiful courtyard and front yard garden I have visited, lives near San Francisco. She made using vegetables for decorative effect popular. I can hardly wait to see her soon-to-be released revision of the original which is soft cover and 380 pages. I especially admire Roslyn's suggestions for visually interesting companion plantings and the use of colorful vegetables like Bright Lights chard and ornamental kale in containers. I wish there was a location in North America as impressive as the Chateau de Villandry, France. This historic estate in the Loire Valley uses vegetables for stunning ornamental effect among intricate parterre beds. Tens of thousands of visitors visit Villandry every year from spring through fall, and few realize that a table on the way out features freshly picked vegetables from the garden, free for visitors to take away. I never saw such fava beans – pods up to 18 inches long, and meaty beans that are delicious. Roslyn's book won an award from the Garden Writers Association.

The Encyclopedia of Herbs & Their Uses (Deni Brown) – My favorite among numerous books about herb gardening. Although written with a British bias the listings are comprehensive and the photography superb. Here you will find descriptions for more varieties of basil than you ever dreamed possible, plus numerous lavenders and mints, and off-beat herbs like licorice, decorative pineapple sage and scented geraniums that impart a variety of fragrances and aromas from coconut to attar of roses.

Melons for the Passionate Gardener (Amy Goldman) – This and her more recent books, The Heirloom Tomato and Heirloom Squash are a beautiful presentation of colorful and often bizarre heirloom varieties with exquisite descriptions, sensitively photographed by Victor Shrager. I saw her lecture about heirloom tomatoes and she is a strong advocate of organic gardening (also a director of the Seed Savers Exchange)

The Pocket Vegetable Expert (Dr. David G. Hessayon) - I met the author at the Royal Automobile Club in London during a reception by the British Booksellers Association who had chosen one of his books and one of mine (*Renoir's Garden*) for special recognition as a Christmas gift. Collectively, his books on all aspects of gardening have sold more books worldwide than any other person. Small in size, but packed with extremely useful information and beautiful illustrations, there is nothing like them for handy reference. His vegetable book is 128 pages, with soft covers and although Hessayon is British, and the text has a British slant, I think it's one of the best book bargains around.

MY PUBLISHED WORK. Following is a list of the publications I have authored since I began garden writing in the 1960's. This list is in addition to numerous wall calendars, art posters and greeting cards. Two asterisks indicate an award winner. The earlier works are out of print but copies can still be purchased second hand over the internet.

Countryside Series of Pocket Garden Books (1974-76). Handy inexpensive reference books on a range of popular subjects, including Greenhouse Gardening, Ferns, Bulbs, Annuals, Begonias, House Plants and other topics.

The White House Vegetable Garden (Exposition Press, 1976). My involvement with a task force to plant a vegetable garden at the White House during the Ford Administration. The text includes a position paper I wrote as chairman of the task force, explaining how home gardening would benefit the farmer, in order to enlist the support of the USDA who initially believed that the American farmer was better able to feed America.

House Plants for Fun & Profit (Countryside Press, 1978). A manual for home gardeners interesting in growing house plants and making crafts to sell for a profit.

How to Photograph Flowers, Plants & Landscapes (HP Books 1980). Instructions on how to photograph horticultural subjects for publication and how to sell the work.

Vegetables, How to Select, Grow and Enjoy (HP Books, 1982). Focus on growing vegetables for home gardeners.

Annuals – How to Select, Grow & Enjoy (HP Books, 1983). Focus on growing annuals for home gardens

Deerfield – An American Garden through Four Seasons (Pidcock Press, 1986). A souvenir book of the late H. Thomas Hallowell's beautiful private garden near Philadelphia.

Trees & Shrubs (HP Books, 1986). A focus on shrubs and trees for home landscapes.

Garden Accents (Henry Holt, 1987). A presentation of garden ornaments and furnishings to improve home gardens.

The One-Minute Gardener (Running Press, 1988). Flower and vegetable gardening made easy through mulching to deter weeds and soaker hoses to water gardens automatically.

Home Landscaping (Simon & Schuster, 1988). A treasury of garden design ideas for home gardeners to improve the appearance of their properties.

Discover Anguilla (Caribbean Concepts 1988). A souvenir book presenting the tourist attractions of Anguilla.

Azaleas, Camellias & Rhododendrons (Ortho Books, 1989). A focus on the three popular families of flowering shrubs, a joint authorship.

The Complete Garden Planning Manual (HP Books, 1989). How to design a pleasant garden space and enhance the value of a property, a joint authorship.

Ornamental Grass Gardening (HP Books, 1989). A focus on the best ornamental grasses for home gardens, a joint authorship.

A Three Year Garden Journal (Starwood, 1989). A day book for gardeners, and a joint authorship.

A Kid's First Gardening Book (Running Press 1989). A book of fun gardening projects for children.

Essential Shrubs (Crown 1990). A focus on hardy shrubs suitable for the home gardener.

Essential Perennials (Crown, 1990). A focus on perennials suitable for home gardens.

Essential Herbs (Crown 1990). A focus on herbs suitable for home gardens.

Essential Bulbs (Crown 1990). A focus on flowering bulbs suitable for home gardens.

Essential Annuals (Crown 1990). A focus on annuals for the home gardener.

Essential Roses (Crown 1990). A focus on roses for the home gardener.

The Essential Gardener (Crown, 1990). A compendium of all the books in the Essentials series.

The Easiest Flowers to Grow (Ortho Books, 1990). A presentation of easy-care annuals, biennials, and perennials.

Renoir's Garden (Simon & Schuster, 1991). A visit to the restored garden of the great Impressionist artist and how it was an extension of his art.

****Beautiful Bucks County*** (Cedaridge Press, 1991). A souvenir book for tourists of Bucks County, Pennsylvania.

550 Home Landscaping Ideas (Simon & Schuster, 1992). Designs for home gardeners to improve the appearance and value of their properties, a joint authorship.

The Encyclopedia of Ornamental Grasses (Rodale, 1992) A presentation of the most useful grasses for home gardens, a joint authorship.

550 Perennial Garden Ideas (Simon & Schuster, 1993). Designs for home gardeners using flowering perennials.

Fell's Floral Encyclopedia (Smithmark, 1993). A presentation of the most useful annuals, biennials and perennials for home gardens.

Garden Guide, Annuals (Smithmark, 1993). Focus on growing annuals for home gardens.

Garden Guide, Perennials (Smithmark, 1993). Focus on growing perennials for home gardens.

Garden Guide, Roses (Smithmark, 1993). Focus on growing roses for home gardens.

Garden Guide, Bulbs (Smithmark). Focus on growing flowering bulbs for home gardens.

The Impressionist Garden (Crown, 1994). A look at gardens of the great French Impressionist painters and how their gardens were an extension of their art, including Monet, Renoir, Cezanne, Caillebotte, Pissaro, Manet, Van Gogh and others.

Flowering Shrubs & Small Trees (Friedman/Fairfax, 1995). Focus on hardy trees and shrubs suitable for home landscapes, a joint authorship.

The Pennsylvania Gardener (Camino Books, 1995). A regional gardening guide.

Gardens of Philadelphia & the Delaware Valley (Temple University Press, 1995). Focus on mostly gardens open to the public, a joint authorship.

Practical Gardening (Friedman/Fairfax, 1995). Essentials of home gardening, a joint authorship.

Shade Gardening (Spring Hill Nurseries, 1996). How to grow in the shade.

Sun Gardening (Spring Hill Nurseries, 1996). How to grow in the sun.

Rose Gardening (Spring Hill Nurseries, 1997). How to grow roses.

Perennial Gardening (Spring Hill Nurseries, 1997). How to grow perennials.

Secrets of Monet's Garden (Friedman/Fairfax, 1997). A visit to Claude Monet's restored garden in Giverny, France. The book reveals the 100 unique planting schemes he used to create what he considered his greatest work of art.

Derek Fell's Water Gardening (Friedman/Fairfax, 1998). How to create a beautiful water garden for a home landscape.

Derek Fell's Shade Gardening (Friedman/Fairfax, 1998). How to create beautiful shade gardens.

Derek Fell's Herb Gardening (Friedman/Fairfax, 1998). How to create beautiful and productive herb gardens.

Derek Fell's Bulb Gardening (Friedman/Fairfax, 1998). How to create beautiful flowering bulb gardens through four seasons.

Impressionist Bouquets (Friedman/Fairfax, 1998). A look at the paintings by famous Impressionist painters and their still life arrangements, and how to re-create them at home.

Let's Investigate Cacti (The Creative Company, 1999). A book for children to learn about the remarkable world of cacti.

Let's Investigate Orchids (The Creative Company, 1999). A book for children to learn about the fascinating world of orchids.

Let's Investigate Herbs (The Creative Company, 1999). A book for children about the wondrous world of herbs.

Let's Investigate Wildflowers (The Creative Company, 1999). A book for children about the colorful world of wildflowers.

Impressionist Roses (Friedman/Fairfax, 1999). A look at the heirloom roses grown or painted by the famous French Impressionist painters like Renoir and Monet.

**Van Gogh's Gardens* (Simon & Schuster, 2000). A visit to gardens that the painter, Van Gogh painted and a look at his gardening philosophy. This book won three awards from the Garden Writers Association, including best writing, best photography and best book.

Herb Gardening for Beginners (Friedman/Fairfax, 2001). How to create a successful herb garden

Water Gardening for Beginners (Friedman/Fairfax, 2001). How to create small-space water gardens.

**A Photographer's Garden Desk Diary (Kodak, 2002). A pictorial photo presentation of the author's garden, Cedaridge Farm.

Campbell Island – Land of the Blue Sunflowers (David Bateman). A souvenir book presenting the rich flora and fauna of a remote Sub-antarctic island.

**Great Gardens of New Zealand (David Bateman, 2003). A visit to the country's most beautiful private gardens open to the public.

Cezanne's Garden (Simon & Schuster, 2004). A visit to the restored garden of this famous Impressionist painter, and an explanation of his garden philosophy.

The Encyclopedia of Hardy Plants (David Bateman 2007). Focus on hardy annuals, perennials, trees and shrubs suitable for zones 6 and colder.

The Magic of Monet's Garden (Firefly 2007). A visit to Claude Monet's restored garden at Giverny, France and an emphasis on the color harmonies, shimmering effects and plants that the gardeners use today to make the garden authentic.

The Encyclopedia of Garden Design & Structures (David Bateman, 2009). An alphabetic featuring of all the design elements that contribute to a creative home garden landscape.

The Gardens of Frank Lloyd Wright (Frances Lincoln, 2009). Focus on the gardens of the great architect, especially his summer home, Taliesin (Wisconsin), his winter home, Taliesin West (Arizona) and his greatest private commission, Fallingwater (Pennsylvania).

Carolyn's Comments:

"Derek has written a lot of garden books and he has helped a lot of aspiring authors get published. His most valuable resource is a library of more than 150,000 images of plants and gardens. He has also helped a lot of garden photographers get establishing, never feeling insecure about possibly setting himself up with a future competitor. He gives advice freely and enjoys spirited debate about art and photography. He reads a lot in libraries and bookstores and has a large book collection, many of the works with a letter from the author taped to the inside front cover, for when he admires a book he often writes to the author to say so. Frequently the author will respond with some interesting particulars about the book. He has also collaborated with a lot of experts on producing books whenever he felt a book project needed a second person's input, for he is a great believer in the axiom that two heads are better than one. When Derek finishes a manuscript he's not content to send it to the publisher until several people – whose opinions he respects – have read it first and given him feedback. He thrives on criticism. Derek is also lucky to have a very good agent – Albert Zuckerman, president of The Writers House, New York. Al has given him very good advice over the years."

CONCLUSION

My objective has been to show you how to grow HEALTHY produce without resorting to chemicals, how to increase YIELDS through variety selection and organically sound growing techniques, and how to SAVE MONEY by being able to grow fresh vegetables through four seasons; and if you are so inclined, to sell your surplus produce.

These nineteen chapters cover the most popular vegetables, herbs and fruits, involving less space and less work than you might have thought possible. Remember that it is the SOIL that is the foundation of a productive plot. The ability of plants to produce abundant yields, giant sizes and to resist pests and diseases starts with a fertile, well drained soil in full sun.

Variety selection is also paramount. One of the advantages of lecturing and travelling to all areas of the US and abroad, is to see varieties perform in a range of climates, and to receive valuable recommendations from other experienced gardeners.

It's quite possible, by following my advice, that you will grow more vegetables than you and your family can consume. Don't let anything go to waste. Locally, there are places to feed the hungry. The website Plant a Row for the Hungry, sponsored by the Garden Writers Association, will tell you how to do so.

Also remember that two ways to consume the right amount of vegetables for a healthy body are to eat lots of fresh salads AND to make a hearty vegetable soup. The soup you can freeze to consume during winter months.

More homeowners should start a compost pile. Think of the tons of kitchen waste that can be converted to a nutritious soil amendment instead of ending up on a dump. Garden residue that you can't eat, like fallen leaves, grass clippings, and spent stalks should be used to make a compost.

It really works!

Derek Fell
Cedaridge Farm

I'll Make You a Gardening Wizard Overnight!

APPENDIX: SOURCES

"You cannot tell quality seeds simply by looking at them, so know your sources."
- from my book, **Vegetables - How to Select, Grow & Enjoy** (Criabooks.com)

I know most of the leading sources for seeds, nursery stock and transplants. During my years with the seed industry I would visit seed trials worldwide and meet seedsmen and nurserymen from all the main mail order companies. The industry isn't what it used to be. Then, seed and nursery companies were largely family owned businesses, handed down from one generation to another. I met Joe Harris, then president of Harris Seeds, and John Stokes, head of Stokes Seeds, and William Park, head of Park Seeds and Otis Twilley who founded Twilley Seeds and died when a roof he was putting up at his residence collapsed on him. Each summer, these innovators would congregate at a barbecue, prior to a tour of trial gardens, cook t-bone steaks and feast on Ambrosia cantaloupe, Big Boy tomatoes, Golden Bantam sweet corn and seedless watermelons. We were all competitors, but friendly.

Conglomerates now own many of the breeding companies, and the emphasis has changed, but there are still enough family owned businesses out there quietly doing their own breeding work for the home garden market. Here's a list of some of my favorite sources for seeds, plants and miscellaneous supplies:

VEGETABLE SEEDS & PLANTS

Baker Creek Heirloom Seeds
2278 Baker Creek Road
Mansfield, MO 65704
(417) 924-8917
Rareseeds.com
Specializing in heirlooms and non-patented open pollinated varieties.

W. Atlee Burpee Co.
300 Park Avenue
Warminster, PA 18974
(800) 333-5808
Burpee.com
Large selection of seeds and plants, many exclusive.

The Cook's Garden
PO Box 5030
Warminster, PA 18974
Cooksgarden.com
Specializes in salad green varieties and lettuce mixes, many from European sources.

Dixondale Farms
PO Box 129
Carrizo Springs, TX 78834
(877) 367-1015
Dixondalefarms.com
Specialists in onion plants.

Dominion Seed House
Box 2500
Georgetown, Ontario L7G 5LS
Canada
(800) 784-3037
Specialists in vegetables suitable for Canada

Gardeners Choice
81961 County Road 687 South
Hartford, MI 49057-8000
(269) 621-2481
Gardenerschoice.com
Specialists in selling plants for giant vegetables and unusual fruit trees

Gurney Seed & Nursery Co.
PO Box 4178
Greendale, IN 47025-4178

Gurneys.com
(513) 354-1491
Large selection of seeds, plants and supplies.

Harris Seeds
355 Paul Road
Rochester, NY 14624
(800) 544-7938
Harrisseeds.com
Vegetable seed specialists, many bred on their farm.

Johnny's Selected Seeds
955 Benton avenue
Winslow, ME 04901
(877) 564-6697
Johnnyseeds.com
Specialists in growing seeds organically, and vegetable breeders.

J. W. Jung Seed Co.
335 South High Street
Randolph, WI 53957-4162
(800) 287-3123
Jungseed.com
Large selection of vegetable seeds and supplies

Nichols Garden Nursery
1190 Old Salem Road NE
Albany, OR 97321
(800) 422-3985
Nicholsgardennursery.com
Specialists in herbs and heirloom seeds

George W. Park Seed Co
1 Parkton Avenue
Greenwood, SC 29647
(800) 213-0076
Parkseed.com
Large selection of vegetables, many exclusive

Pinetree Garden Seeds
PO Box 300
New Gloucester, ME 04260
(207) 926-3400

Superseeds.com
Large selection of vegetable seeds at low costs

Seed Savers Exchange
3994 North Winn Road
Decorah, IA 56101
(563) 382-5990
Seedsavers.org
Specialists in offering heirloom seeds and non-patented open pollinated varieties

Seeds of Change
(888) 762-7333
Seedsofchange.com
Specialists in organically grown seeds and plants

R. H. Shumway
334 West Stroud Street
Randolph, WI 53957-4162
(800) 342-9461
Rhshumway.com
Large selection of heirloom and other vegetable seeds

W. Robinson & Son
Sunny Bank
Forton
Nr Preston
Lancashire PR3 0BN
UK
info@mammothonion.co.uk
Specialists in seeds for giant vegetables.

Stokes Seeds Inc
PO Box 538
Buffalo, NY 14240
(800) 396-9238
Stokeseeds.com
Wide selection of vegetable seeds with extensive trial gardens in Canada

Territorial Seed Company
PO Box 158
Cottage Grove, OR 97424
(800) 626-0866

Territorialseed.com
Specialists in vegetable seed for the Pacific Northwest

Thompson & Morgan
PO Box 4086
Lawrenceburg, IN 47025
(800) 274-7333
Tmseeds.com
US branch of a British seed company that once sold seeds to Claude Monet and Charles Darwin

Tomato Growers Supply Co
PO Box 60015
Fort Myers, FL 33906
(888) 478-7333
Tomatogrowers.com
Offers more than 500 varieties of tomato, pepper and eggplant seeds

Totally Tomatoes
334 West Shroud Street
Randolph, WI 53956
(800) 345-5977
Totallytomato.com
Specialists in the supply of tomato seed

Vesey's Seeds Ltd
PO Box 9000
Calais, ME 04619
(800) 363-7333
Veseys.com
Specialists in vegetable seeds for northern climates

FRUITS & BERRIES

Aaron's Nursery
PO Box 800
Sumner, GA 31789
Aaronsfarm.com
Fruits and berries for the south

Adams County Nursery
26 Nursery Road
Aspers, PA 17304
(717) 677-8105
Acnursery.com

Fruit-tree.com Nursery
19132 SW Neugebauer Road
Hillsboro, OR 97123-9464
Fruit-tree.com

Hartmann's Plant Company
310 60th Street
Grand Junction, MI 49056
(269) 253-4457
Hartmannsplantcompany.com
Specialists in blueberry bushes

Miller Nurseries
5060 West Lake Road
Canandaigua, NY 14424
(800) 836-9630
Millernurseries.com
Specialists in apples, peach, grapes and other fruits

Raintree Nursery
391 Butts Road
Morton, WA 98807
(360) 496-6400
Specialist in fruit trees
Raintreenursery.com

Stark bros Nurseries & Orchards
PO Box 1800
Louisianna, MO 63353
(800) 325-4180
Starkbros.com
Extensive listings of apples, peaches, grapes and other fruits

GARDEN SUPPLIES

BioWorks Inc
1100 Rawson Road
Victor, NY 14564
(800) 877-9443
Bioworks.com
Suppliers of biofungicides

CompostTumbler
1834 Freedom Road
Lancaster, PA 17601
(800) 880-2345
Compostumber.com

A compost system that can make useable compost in 14 days.

Gardens Alive
51 Schenley Place
Lawrenceberg, IN 47025
(513) 354-1482
Gardensalive.com
Organically friendly pest controls and other garden products

Kinsman Company
PO Box 428
Pipersville, PA 18947
(800) 733-4146
Kinsmangarden.com
Suppliers of container gardening and vertical gardening systems

Monterey Lawn & Garden Products
PO Box 35000
Fresno, CA 93745
(559) 499-2100
Organic lawn and garden pest controls

Nitron
Fayetteville, AK
(800) 835-0123
GardenIQ.com
Suppliers of organic fertilizers

Skyscraper Gardens
The Cedar Store
5410 Route 8
Gibsonia, PA 15044
(888) 293-2339
Cedarstore.com
Suppliers of vertical gardens and other garden structures made from Western red cedar

Spray-N-Grow
PO Box 2137
Rockport, TX 78382
(800) 323-2363
Suppliers of organic fertilizers

ASSOCIATIONS

American Community Gardening Association
1777 East Broad Street
Columbus, OH 43202
(877) 275-2242
Communitygarden.org
Promoters of community gardens

Feeding America
35 East Wacker Drive
Chicago, IL 60601
(800) 7711-2303
Feedingamerica.org
Large domestic hunger-relief charity

Green Education Foundation
1412 North Street
Walpole, MA 02081
(888) 668-2298
Greeneducationfoundation.org
Promotes school education programs for children

National Gardening Association
1100 Dorset Street
South Burlington, VT 05403
(802) 863-5251
Provides grants to schools and community groups for children's gardening education

Plant-a-Row-for-the-Hungry
10210 Leatherleaf Court
Manassas, VA 220111
(703) 257-1032
Gardenwriters.org
Administration for the Plant a Row hunger relief program

I'll Make You a Gardening Wizard Overnight!

INDEX

Acorn squash, Ace, xi
Activator, 50
African violets, 245
Agri-chemical industry, 2
Air layering, 255, 259
Alaska, 4
Alaska State Fair, 88, 110
Alkalinity, 6, 29
All America Selections, x, xi, 61, 87106, 110, 117, 121, 134, 135, 151, 152, 164, 175, 266
All season harvest, 219
Allegheny mountains, 4
Almond, 232
Aloe vera, 190
Altzheimer's disease, 2
Aluminum foil, 6
Amaryllis, blue, 87
American Community Gardening Association, 184
American Seed Trade Association, 36
Amish, 3, 48
Ammonia, 261
Angel's trumpet, Charles Grimaldi, 245
Anise, 2, 190
Anise hyssop, 190
Antheus, 49
Anthracnose, 85
Anti-oxidants, 94, 168
Aphids, 35, 79, 82
Apple, 219, 242, 255
Apple, Bramley's Seedling, 219
Apple, Fuji
Apple, Golden Delicious, 221
Apple, Granny Smith, 223, 251
Apple, Honeycrisp, 220, 223
Apple, Jumbo, 221, 223
Apple, Red Delicious, 221
Arbors, 25
Arches, 25
Architectural Digest, 32, 71, 184
Arctic, 4

Arkansas, 3
Aromatherapy, 216
Artichokes, 10, 94, 100
Artichoke Green Globe, 95
Arugula, 95, 100
Ascutaquash, 149
Asparagus, 75, 96, 178
Asparagus beans, 106
Asparagus, Jersey Giant, 96
Asparagus Purple Passion, 97, 100
Associated Press, 139
Assyrians, 61
Australia, 152, 265
Australian tree fern, 245
Avocado, 254, 257
Babylonians, 61
Back pack sprayer, 40
Bacteria, 69, 84
Bailey, Dick, 138
Ball Seed Company, 136
Bamboo, 25, 41
Banana, 241, 245 249
Banana skins, 51
Baobab tree, 184
Bartholomew, Mel, 8, 9, 65, 266
Basil, 2, 187, 194, 242, 244
Bat guano, 50
Bath tub, 242
Bean, bush snap, 2, 67
Bean, bush Romano, 99, 100
Bean, edible soybean, 2, 178
Bean, Excalibur runner, 265
Bean, fava, 79, 178
Bean, hyacinth, 74, 76
Beans, Lima, 2, 178
Bean Lima, King of the Garden, 98
Bean, Navy, 106
Bean, pole, 25
Bean, pole Blue Lake, 98
Bean, pole Lazy Wife, 63, 99
Bean, pole Romano, 21 98
Bean, red Kidney, 106
Bean wig wam, 256

Bean, Wren's Egg, 106
Bean, Yard long, 178
Bee, mason, 233
Bee skip, 191
Bees, 233, 252
Beets, 107
Beet Burpee's Golden, 103, 107, 178
Beet, Chiogga, 107
Beet, Cylindra, 103, 107
Beet mixture, 178
Beneficial insects, 82
Beta carotene, 168
Better Boy hybrid tomato, 89
Bevin, Lawrence, 109, 122, 135
Big Boy tomato, x
Big Rainbow tomato, 92
Bill's Perfect Fertilizer, 52, 70
Bismarck palm, 245
Black figs, 32
Blackberries, 178, 223, 255, 258
Blackberry, Thornfree, 222
Black-eyed beans, 102
Black plastic, 177
Black walnut, 76
Block planting, 14
Blood meal, 50
Blood sugar, 2
Blossom end rot, 85, 158
Blue Lake snap bean, 67
Blueberries, 2, 178, 224
Blueberry, Blueray, 224, 227
Blueberry Hill Inn, 215, 217
Bone meal, 41, 51, 69
Bones, 76
Books by Derek Fell, 268
Borage, 206
Borers, 82, 223
Bottom heat, 58
Boxwood, 186
Brand names, 92
Bright Lights chard, xi, 267
Britain's Best Seed Catalog Contest, x

British Isles, 4, 265
Broccoli, 108
Broccoli, Green Comet, 108
Broccoli, Premium Crop, 103, 108
Broccoli, Romanesco, 105, 108
Brown, Deni, 268
Brussels sprouts, 29, 79, 109
Brussels sprouts, Jade Cross, 104, 109
BT (Bacillus thuringensis), 81, 93, 108
Bucket, 41
Burbank, Luther, x, 87, 130, 159
Burns, Robert, 79
Burpee, David, x, 123, 159
Burpee Seeds, 63, 130
Butterbeans, 97
Buttercrunch lettuce, 14
Buttermilk, 261
Butternut, 232
Byrd, Bill, 63, 99
Cabbage, 1, 54, 110
Cabbage, OS Cross, 110, 111, 253
Cabbage, Red Head, 116
Cabbage, Savoy Ace, 104, 116
Cabbage, Savoy King, xi
Cabbage, Stonehead, 104, 110
Cabbage worms, 83
Calcium, 69, 85
Calendula, 206
Calendula salve, 215
Caliche, 6
California, 4
Cherries, 224
Campbell Island, 184
Cantaloupe rinds, 51
Cantaloupe, Ambrosia, 126
Cape gooseberry, 162
Cardin, Pierre, xii
Carnations, 205
Carter, President Jimmy, 33
Carrot, 29, 116
Carrot, Chantenay Red Cored, 117
Carrot, Kaleidoscope, 117
Carrot mixture, 178
Carrot, Nantes, 117, 124
Carrot, Scarlet Wonder, 117
Caucusus Mountain, 1
Cauldron, 239
Cauliflower, 117, 124
Cauliflower, Snow Crown, 124

Cavitt, Dick, 175
Cedar bark, 41
Cedaridge Farm, iii, xii, 5, 7, 16, 25, 43, 47, 71, 174, 179, 189, 239
Cedaridge South, xii
Celeriac, 117, 124
Celery, 118
Celery, Golden Self-blanching, 118, 124
Certified organic, 177
Chamomile, 196, 215
Chandoha, Walt, 266
Chateau Eze, 234
Chayote, 118
Chard, 29, 244, 267
Chard mixture, 178
Chelsea Physic Garden, 47
Chemical controls, 2
Chemical fertilizer, 8, 48, 49
Chemical-free vegetables, 6
Chervil, 194
Chia pets, 256
Chestnut, Chinese, 233
Cherries, 223
Cherry, Stella, 224, 228
Chervil, 197
Chesapeake Bay, 35
Chicago Flower Show, 122
Chinese vegetables, 177
Children's gardens, 251
Chitting, 59
Chives, 2, 187, 194, 206, 214, 242, 258
Churchville Giant Pumpkin Contest, 138
Cilantro, 194, 202
Cinder blocks, 25
Citrus rinds, 55
Clay, 7, 54, 77
Clean-up, 68
Climbing plants, 18, 27
Coco fiber, 240, 242
Coconut palms, 4
Coffee grounds, 51, 55, 65
Coleman, Eliot, 267
Coleus, Saber, 241
Collard greens, 104, 116
Colorado potato beetle, 82
Companion planting, 262
Compost, 6, 8, 10, 35, 48, 49, 50, 52, 74, 176, 273
Compost, commercial, 52
Compost bin, 41, 47, 53
Compost materials, 50, 51

Compost tea, 52
Compost Tumbler, 53
Community garden, 183
Container, 239, 240, 241
Container Gardening, 240, 244
Cook's Garden, The, 121
Cordon, 24
Coriander, 187, 202
Corn earworm, 83
Corn salad, 118
Corn salad, Bistro, 119, 125
Corn smut, 151
Corn stalks, 51
Cornell, John, 138
Cornell Pumpkin Contest, 139
Cornell University, 144
Country Gentleman sweet corn, 92
Courgettes, 149
Cow manure, 41
Crab meal, 35
Crabgrass, 51
Crane, Oliver, 130
Crawford, Pamela, 240
Creasy, Rosalind, 10, 267
Cress, 258
Cress, American, 164
Crop rotation, 54
Cucumber, 20, 54, 119, 178
Cucumber beetle, 84
Cucumber, Burpee Hybrid, 119
Cucumber, indoors, 246
Cucumber, Lemon, 119, 125
Cucumber, Orient Express, 120
Cucumber, Salad Bush, 120
Cucumber, Snake, 119
Cucumber, Tall Telegraph, 119
Cucumber, Yard Long, 119
Currants, 224
Cuttings, 255
Cutworms, 83
Damrosch, Barbara, 267
Darwin, Charles, 134, 263
Deer control, 40, 80, 81, 85, 239, 265
Delaware Valley Agricultural College, 160
Delaware River, 31, 43
deVenzio, Dick, 18
Diatomaceous earth, 81
Dill, 187, 194
Dinghy planter, 242
Disease control, 79, 84
Dolichos lablab, 74
Domain Botanical Garden, 37

INDEX

Dorrian-Smith, Robert, 32
Double dig, 8
Doylestown Merchants' Association, 179
Drainage, 6
Drake Hotel, 122
Drip irrigation, 176
Edible flowers, 205
Eggs, 51
Earliness, 88
Earthworms, 54
Easter egg plant, 257
Eaton, John, 152
Echinacea, 194
Ecuador, 1
Earthworms, 48
Earthworm castings, 51
Edible Landscape garden, 10, 11
Edible Landscaping, 267
Egghead, 258
Eggplant, 83, 120
Eggplant, Black beauty
Eggplant, Dusky Hybrid, 120, 125
Ellison, Dr Howard, 96
Encyclopedia Britannica, 71
Encyclopedia of Herbs and their Uses, 268
Epsom salts, 262
Espalier, 24, 76
Evans, John, 110
Example vegetable and fruit garden, 76
Extension service, 85
Family Food Garden, 99
Farmers markets, 177, 179, 182
Fava beans, 76
Feathers, 51
Fennel, 121, 125
Fertilizer, 47, 50, 68, 69, 176, 241
Fertilizer, timed release, 73
Field, Xenia, 106
Figs, 234, 245, 255, 259
Filbert, 233
Filbert, Casina, 233
Findhorn Community, 185
First Lady, 2
Fish emulsion, 51 176
Fish scraps, 51
Fiskeby edible soy bean, xi, 103, 106
Flavorful vegetables, 165
Flea beetle, 83, 120

Floating row covers, 79
Florida, 4
Flower & Garden Photography, 71
Flower Gardening, 244
Flusser, Alan, xii
Food Factory, 12, 13
Ford White House vegetable garden, 2, 33, 35
Fordhook Farm, x, 123
Fordhook zucchini squash, x
Foundation plantings, 28, 29
Four Seasons Harvest, 267
Free plants, 255
FreezePruf Protector, 60
Freezing, 170
Frequently asked questions, 74
Frost dates, 4
Frost protection, 59, 60, 75
Fruit trees, 77, 241
Fungi, 84
Fungicide, 40
Galetta, Dr Gene, 231
Gallup Jr, George, 3
Garden books, 265
Garden budget, 41
Garden cart, 39
Garden Design, 44
Garden fork, 41
Garden gloves, 41
Garden hoe, 41
Garden hose, 40, 41
Garden myths, 261
Garden Primer, The, 267
Garden rake, 41
Garden remedies, 261
Garden shovel, 41
Garden Writers Association, xi, 33, 37, 184, 263, 273
Gardeners Question Time, 74
Garlic, 2, 55, 195, 79, 198
Garlic chives, 199, 195
Garlic spray, 81, 83
Garlic-pepper spray, 40
Gauguin, Paul, xii
Genetically modified seed, 93
Geranium, scented leaf, 195, 242
Germander, 186
Germination, 263
Germination test, 252
Giant vegetables, 53, 88, 253
Gillman, Jeff, 261
Ginger, 195, 200
Ginseng, 201, 202

GMO seed, 93
Golden Bantam sweet corn, x, 63
Golden beets, x
Goldman, Amy, 92, 123, 268
Goldsmith, Glenn, 62
Good Gardeners Association, 3, 8, 81
Google, 92
Goose Cove Lodge, 218
Gooseberries, 224
Gourds, 25
Government grants, 181
Government Printing Office, 170
Government subsidies, 183
Graft, 255
Granular feed, 69
Grape, Cayuga, 247, 249
Grape, Concord, 249
Grape, Fredonia, 249
Green Education Foundation, 41
Green manure, 53, 54
Greensand, 35, 51
Grow Light, 246
Gulf of Mexico, 4
Haggis, 79
Hand fork, 41
Hand trowel, 41
Haney, Dale, 34
Hanging baskets, 241, 244
Hardiness zones, 4
Harris, Joe, 275
Harris Seeds, 275
Hastie, J. Drayton, 43, 44
Hastings Seed Co, 62
Hazel nut, 233
Hazelnut, Barcelona, 233
Heating mat, 58
Heirloom Squash, The, 268
Heirloom Tomato, The, 268
Heirloom varieties, 92, 178
Henderson, Peter Seed Co, 98
Herb garden, 5, 187, 185, 188, 190, 191, 241
Herb garden design, 186
Herb garden, Colonial quadrant, 185, 188, 189
Herb infused oils, 215
Herb knot garden, 186, 187
Herbal soaps, 216
Herbal vinegars, 216, 217
Herbs, cooking, 2, 187, 245, 246

Herbs, dried, 193
Herbs, preserving, 187
Herbs, useful, 187
Hercules, 49, 255
Hessayon, Dr David G., 268
HGTV, 32
Hibiscus, 205, 245
Hobby gardening, 181
Hobby Greenhouse Association, 245
Holmberg, Swen, 106
Home canning, 170
Home Grown Vegetables, Fruits & Herbs, 266
Honey & Pearls, 63
Horseradish, 202
Horticulture, 3
Horticultural fleece, 4, 60, 79, 177, 232
Howard's End, 74
Hubacek, Steve, 110
Humus, 49
Hurst Seeds, x, 109, 122, 135
Hybrid seed, 60, 61, 62, 177
Hydra, 255
Hydroponics, 262
Iceberg lettuce, x
Impatiens, New Guinea, 241
Impressionist gardens, 184
Indoor harvests, 245
Innoculant, 40
Insect control, 79, 84
Insect traps, 82
Insecticidal oil, 81
Insecticidal soap, 81, 177
Intercropping, 31
IRS, 181
Irrigation, 41, 70
Irrigro, 70
Isles of Scilly, 32
Japan, 4
Japanese beetles, 35, 81, 83
Johnny's Seeds, 152, 177
Johnson, Rob, 152
Joseph, Stanley, 218, 267
Kale, 29, 116, 244
Karlin, Lynn, 218, 267
Kass, Sam, 34
Kelp meal, 51
Key West, 4
Kilbride, Bert, 71
King of the Garden lima bean, 19, 101
Kinsman Company, 239, 240, 244

Kinsman, Graham and Michelle, 239
Kiwi fruit, 32, 225
Kiwi, Arctic, 229
Kiwi, New Zealand, 229
Kiwi vine, 228, 259
Klein, Calvin, xii
Known-You Seed Company, 165
Kohl-rabi, 121
Kruger National Park, 184
Ladybugs, 35, 82
Lamb's lettuce, 118
Lanza, Pat, 8, 9, 266
Lasagna garden, 8, 9
Lasagna Gardening, 266
Lateral growth, 53
Lavender, 202, 206, 207, 215
Lavender cotton, 186
Lawn, 10
Laughman, John, 151
Lazy Wife bean, 60, 92
Leafhoppers. 84
Leeks, 29, 121
Leeks, Titan, 126
Lemon balm, 187, 203, 208
Lemon grass, 203
Lemons, 255
Lettuce, 15, 17, 32 35, 62, 121, 122, 242
Lettuce, Bibb, 122
Lettuce, Black-seeded Simpson, 122, 123
Lettuce, Buttercrunch, 122, 126, 178
Lettuce, Deer Tongue, 122
Lettuce, Forellenschluss
Lettuce, Green Ice, 122
Lettuce, Lollo Rossa, 122, 244
Lettuce, Simpson Elite, 123
Lettuce, Tom Thumb, 29
Lewis and Clark Expedition, 246
Lima bean, 19, 97
Lima bean, Fordhook,
Lime, 7, 8, 41
Liquid feed, 69
Liquid Fence, 85
Living the Good Life, 218
Livingston, Alexander, 153
Loam, 6, 49
Lowenthals, Jeff, 263
Lloyd, Christopher, 106
Lowe's, 41
Lycopen, 168
Mache, 118

Magnolia Plantation, 43, 44
Mail order seed companies, 40
Maine Farm, 267
Malabar climbing spinach, 22
Manure tea, x, 73
Marigolds, 83, 206
Marjoram, 203
Meader, Elwyn, 106
Melon, Ambrosia, 123, 126, 130, 178
Melon, Charentais, 127
Melon, Early Crenshaw, 130
Melon, Fastbreak, 178
Melon Ha'ogen, 130
Melons for the Passionate Grower, 123, 268
Mendel, Gregor, 61
Mesclun mix, 121, 126, 153
Michigan State University, 226
Micro climates, 31
Micro-organisms, 49, 261
Mid-America CropLife Association, 2
Milk cartons, 57, 73
Milky spore (Bacillus papillae), 81
Mini greenhouse, 57
Mint, 187, 203, 204, 211
Mint, Chocolate, 204, 211
Molt, Ted, 73
Mondale, Walter, 33
Monet's garden, 265
Moneymaker vegetable garden, 45, 46
Moon and Stars watermelon, 92
Moon planting, 263
Mount Fuji, 136
Moriary, Dr George, 144
Mulch, 6, 41, 65, 67, 74
Murray, David, 132
Mushroom 246, 249, 257
Mushroom, button, 246, 248
Mushroom, Portobello, 206, 246
Mushroom, shitaki, 246
Mustard, 116
Mustard, Osaka Purple, 114
Mycoplasmas, 84
Nasturtiums, 206
National Garden Bureau, x, xi
National Parks Service, 34
Nearing, Scott and Helen, 218
Nematodes, 83, 84
Neophobic, 80
Netting, 25

INDEX

New Zealand, xii, 1, 36, 37, 152, 184, 223, 250
Nitrogen, 8, 40, 48, 50, 51, 68, 69, 77, 176, 261
Nitron organic fertilizer, 53
No-dig gardens, 8, 39
Nutrient analysis, 50, 51
Nutritional advice, 168
Nuts, 232
Oak leaves, 51
Obama, Michelle, ix, xi, 35
Obama White House vegetable garden, 34, 35
Ogden, Shepherd, 121
Ohio Valley Giant Pumpkin Contest, 139
Okra, 130
Okra, Annie Oakley, 131
Okra, Clemson Spineless, 128, 131
Onion, 251
Onion, Ailsa Craig, 132
Onion Cippolini, 131
Onion, Egyptian Walking, 132
Onion, Giant Walla Walla, 128, 132, 177
Onion, Mammoth, 112
Onion, Texas Supersweets, 128
Onion, Vidalia, 131
Open pollinated seed, 60
Oranges, 255
Oregano, 2, 187, 209
Organic fertilizer, 35, 41
Organic farming, 175
Organic gardening, 2, 175
Organic Materials Review Institute, 177
Organic Seminar, 3
Pakistan, 1
Pane, Thomas 263
Pansies, 206
Parade, 159
Parasite, 84
Park, George, 275
Park Seeds, 275
Parsley, 2, 30, 187, 204, 242, 244, 258
Parsley, Hamburg, 204
Parsnips, 29, 132
Parterres, 10
Patio planting, 28
Paw paw, 225, 230
Pea, 133
Pea, Black-eyed, 133
Pea, Green Arrow, 135

Pea, Sugar Snap, xi, 35, 129, 133, 134, 152, 251
Peach, dwarf, 242
Peaches, 223, 226, 255
Peach, Flamin' Fury, 226
Peaches, Redhaven, 223, 226
Peanuts, 76, 133, 172, 256
Pear, 225, 255
Pear, Bartlett, 225
Pear, Bosc, 225
Pear, Asian, 225
Pear, Moonglow, 225, 235
Peat moss, 8, 10, 41
Peat starter pots, 41
Pecan, 233, 238
Pecan, Missouri, 233
Penn, William, 43
Peppermint, 241
Peppers, 35, 76, 135, 136, 242, 245
Pepper, Big Bertha, 129, 136
Pepper, Big Jim Chili, 137
Pepper, Golden Goliath, 136
Pepper, Gypsy, 61, 88, 129, 136
Pepper, hot, 2
Pepper, indoors, 246
Pepper, Islander, 136, 137
Pepper, McMahon's bird, 246
Pepper, Rainbow, 136
Perlite, 41, 52, 58
Pests, 79
Peter Henderson Seed Company, 160
Petoseed Co., 160
Pheronome lure, 82
PH buffer, 8
Phosphorus, 49, 50, 51, 68, 69, 249
Pickles, 170
Pieri, Peter, 132
Pine needles, 51
Pine Tree Seed Co, 62
Pineapple, 2, 250, 254, 256
Pironti, Bud, 159
Plant a Row for the Hungry, 273
Plant labels, 41
Plant patents, 93
Plant pots, 41
Plant Variety Protection, 60
Planter box, 25,
Planter, rack, 239, 242
Planting plan, 6
Plastic, 68
Plums, 223, 226
Plum, English Damson, 226, 234

Plum, Shiro, 226
Pocket Vegetable Expert, The, 268
Poisonous parts, 75
Pollination, 233, 254, 261
Potash, 49, 51, 68, 69
Potatoes, 137
Potato, blue, 178, 253
Potato, French Finglering, 138
Potato, King Edward
Potato, Red Pontiac, 159
Potato Yukon Gold, 129, 138
Potpourris, 216
Potting soil, 8, 41, 58, 241
Powdery mildew, 84
Praying mantis, 35, 82
Pre germinating seeds, 40, 59
Premium Crop broccoli, xi
Preservative, 18
President Ford, xi, 33, 36
Prince Charles, 261
Pumpkin, 88, 138, 139
Pumpkin, Big Max, 139
Pumpkin, Cinderella, 142
Pumpkin, Jack o'Lantern, 142
Pumpkin, New England Sugar, 142
Pumpkin, Prizewinner, 139, 140
Pumpkin, Rouge Vif d'Etampes, 142
Punta Gorda, 177
Pyrethrins, 82
Pyrethrum, 82, 177
Quaker, 3
Queen Anne's lace, 55
QVC, 65, 77
Radish, 142
Radish, Cherry Belle, 142
Radish, Daikon, 142
Radish, Easter Egg Mix, 142, 143, 148
Radish, French Breakfast, 142
Radish mixture, 178
Radish, Red Meat, 178
Radish, Sparkler, 142
Radish, Watermelon, 142
Ragweed, 51
Rake, 39
Rainbow vegetables, 93
Raised beds, 6, 8, 15, 16, 17, 27, 28, 31, 65, 76
Raleigh, George, 122
Raspberries, 178, 231, 255, 258
Raspberry, Titan, 231

Recommended reading, 265
Renoir's Garden, 55
Reynoldsburg, 153
Rhubarb, 75, 91, 143
Rhubarb, Canada Red
Robinson, W and Son, 88
Rock phosphate, 51
Rodale, J. I., 2, 175
Rodale, Robert, 2, 175
Rodgers Bros, 151
Rogers, Desiree, 33
Rolston, Larry, 152
Romano bean, 21
Rooftop garden, 27
Root cellar, 170
Root crops, 54
Rosemary, 2, 187, 204, 213
Rosemary, weeping, 213
Roses, 206
Rotenone, 81
Round Up, 68
Rutabaga, 30, 166
Sangster, Keith, 134
Sakata, Takeo, 106
Saks of Fifth Avenue, 55
Salad greens, 242, 251
Salt deposits, 8
Sand, 6, 7, 49, 54, 68
Sangster, Keith and Bruce, 106
Sanibel Island, xii, 175
Savings, 41, 42, 43
Savory, 204
Sawdust, 77
Scurvy, 168
Seasonal differences, 29
Seaweed, 51
Secrets, Top Ten, 73
Seed, 40, 41, 60, 147
Seed, coated, 40
Seed, days to maturity, 73
Seed, mail order, 62
Seed packets, 40, 41
Seed, patented, 61
Seed, pelleted, 40
Seed, pre-germinating, 40, 59
Seed rack, 62
Seed saving, 62
Seed Savers Exchange, 92, 106, 268
Seed starting supplies, 57
Seed tape, 40
Selling tips, 177
Shade, 6
Shallots, 132

Shewell-Cooper, Dr. W. E., 1, 3, 8, 81
Shifriss, Oved, 160
Shredder, 50
Shrewsbury Chronicle, x
Shrewsbury Flower Show, x
Silverbeet, 152
Skin cleansing lotion, 215
Skyscraper gardens, ix, 8, 27, 28
Slug, 79, 80
Smith, Harry, 71
Snow Crown cauliflower, xi
Secret soil formula, 47
Soaker hose, 28, 40, 41
Soil, 41, 49, 273
Soil amendments, 41
Soil crusting, 7
Soil experiment, 252
Sol layering, 258
Soil test, 7, 41
Soy beans, 106
Spade, 39
Spearmint, 210
Sphagnum moss, 41, 242, 244
Spinach, 30, 58, 143
Spinach, Malabar climbing, 22, 143
Spinach, New Zealand, 149
Spray bottle, 41, 57
Spray nozzle, 41
Spray-N-Grow, 52, 70, 156, 249
Sprinkler, 40, 41, 70
Sprouts, 249
Square Foot Gardening, 8, 9, 10, 65, 266
Squash, 35, 144, 149
Squash blossom, 206
Squash, Vegetable Spaghetti, 144, 145, 146
Squash, Summer Early Prolific Crookneck, 144, 146
Squash, Winter Delicata, 144, 146
Staking, 74
Starbucks, 58, 65
Starter pots, 57
Step-by-step Gardening, xi, 77
Stokes, John, 275
Stokes Seeds, 275
Storage, 170
Stout, Ruth , 6, 8, 9, 262
Straw bales, 41
Strawberry, 73, 178, , 231, 251
Strawberry, Brighton, 87, 231

Strawberry, day neutral, 231
Strawberry, Earliglow, 74, 237
Strawberry, Tri-star, 231
Striped German tomato, 92
Succession planting, 30
Sugar cane, 249
Sugar cane, Pele's Smoke, 250
Sunflower, 145
Sunflower, Mammoth Russian, 147
Sunlight, 6
Sunscald, 84, 158
Surplus, 175
Sweet cicely, 205
Sweet corn, 92, 145, 150, 151, 154
Sweet corn, County gentleman, 92, 150
Sweet corn, Early Xtra Sweet, 154
Sweet corn, Golden Bantam, x, 150, 275
Sweet corn, Illini Xtra Sweet, 151
Sweet corn, Jubilee, 151
Sweet corn, Silver Queen, 151, 169
Sweet corn, Stowell's Evergreen, 150
Sweet corn, Sugar Enhanced, 151
Sweet corn, Supersweets, 151
Sweet leaf, 205
Sweet potato, 151
Sweet potato, Beauregard, 152, 155
Swiss chard, Bright Lights, 31, 152, 155, 241
Swiss chard, Five color
Swiss chard, Fordhook Giant
Tahiti, xii
Takii Seeds, 110, 117
Tarragon, 205
Tax deduction, 181
Tea leaves, 51
Tee-pee support, 23, 24
Tent support, 24
Terracotta pots, 242
Territorial Seed Co., 62
The Sower, 47,
Thompson, Emma, 74
Thompson and Morgan, 106, 134, 161, 249
Three Sisters, 150
Thyme, 205, 213

INDEX

Today Show, 139
Tomatillos, 153
Tomatoes, 6, 26, 35, 52, 74, 75, 89, 92, 115, 153, 178, 241, 242, 251, 255, 261
Tomato, Beefsteak, 156, 159
Tomato, Better Boy, 88, 89, 160, 239
Tomato, Big Boy, 61, 156, 157, 275
Tomato, Big Rainbow, 115, l60, 163
Tomato, Burpee's Big Early, 161
Tomato, Bushelmaker, 160
Tomato cat faces, 158
Tomato cracking, 158
Tomato, Delicious, 156, 160
Tomato, Early Cascade, 88, 156, 161, 163, 239, 242
Tomato, Early Girl, 156
Tomato, Flame, 91, 160
Tomato, indoors, 245
Tomatoes, late ripening, 156
Tomato, low yields, 156
Tomato, Paragon, 153
Tomato, Pineapple, 160
Tomato, Pixie, 245, 250
Tomato, Polbig, 161
Tomato-Potato, 158, 159, 163, 173, 243, 253, 255
Tomato, red plum, 242
Tomato, Striped German, 160
Tomato, Sub-Arctic, 159
Tomato, Sungold, 153, 161, 163
Tomato, Supersteak, 159, 162
Tomato, Sweet 100, 153, 161
Tomato troubleshooting, 156
Tomato, Tumblin' Tom
Tomato, yellow cherry, 242
Tools, 39, 41
Topsoil, 41, 50, 77
Topsy-Turvy planter, 242, 244
Torrey, Ted, 120, 123, 159
Trace elements, 69
Transplants, 41, 60
Transplants, root bound, 59
Treated lumber, 18
Tree wrap, 223
Trellis, 25, 26
Tresco Island, 32
Trombone zucchini, 92
Trowel, 39
Trug tubs, 244
Tubers, 41
Turnip, Blanc de Crossy, 164

Turnip, Purple Top Globe, 164
Turnip, Purple Top Milan, 164
Turnip, Tokyo Cross, 113, 166
Twilley, Otis, 275
Twilley Seeds, 275
Twine, 41
Twist-ties, 25
University of Florida, 51, 177
University of Illinois, 151
University of Louisianna, 152
University of Minnesota, 223, 261
University of New Hampshire, 106
USDA, 2, 33, 85, 92, 134, 170, 176, 183, 231
Vahe, Gilbert, 265
Van der Kemp, Florence, 265
van Dyke, Henry
Van Gogh, xii, 47
Variety selections, 87
Vegetable garden, iii
Vegetable spaghetti, 144, 177
Vegetables – How to Select, Grow & Enjoy, xi
Vermiculite, 9, 10, 41, 52, 58
Vermont Life, 217
Versailles planter, 242
Vertical gardens, 18, 27
Villandry, 10, 267
Vines, 73
Viola, 206
Viruses, 84
Walla Walla onions, 52
Walnut, Black, 232
Walnut, English, 232
Watercress, 30, 164, 166
Watering, 70
Watering can, 41
Watermelon, 164
Watermelon Jubilee, 166
Watermelon, seedless, 165, 275
Watermelon, seedless Sangria, 165
Watermelon, Yellow Baby, 165, 167
Weeding, 65, 68
Western red cedar, 18
Wheelbarrow, 39, 41
Whisky half barrel, 239, 241, 242
White House, ix, xi, 33, 35, 36
Wilbur, Charles H., 79, 160, 239
Wilson, Jim 266

Wilts, 85
Window box planter, 41
Winter vegetables, 29
Wolmanize wood treatment, 18
Woman's Day, 87
Wood ashes, 49, 51
Worden, Chris and Eva, 176, 179
Worden Farm, 176, 177, 179
World records, 110
Worm farm, 54
Yahoo, ix
Yale University, 176
Yam, 151
Yard Long beans, 106
Yorkshire Dales, xii
Yucca, 206
Zaan, Dr. Molly, 144
Zone 11, 4
Zucchini squash, x, 74, 90
Zucchini squash pollination, 254
Zucchini Squash Richgreen, 90, 146, 149
Zucchini, Trombone, 92, 149, 150
Zuckerman, Al, 272